The Limey Project

"Frequently hilarious, often informative, sometimes surreal, this journey of discovery across America - that intimately reveals the land and its people - is only made possible thanks to the power of the bicycle to enrich ourselves and connect with others." - **Maud de Vries, CEO, BYCS cycling agency**

"It's really good. Very witty, pacy, well-crafted writing with a nice balance of cheeriness and irony and some excellent flashes of observation and insight." - **James Spackman, Profile Books**

"What happens when two comically under-prepared young Brits try to cycle across America, pursued by gun-toting rednecks and protected only by an imaginary bear? The Limey Project is a brilliantly wild, fantastic and big-hearted adventure, a love letter to the joy of taking on something much, much bigger than yourself. An amazing journey and an equally great book. Loved it." - **Nick Parker, author of *The Exploding Boy***

"The Limey Project is both a timeless, coming of age adventure and a poignant record of the unfolding, wild America of George W Bush at the beginning of this century. It's a funny, fresh story that reveals the incredible things that can happen when you just ride your bike." - **Roos Stallinga, author of *Ride With Me* cycling guide series**

"Enjoyable and well-researched. Two friends with the combined cycling experience of a tortoise take off on an adventure of discovery across America. Like a modern day Lewis and Clark, they discover the landscapes and people. Ride with them with each turn of the page and discover America without the saddle sores." - **Tom Kirkendall, author of *Bicycling the Pacific Coast***

"This incredible and timeless journey - completed with unrivalled, naïve enthusiasm, and with zero technology for navigation or communication - will alight your wonder and inspire you to take to the road. It's an important reminder that we are all much more capable than we deem ourselves to be." - **Lee Feldman, co-founder of the global Bicycle Mayor Network**

"It's a coming-of-age pedal-powered road-trip travelogue like no other. An oddball cycling odyssey. Stones has a marvellous way with words and keeps up a zippy pace. The reader delights in discovering the myriad pearls, pitfalls, and peculiarities of America." - **Felix Lowe, Eurosport cycling writer and author of *Climbs and Punishment***

THE
LIMEY
PROJECT

A long, weird cycling odyssey
into the heart of the USA

Adam Stones

Published 2020
Beaumaris Books

ISBN: 978-1-8381401-0-6

For Sylvia and Noah

The prefacey bit

I have tried to write this story a number of times. Each time, I stalled as I didn't feel I had captured the full bizarre, surreal brilliance of the experience. Just how do you explain meeting a philosophical (and flatulent) bear, a murderous woodsman and a shape-shifting do-gooder? (Don't worry, it will all become clear…) And how to convey the incredible transformative power of the journey? Or its constant gut-aching hilarity? So I put it aside, hoping that one day I would have the time required to do it justice.

When that opportunity came a couple of years ago, I then worried too much time had passed. Was this still of interest 15 years later? As I revisited my diaries and my early book attempts, I saw that it has actually never been more relevant or interesting. I see the handprints of history all over the pages of this book; the building blocks of the world we see - and perhaps watch with confusion - today. By revealing the seeds, this book helps make sense of some of that. I also realised that the books on adventure that I have most enjoyed (and I mention some of them in this book) all took place many, many years ago. Because a good story doesn't age. Lastly, only the passage of time has allowed me to see what this journey really was, and to bring all its elements together into one story.

Our journey takes place between September 2003 and January 2004. At this time, America was adapting to Bush's new form of post-9/11 patriotism; a culture of fear of the 'other' amidst his new global War on Terror. We met proud Republicans trying to find their place in this world, concerned Democrats that did little about it, we met people in public office that were openly racist, homeless people who blamed immigrants for not being able to get a job, Hollywood people attuned to luxury, a Marine fighting Bush's war who wanted to drink himself (and me) to death, and a hotel owner who tried to sell us prostitutes like they were happy hour cocktails. We saw polarisation in the news and unfolding natural disasters that were brightly burning warning signs but which went ignored. We might also have been the last two people to journey across the USA with such an immersion; free from technology, phones and social media, at precisely the time Mark Zuckerberg was writing the code that would change it all. It was a unique time to discover America. And so many of our experiences had a freaky serendipity to them. It was like someone was writing the script of our adventure as it occurred, knowing it would make one hell of a book one day.

The adventure then - it obviously takes place on two wheels. And that was quite something in itself. Cycling in the UK did not then enjoy the booming enthusiasm it does today. This was pre-Wiggins, pre-cycle superhighways and Boris bikes. And in the USA it was even more of a rare quirk. A 4,500-mile journey by bike across America by two inexperienced Brits may come across as an unlikely achievement reading it today. Back in 2003 it was nothing short of a miracle. In some ways, the book celebrates the opportunities that arise when you open yourself up to such miracles.

But this book is not just for anyone that, very wisely, rides a bike. You won't find any instructions on how to change a puncture or suggestions for the best kit for a cycle tour. (OK, one tip: pack more Vaseline). The bikes were what gave us the behind the scenes access to America, as well as to ourselves, and that is what you'll read about. A journey that is both physical and mental. The one providing a sort of sweaty, sweary, smelly, visual representation of the other.

The two passions that developed on the journey - writing and cycling - have since become significant focuses of my professional and personal life. The journey gave me a clarity of ambition and the confidence to pursue it. I have since written for a number of national newspapers and magazines, and I have supported a large number of campaigns and organisations that champion everyday cycling for all. Last year, I gave a TED talk on the incredible ways cycling transforms people and places (appropriately, I gave this talk back in the home town that is the setting for the start of this adventure). Cycling improves mental and physical health, it supports the environment, and it builds stronger, closer communities. I learned these lessons first on this adventure. And, of course, my realisations weren't exclusive to cycling - this journey also taught me a lot about friendship, love, and our connection to - and responsibility for - the natural world. Sounds clichéd? Yeah, well I'm afraid it's the truth. And that might be the last sincere thing you hear from me for a while. It's nearly time to pass back to '2003 me' and he doesn't do much of that. Not at first.

This book was written before the world changed profoundly due to Covid-19. As we locked ourselves away and cities shut down, the humble bicycle emerged as the vehicle for ensuring we could maintain, and even rebuild, society. Bike lanes popped up overnight and millions of people reconnected with life on two wheels. In my TED talk, I outlined how any place can become bike-friendly - and so human-centric - in just five years. What we learnt in 2020 is that, when we need to, we can make changes much faster than that.

The story in this book is all true. You'll get to points and shake your head at the incredulity of it, but it's true. We kept very detailed diaries, even recording quite extensive conversations with each other and with the weird and wonderful creatures we met (including with the imaginary ones). In some instances, I have filled in some of the dialogue from memory or I have tried to find words that best convey the truth of the situation. And I have changed the names of a couple of people, as I am sure they didn't know I would be committing their after-hours habits to ink one day.

And committed to ink it is, finally. I hope you enjoy reading this as much as I did writing it. And if you don't cycle already, I hope this book will encourage you to get that old bike out of your shed and go for a ride. Just see where the bicycle can take you.

ABS

The Limey Route

Washington

Oregon

California

Arizona

New Mexico

Texas

Louisiana

Mississippi

Alabama

Florida

1. 'Raring' to go

Life is like riding a bicycle.
To keep balance, you must keep moving.
Albert Einstein

"Whose idea was this anyway?" This was the common question we asked each other the first few days out of Seattle, with logging trucks bearing down on us, rain like meatballs, hills like steeples, wild beasts stealing our food, and at every stop crackpots, oddballs and outcasts. No one had believed we would survive this adventure and it was immediately obvious they may be right. 'Whose idea was this?' It had started with Killer.

"Wouldn't it be great to cycle across America," he'd said cheerfully one evening, cracking open a can of lager and lighting a cigarette.

"What do you mean, like from one coast to the other?"

"Too easy. I was thinking from Miami in the bottom right hand corner to Seattle in the top left, finishing in the home of grunge rock."

"Really? America?"

"Yes, the land of Nirvana, Pearl Jam…"

"Cars, guns, burgers…"

"Yes, yes, but also Hollywood, cowboy hats, the Mississippi, and er," he reached for something he thought I might connect with, "…Arnold Schwarzenegger? And I don't think it would be very far."

"Well, it does *sound* far. Do you even own a bike?"

Killer did not own a bike. And my own was a seven-speed mountain bike purchased from a garden centre in Dorset. The furthest I had ridden it was a 15 mile loop around the local villages, pausing to catch my breath behind the occasional cow. I cycled in jeans, with a few coins in my pocket for a pint and a pork pie at the end. At one point on the loop I'd sit on top of the biggest hill and look out across the levels, looking, but not sure what for.

"We need to *do* something, Bone. We can't stick around here forever."

Killer knew what was on my mind. After university we'd found ourselves working back in our home town. It's a beautiful place. Idyllic, really. 9,000 people, two castles, a medieval Abbey, and there's a stream threading through it whose clear water gives the town its name, 'Sherborne'. I would intentionally bore my friends by reciting its history, from its Saxon roots to its ascent in the 8th Century as a centre of the Kingdom of Wessex, and onwards. "Did you know that Sir Walter Raleigh lived here after he brought back tobacco from South America? The castle was a gift from Queen Elizabeth the First. He smoked by the lake one day and his servant, who'd never seen a pipe, thought he was on fire so threw a bucket of water over him, ah ha ha ha!"

"Yes, you told us that one."

Sherborne was a place people settled in. And yet, I was restless. I was letting life happen to me rather than seeking it out. I was allowing myself to be constrained by complacency and by my own fears of my abilities. But here, Killer was suggesting a way to stand up to that. Maybe I should be 'more Raleigh', I thought. I imagined myself in a high-twilled collar presenting the current Queen Elizabeth with bounties from a modern day trip to the Americas. "It's called a 'Big Mac' Ma'am." She takes a bite then winces before removing a gherkin and tossing it to the corgis. Hmmm, if I was to cycle anywhere, across any land mass, I probably wouldn't have chosen the USA. My assumptions of what it offered were limited by cliché. But I didn't know anyone else crazy enough to join me on such a journey and for Killer, it had to be America. Well, at least I did like Arnie.

A week later I placed my *Times Atlas of the World* on Killer's dining table and opened it up.

"We'd have to start in Seattle of course," I said, jabbing my finger then sliding it down along the page. I've read that the winds are more encouraging if you travel south, and if we planned to leave in the next few months then it would be an even more acute form of madness to set off *towards* the north during winter."

"Oh, you've... been looking into this."

Killer had assumed it was one of those ideas we'd always talk about, like winning a Grammy, but which would reside firmly within the confines of pub banter fantasy.

"Yes, the best route would be to follow the coast - apparently it is famously stunning, the sort of roads you can film a car advert on - follow it all the way down to the Mexican border - pausing briefly for a guest appearance in Baywatch - and then hang a left and basically keep going until we reach Miami."

"Interesting. You're suggesting a *double* continental crossing…"

"Indeed."

"How far is that?"

I pulled out some notes I'd made.

"Er, about 5,000 miles."

"Jeez. How long will that take us?"

I smiled. "I have no idea."

Killer traced the approximate journey with his own hand, crossing rivers, deserts, forests and mountains, resting finally at the tip of Florida. He turned to me.

"Well let's bloody well do this thing then."

We laughed the deep, giddy laughter you'd expect from two men who'd just announced they planned to fly to the moon in a saucepan.

We had no idea how big America was. Or what 5,000 miles even meant. To put it into perspective, you can lay the map of the United States almost exactly over Europe. Seattle to Miami, via San Diego would be like riding from Dorset to the North African coast and then following it east, all the way to Cairo. Or stretch it out straighter and you could get to India. How long does it take to cycle that far if you are unfit and inexperienced, stopping in the occasional city for respite and ale?

"Maybe we could do 50 miles a day, five days a week, something like that?" Killer suggested.

"Five months, a month per thousand miles? Yeah, that sounds like it could be right-ish."

We didn't have a clue.

To make it harder to back out we started telling friends and family of our plans.

"We may be gone some time."

For years I had loved adventure stories; not comic book heroes but real ones - people like Shackleton and Mallory, and books like *Seven Years in Tibet* and *Touching the Void*. A favourite book shared by both Killer and I was *The Long Walk*. Polish cavalry officer Slavomir Rawicz escapes from the Russian gulag and walks across Siberia, the Gobi Desert and the Himalayas, before finally finding freedom one year later in northern India. We discussed his trip so extensively he even found his way into our vocabulary; going for a long walk became known as 'taking a Slavomir.' What sort of person might I be if I were to succeed in an epic voyage of my own? And what limits would I always find in life if I passed up this opportunity because of fear of failure? Maybe I should be 'more Slavomir'.

Something was awake in me. I wrote to bike shops, map providers, and bag makers (I eventually learned bike bags are called 'panniers') asking all for discounted or free kit for what I was now romantically calling the 'expedition' but which many people might more accurately call 'a bike ride'. I'd contacted the charity Cancer Research UK saying we wanted to undertake this challenge for them and they sent us fundraising materials and ideas. I created a website outlining our plans and detailing ways to sponsor us, and I quit my job.

As progress accelerated, I suggested to Killer that our expedition would need a name. Something to capture the spirit of heroic adventure ahead.

"Yes, I was thinking of 'The Limey Project'," he replied decisively.

"Oh that's good. And for very obvious reasons."

"Yes, people will see that and understand everything immediately. It's very obvious that it is a great name."

"Very obvious," I repeated, immediately purchasing the web domain.

"Speaking of names, I'm going to need a new one too, of course," said Killer, who at the time was still walking around as plain old 'Nick'. "You have a cool nickname already - Bone - but we can't be a duo of daring badasses as Bone and *Nick*. It simply won't do."

Indeed, by then most of my friends knew me as Bone; the result of a drunk man mishearing my surname and then me 'forgetting' to correct him because it sounded so cool, and then me 'forgetting' not to use it as if it was my real first name.

It was my turn to be decisive.

"What about Killer?" I suggested, summoning a name that would surely protect us on the adventure ahead. "We are sure to meet a killer on the journey so isn't it better to be *the* Killer?"

"I like Killer," said Killer.

And with that we were ready.

The plane stopped to refuel at Dallas Fort Worth. Looking out over the endless, unimaginative, prefabricated, dusty-coloured housing estates of the city I got a sinking feeling that America would be a disappointment. And whilst Seattle was only another four hours flight away, we suspected it would take us maybe another three months before we would pass this way again on our bikes. We ordered more gin.

"How are you feeling?" asked Killer.

"A bit better after that Imodium, thanks," I said.

"Um, yes, but I meant the other thing?"

'The other thing' was more of an internal ailment. But Killer didn't know that. He was only aware of the physical symptoms. Two weeks before we flew I had become unwell. My glands were swollen, I was tired, I had headaches. The more I worried that I was too unwell to attempt the journey, the more sick I became. The night before we were due to leave, we had a crisis meeting in the pub, naturally, discussing to delay the departure by a couple of weeks to allow me time to recover. But I suspected a delay would just make it worse. Various childhood illnesses and experiences had left me with a legacy of background nerves and obsessive thoughts. An anxiety that occasionally gnawed at me. And I felt that something beyond the conscious level, related to the enormity of the challenge ahead, was now working away at me.

"No, let's go. Let's just get out there and do our best," I said.

We flew into Seattle over a thick pine forest. It was the first day of autumn and the air was crisp. We took our bearings from the top of the Space Needle (I quickly discovered the US does not do modesty well), looking out over Washington State in 360 degrees. The city had a modest downtown skyline, backdropped by the distant Cascade and Olympic mountains. The colossal Mount Rainier over 50 miles away appeared graceful, like a white bell on the horizon. The city's harbour framed the expansive deep and pleasing blue of the Puget Sound that moved north and crossed into Canada. From our elevated perch the giant shipping tankers, which had gathered from ports around the world, dotted the water like sailboats. We spied the first part of our trip and looked out over what we imagined might be the first few days' ride. It all looked so serene from up high.

The calmness continued on street level. At the famous Pike Place fish market, a toothless man with a long handlebar tash and a possum on his shoulder played guitar. His hat read 'Vietnam Vet & Proud Of It'. Outside, a giant sign on the side of a building said, 'The world is your pork chop'. I had no idea what it meant but in my desperate search for good omens I took this as one. At the aquarium, the richness of life from Puget Sound and the Pacific was on display. We encountered an array of deadly looking sea urchins and Killer remarked that he wouldn't want to get on their wrong side. I agreed.

"Yes, keep your friends close and your anemones closer," I said offhand. This pleased Killer and so began a regular feature of our trip that was to be called *Bone's Quote of the Day*.

We gradually ticked off the staples of American iconography known to us through films and TV; the 'Walk / Don't Walk' street sign, the coin-operated newspaper vending machine, the cop cars and taxis. Along wide sidewalks, people strolled with vast thermos beakers of coffee, clasped in purposeful hands while they presumably discussed coffee and coffee shops. This was the city of Starbucks and the coffee culture was still evolving fast to stay ahead of the global trend. We got lost in the options for added themed flavours.

"Um, can I maybe just get a white coffee?"

The server laughed, hands on hips. "Ok, where's that on the menu sir?"

I'd perhaps not expected Seattle to be so civil and still. Only four years before, 40,000 people had taken over the city to protest corporate power. The streets filled with tear gas and smashed windows and the US media started talking for the first time about 'anti-globalization'. But even in sleepy Seattle, the movement's momentum had been derailed by the new powerful narrative of patriotism and terrorism. *You're worried about corporations? Let me really give you something to worry about.* We were in Bush's America now and we would find out much more about that from the Americans we'd meet on the road.

But for now, we settled in. We'd allowed ourselves three days to acclimatize and prepare. I took afternoon naps and we had early nights as I still didn't feel well. There were two other British guys in our dorm room at the hostel. They were our age and appeared almost identical in dress and behaviour to us, except they were a gay couple. And instead of cycling south, they were taking a convertible mustang.

"I'm quite jealous of your trip. I'm not sure we'll survive ours," I told them lightheartedly.

"Well, we might not survive either. Rednecks do not like gay people."

I hadn't considered that. I immediately became pleased with the fact we had opted for a tent each. And that I had a Swiss Army penknife. But it wasn't enough. We had arrived in America with Imeldamarcosian levels of kit but still felt vastly unprepared. We had reckoned on being able to buy things cheaper and in more variety in Seattle than Dorset but we didn't know what we needed. We'd never read any books or articles about anyone cycling this far, or discussed with anyone smarter than the local drunks how many ways America and its wilderness might try and defy us. These beer-fueled geniuses predicted our demise like it was a game of Cluedo. Invariably, it was the crazed woodsman, with an axe, in the campsite (and how right, they almost were).

And so it was that we found ourselves in a state of salvation and salivation at the outdoor megastore REI. I commented on how impressively massive their range of stock was and an enthusiastic worker jumped on the opportunity to tell us the full history of Recreational Equipment Inc, from small Seattle dockside stall selling imported Austrian ice axes to becoming one of America's largest retail cooperatives and all-round advocate for the great outdoors.

"And do you know what, today is the anniversary of the founder's death. Isn't that funny?" He chuckled, shook his head and led us off to find more 'stuff'. Killer and I were confused by this man. Unsurprisingly, given the bounty of natural beauty bounding Seattle, the locals here have a strong connection with getting outdoors and at REI they cater well for this. We loaded our basket with essentials like sunglasses, woolly hats and lightweight fleeces, as well as perhaps just one or two items only purchased by the naive adventurer.

"Look Killer, this 3-in-1 liquid promises to wash clothes, pots AND your body, all effectively and without noticeably harming any of them!"

"It sounds essential. Let's get it."

When we arrived at the 'technology' section our merry guide asked us what sort of cycling computers we had in mind.

"Sorry, *computer*?" said Killer.

"Yes, for showing your distance each day, speed, time and so forth and so forth. So you know where you are and how fast you're going. It's, er, kinda essential."

"Oh, then perhaps one that let's off a small triumphal firework whenever I cover one mile, accompanied by a short blast of 'Eye of the Tiger'."

It was the man's turn to look confused.

"Or the cheapest one will also do," Killer added.

It would have been obvious to any observer that two such inexperienced people should not be allowed to set off on the adventure we had in mind.

There were two things we were learning very quickly about these Americans, or at least these Pacific Northwesterners. They didn't get our jokes, yet, but they were seemingly the most polite and enthusiastic race of humans on the planet. The bus driver that had dropped us off from the airport had taken the time to give us detailed directions to the hostel, even drawing us a small annotated map. This was in acute contrast to the acerbic ass that had thrown us off at Heathrow with a grunt and a barely disguised mutter of 'wankers' as we wrestled with the bikes and held up his precious day. The benevolence extended itself through all spheres of life, from this driver to shopkeepers and fast food vendors – simply everyone. Every interaction with a Seatolian became a tennis match of courtesy. They were almost competing in kindness, but it was all wholly sincere and expressed wide-eyed and intently. A typical exchange between two strangers went as thus:

American 1: "Hi! How are you doing?!"

American 2: "I'm just fine, how are *you* doing?"

American 1: "I'm fantastic, thank you so much for asking!"

American 2: "Oh, you're totally welcome! Have a wonderful day!"

It was quite frightening to behold. This openness could also lead people to confuse courtesy with familiarity. In a pizza place in the student quarter the patron greeted me warmly.

"Oh hey, how was your summer?"

"Er, yes, good thanks."

"Great, great, well it sure is great to see you."

"Yes, um, you too. Do we, er, do we know each other?"

Our diet then started as it went on. That's to say appallingly. We ate McDonalds and Subways, believing that adding extra olives to a three-meat cheese melt would keep us regular. And we enjoyed bagels, croissants, bananas and other provisions from the generous breakfast buffet in the hostel that found their way into our deep pockets for later snackage. One night, we did try a restaurant, The Pink Room - what better place for two happening young lads about town. There was a piano in the corner and I wouldn't have been surprised if local fictional radio psychiatrist (a very Seattle profession I was fast learning) Frasier Crane had been sitting across from us. We settled in before we saw the prices and then quickly decided on a light dinner of a starter each, which threw the waiters.

"I'd love to try the soup, please," said Killer.

"And for you, sir?"

"Yes, I think I'll haaaave…[I pretend to look at the menu]... the same. Yes."

By then our thoughts should have been turned to the route ahead, discussing various strategies, directions, plotting our rest stops, confirming our nutritional plans. But we did none of that. This may have had something to do with the fact we could not fathom surviving more than a few days, but it may also have related to the fact that, as man-boys, we enjoyed elevating irrelevances as if they were matters for urgent debate. Over our last meal in Seattle we contemplated the constitutional differences between soups, sauces and dips. We reached an impasse when trying to agree when does a soup become a sauce and can you make a dip from a sauce or must it have a different make-up from its initiation.

"What about marinades?" asked Killer a little later.

"Oh, I don't think we're ready for that." I said.

We were, of course, not ready for much, but we could put it off no longer. In the basement of the hostel - which seemingly doubled as Satan's boiler room - we laboured shirtless, sweaty and swearing over the bikes we had bought in England, which had been disassembled to wedge into cardboard boxes to fly with. The nuts didn't thread, the racks didn't fit, the panniers didn't hook up and a litany and tyranny of slander and curse was heaped upon Topeak, Ortlieb, Marin and any other manufacturer's name we could see about us. When they finally somewhat resembled bicycles, we attempted to pack our possessions into the panniers. In hindsight we perhaps should have tried this back in the UK.

We had four panniers each, two astride the front wheel, and two larger ones at the back. Before we became more seasoned and some sort of packing logic was established, they acted as mere buckets for our belongings. We also had a rear rack for the tents and handlebar bags for everyday essentials. But this was not enough.

"We'll have to leave a lot of stuff behind," I observed.

"What about this?" asked Killer, holding up a head torch.

"Negative. Essential for fending off nighttime attackers and for general nocturnal urinations."

"Ah ha, I'll leave a few of these then." Killer then pulled out a small library, consisting of Moby Dick, Jaws and The Great Gatsby. He sensed my look. "Well, I've always wanted to read them." I didn't blink. "OK, I'll just take Jaws. And Moby Dick. I guess we can swap and trade or buy books along the way, or something."

"Yes, I guess we can," I agreed, as if it were a stroke of inspiration.

We formed a collection of belongings, which also included spare trousers and jackets, and filled a whole travel bag with our rejects, which we gifted to the hostel manager.

"Thank you *so* much," he said.

"Oh you're *totally* welcome," I replied, confirming immediately I was ready to venture further into America.

Straddling the bikes for the first time, there were a few audible creaks from the metalwork, a little like a whimper, and the tyres looked flat from the effort.

"We're going to need bigger bikes," Killer concluded.

We boarded the ferry across the Puget Sound to Bremerton, from where we believed we could pick up the route south. The sun was bright, the water shimmered. We laughed again at the thought that a passing comment from Killer in his living room had led us here.

"Do you think we've taken this joke too far now?" he remarked.

And then I thought of something.

"Killer, I saw you with two of our paraffin bottles outside the hostel. What did you do with them?"

"Oh I got rid of them Bone. No space. We'll just have to source fuel for cooking when we need it. We have enough for a few days. Possibly."

"So you binned them?"

"Well, the bin wasn't immediately to hand so I, er, left them on the side of the road."

"In the midday sun?"

"Uh huh…. And I can see now that was the wrong thing to do."

I turned back, imagining I'd see downtown Seattle in flames. I pictured the hostel owner, soot-faced like in a cartoon, telling the cops, "It was two limeys what did it. You can't miss them, they're heading south, and something tells me they ain't going very far." We mounted the bikes at Bremerton, took a deep breath and nodded to each other as if to acknowledge the true beginning of the mission. Months of planning were finally being put into action. We then simultaneously realised we had no idea in which direction to cycle.

2. Two go mad in Washington

I'm so happy because today I found my friends.
They're in my head.
Kurt Cobain

The roads were virtually empty and each time we saw another cyclist we made a point of signaling them. A knowing nod and a wave that showed we were 'in the club'. But why was no one else heading in our direction? We joked that they must all be lost. That was a much more enjoyable thought than that we might have set off alarmingly late in the season. "Miami is this way!" I would shout, pointing ahead of me as the cyclists frowned in a combination of confusion and irritation.

We'd been riding just a few slow, happy miles when one of these cyclists crossed over to enquire about our journey. I hadn't even launched into my joke yet - he must have seen these bikes, loaded like pack mules, mirror-like in their shiny newness, steered by men in crisp, clean T-shirts and emanating enthusiastic naivety and, strangely, thought we needed help.

"So where are you guys heading?"

"Er, Miami?" I suggested, looking at Killer for affirmation, having realised how implausible it sounded from the opposite corner of the continent.

It was a question and answer routine we would experience a multitude of times daily. In my diary I kept a 'yes, we're honestly going to Miami' count (which I tried to make sound more affirmative as the days passed) but decided to stop when I had exceeded 40 before the week was out. Invariably, the questioner would not be on a bike. In fact, we wouldn't encounter another cyclist for more than a week. The question was typically vollied at us by a driver at a store or rest stop, and would often be followed by a guffaw of, "Wouldn't it be faster in a car?!"

"Miami huh. Well you got a ways to go I guess. What's your rowt?" said the cyclist.

"I'm sorry?" I said.

"Rowt…?" He kept repeating the word as Killer and I looked increasingly quizzical. "You know... *rowt,* ROWT," he was shouting now, "… your direction."

"Oh, our *route!* Rowt is route. Right, rowt, er, well, we actually don't really have one."

This exchange perhaps isn't worth the ink I am giving it here but at the time, I was dumbfounded that having been so well versed in the difference between a tomato and a tomayto, and growing up on a diet of Friends and Seinfeld, I had never noticed this particular phonic yanky-twist.

"You have no rowt?!" The guy was almost angry now at our professionalism, like we were letting down cyclists everywhere.

"Oh well we have maps," I assured him, "and plan to follow the coast all the way down. It's just that we don't know how far we can cycle so haven't planned where we will stay tonight. Or, well, any night."

He sighed, and pulled a local road map from his handlebar bag.

"Head to Twanoh State Park. It's about 30 miles away. Beautiful park. Great spot to pitch a tent and light a fire."

He pressed the map into my hands and then, satisfied with his good deed, buggered off. As he disappeared down the road, Killer and I simultaneously turned to each other and exclaimed, "30 fucking miles?!"

Through the conversation, Killer had been silent. I asked him what was going on.

"Did you not see that big can of mace in his handlebar bag, Bone? Yeah I was keeping an eye on him in case he used it on us to try and mug us or something."

"Oh, I think that's to fend off bears, not Englishmen," I suggested. This satisfied us both for a moment, until the implication finally resounded, like striking a bicycle bell with a hammer.

"Um, what are *we* using to fend off bears?" Killer asked.

We thought for a while. Even our deodorants were ineffective - we'd chosen roll-ons, so we could preserve space, and an intimate application of Lynx Africa was hardly going to save us.

"Er, the penknives?" I finally suggested.

"We only have one penknife. Yours," said Killer dejectedly.

"Oh well, I read the chances of being attacked by a bear are, like, very small. We just need to keep our food locked up at night apparently. And anyway, they'll probably start hibernating soon."

I was making this up but it seemed to reassure Killer and we cycled on. I would have been worried myself, had I not been the holder of our only form of defence. At least I will have a Swiss-army-shaped chance, I thought, as I contemplated whether the blade, mini saw or bottle opener would be most advantageous in a bear fight.

The maps I had referred to were special cycle touring maps produced by the ACA, the Adventure Cycling Association. They had taken a number of rowts across the USA, including the entire Pacific coast and the Southern Tier, and divided the journey into several sections. Each of these was then cut into chunks that most people - not us, yet - would be able to cover in a day or so. These chunks were detailed on small rectangular pages, designed to fit perfectly into the average clear, weather-proof plastic map holder, such as the one velcroed to the top of my handlebar bag. And they were excellent. Each section detailed bike shops for repairs, campsites, stores for provisions and, alongside the directions, an elevation profile to warn you of the hell ahead. They also had short texts to alert you to expected hazards or to indicate where even water was not available for entire days. It was clear to us very early on that these maps would be a life-saver. How curious then that only a few miles into the journey and we were veering off course to find a campsite we knew nothing of. Perhaps it was the small reflective flag thrusting out from the side of his bike that, although ridiculous looking, suggested the cyclist who had advised us of this course knew what was best for us.

Mercifully, the road to Twanoh was splendid. In what was to become typical of the first few days, the road was gentle, quiet and lined with conifers, often fringed by cool rivers and lakes. In the more affluent communities, wooden cabins and mansions dotted the waterside, sun-dappled, but in many places the homes were more shed-like, beaten by weather and time, and seemingly dropped poetically into the middle of scraps of untethered land. Typically there was a faded stars and stripes flying in the front yard, a lazy dog on a chain and a bashed metal postbox by the road.

We cycled at a gentle pace, taking it all in wide-smiled, and my happiness manifested itself in bursts of badly-sung *Les Miserables* numbers, allowing the struggles of Jean Valjean to reverberate through the woodland. In the fresh Washington air, all the worries seemed to fade, like a convict slipping his captors. It was such a relief to be gathering momentum through this scenery that we entertained thoughts of continuing on past Florida to go up the east coast and complete the circumnavigation. In the afternoon sun a false sense of security bloomed in our breasts.

"If the next 4,990 miles are as easy as the last ten, we'll be in Miami by Christmas," Killer remarked fatefully.

We arrived at Twanoh having ridden further in one day than we had ever before in a week. By anyone else's standards this might have been considered a rest day, but for Day 1 - noted in the annals as 'TLP 1' - we couldn't be more pleased.

"What sort of training are you doing?" people had asked us back home.

"We are going to start fairly slow and build up our strength on the journey," was our deflectory response. I'd sat on the exercise bike at the gym a few times but the occasional 45 minute spin while I watched MTV didn't really emulate the conditions of the road, or prepare me for the weight of the load. I might as well have followed Killer's regimen of no exercise.

"Nothing can prepare us for this trip Bone," he'd remarked one day.

"Except perhaps... preparation?" I'd suggested.

We hadn't even attempted to put up the tents before. They were the lightest and simplest one-man tents I could find. The Vango Phantom 150 - weighing in at under 2kg and rolling up small enough to rest on the rear rack, they were perfect. They consisted of an inner tent for sleeping, suspended by a single arching pole, and this was then covered with a larger, forest-green coloured outer skin that extended the footprint beyond the inner tent door to create a small vestibule for protecting belongings from the elements. With just the one pole, good pegging and the use of the guide ropes were essential in keeping the tent upright. The guide ropes also ensured the two tent layers didn't touch each other and create condensation. It took us a few days of nocturnal flapping and water dripping onto our foreheads to work that bit out...

We started the assembly procedure and soon laughed as we saw our tent doors were pressed so tightly together we couldn't get in. We tried again, only to realise we had pitched on a slope meaning we would be rolling into the fire pit in the night.

"You learn something new twice a day," I concluded, just managing to get my daily quote in before nightfall.

We laid out our sleeping mattresses inside the tents, spread out the sleeping bags (also from Vango) and made cosy nests. I stepped back and nodded to myself. This would be my home for the majority of the coming months and I liked it enormously. And the mad macey cyclist was right - it really was a beautiful place to pitch a tent. Tall trees surrounded our clearing like dutiful apostles, and walking paths led into the woods where we found sticks for our fire. We signed the self-registration and paid the $16 for our site. As I did so, I noted a sign celebrating the park's construction by members of the Civilian Conservation Corps (CCC). And if there's one thing I like, it's a good information board.

I read that in the 1930s Franklin D Roosevelt had launched the CCC as part of his New Deal. Young, unemployed, unmarried men were invited to work on a range of public improvement programmes in return for a wage at a time when the country was falling into the Great Depression. Over the CCC's nine-year span, three million people took part. They got food, shelter, clothing, money. And in return the country got three billion more trees, improved public roads, trails and lodges and 800 parks were updated or installed. The work of the CCC was credited with radically transforming the public's association with the natural wonders on their doorstep. People understood they should treasure these places and escape to them when they needed to reconnect. People, perhaps, like James and Sharon.

"Hey, have you guys eaten?" a man called over from a nearby camp spot, brandishing a barbecue spatula. "I got burgers here with your name on them. I saw you struggling with your tents so figured I'd throw a couple more bits of meat on." The woman next to him waved us over in confirmation.

James and Sharon were in their early to mid 30s, were rotund and ruddy faced. They had parked their car, pitched up a huge tent and unfurled a giant gas barbecue, drinks cooler, camping lights and rain covers. They were Twanoh veterans but hadn't so much come for the camping as to relocate their living room.

Once we had hilariously navigated the question of our destination and the comparative speeds between motorised and pedal-powered transport options for such an endeavour I took over the cooking from James, which left Killer pressed up against

Sharon's bare, sticky thighs on the picnic bench. She turned to him, held his hand and then began her story.

"They took my children," she said airily.

What had we let ourselves in for? It wasn't a conversation so much as a two hour lecture on the hardships of a down-trodden working class American family. They had four kids but each one had been taken away by the Child Support Agency when Sharon was still in the hospital and they'd been fighting to get them back since the first was born 18 years ago. She wouldn't elaborate on why but just kept crying and saying it was unfair.

"I'm a good mom," said Sharon, who'd never had the chance to even be a mom.

Just when I thought we were getting to the happy bit, James shared that eight years before, burglars had broken into their home and beaten him so badly with baseball bats that he'd spent a year in a coma. They were both taking a range of medication for pain relief and depression, and getting ongoing help. They looked beaten down and seemed to have lost the ability to speak coherently - their story was shared in random order, with frequent sidetracks. At one point Sharon offered, "The other day I was walking down the street with an angel, well, not a real angel but, you know, my sister…" and she spent considerable time describing directions to a tobacco store in Bremerton that sold very good quality, cheap bracelets. Our not needing bracelets or a vast detour was unimportant. And yet, through it all, James managed to keep smiling, perhaps buoyed by his fascination for the exotic foreigners amongst them.

"Hey, have you guys got the internet in England?" he asked.

"Yes, of course," I laughed, thinking he was joking.

"Oh great. Give me your email address - I want to see if I can get an email all the way over to England. Wouldn't that be something."

We slipped away back to our tents and quickly fell asleep. But rest was short-lived. The burgers caused an almighty drama in my duodenum, the performance awaking me and sending me on a 2 am dash to the camp facilities, running desperately with my head torch lit as if being chased by the Blair Witch. I arrived too late.

"They took my boxer shorts," I said to Killer in the morning, feeling immediately guilty for offering humour above humanity.

One of the few books on cycling I had managed to flip through before we left did little to prepare for me such incidents. Perhaps it was a *little* outdated. *Bicycling 1874* was the first attempt to catalogue the exciting new ways people were taking to biking in both the UK and USA, and to convince many others to try it. 'There seems to be little doubt that the practical utility of these machines will lead to their speedy adoption for many purposes of business, or pleasure,' it prophesied. It was a little depressing to think these high ambitions were so far from being realised in this country, despite such clear reasoning. 'You command the most varied scenes. From town to country, from country back to town, you skim along freely, easily, quickly…' It went on: 'The Bicycle is more useful than the cleverest nag man ever bestrode, with the additional advantage that a bicycle consumes nothing but a little oil.' In many ways, nothing had changed at all for this timeless wonder. In some ways, a lot had. 'Never use any oil but the best sperm…' It also suggested we would be foolish to depart without 'a light gun'. As it turns out, we would have been wise to follow this advice. And we might as well have been following their guidelines on attire, for all the practical sense our own choices made. 'For a long journey riders will find knickerbockers more comfortable than trousers and gaiters. A flannel shirt and short yachting coat will complete the costume'.

In fact, our clothing was the most obvious immediate visible clue that we were not seasoned adventurers, and the curious arrangement we set off with was to go largely unchanged for the rest of the trip. The only major switch was that halfway through TLP 2 we developed a profound and painful appreciation for the necessity of wearing the padded lycra cycling shorts that were stowed in our pannier buckets and made a commitment to switch from boxers (already in low supply) the next day. However, we also vowed to always keep this lycra covered with our baggy hiking shorts - clown-like in their lack of aerodynamism - so as not to trouble the redneck's rifle. These shorts could be extended into trousers with zips at the knee, in pleasing geeky versatility, when cold. And we would layer up further with lightweight fleeces. When it rained we had non-breathable, large rain jackets that caused further sweat and stickiness and caught the breeze like windsocks. Killer's was in cool dark hues, while I'd chosen lurid dayglo yellow, hoping it would fend off lazy drivers.

On our feet we sported simple trainers, unable to fathom why anyone needed especially-designed-for-cyclists clip-in cycling shoes. Killer's trainers even had air vents, perfect for those approaching winter days. Our heads were protected by helmets of course, but not the ergonomic, lightweight kind enjoyed by normal people. Mine was a shiny purple dome that my mum had given me nervously before I left - it was too big and rattled around my cranium at the whim of the winds but I had made a promise to wear it every day. Killer's, in contrast, was a tight-fitting black helmet, designed for BMX stunt riders, offering protection all round and even down the back of his head. This resulted in some extensive head sweat and, before we left Twanoh, Killer attacked the helmet angrily with the penknife to cut wide ventilation holes, no doubt thereby also destroying its protective architecture.

We had a couple of tight cycling shirts but often we wore our matching white T-shirts, on to which I had transferred the logos of our 'expedition sponsors'. I had seen adventurers in glossy magazines with global brand names bedecking their Gore-Tex jackets, and decided that if no one was going to give me one, I'd make my own, cheaper, alternative. It may have looked like an exercise in self-aggrandisement but it was quite the opposite, and I delighted in knowing very few people would understand. I wanted someone to say, "Oh, you're being supported by Tropicana Orange Juice?" and

I would then say, "That's right, they sent me a small booklet of discount vouchers that expire in a week."

Amongst the logos was the genuinely brilliant ACA, that had gifted maps for the entire journey, as well as Ortlieb and the local bike shop BikeLab, that had respectively provided cost-price bags and bikes. I also added Vango, despite not having given us any special deals, just for having 'supplied' us, to make up the numbers. And I added Killer's employer, a regional news weekly called the Blackmore Vale Magazine, for letting him keep his job while he went away on sabbatical in return for us writing articles from the road every few weeks. I also added the logo of our incredibly awesome band, Stonegarth (but more on that one later...)

"Where. Are. We. Camping. Tonight?" wheezed Killer at the top of another arduous ascent, both of us pausing to gently prod our buttocks to gauge the severity of the chafing. The day had started with singing but after 40 miles had found the silence of pain and exhaustion, as well as a profound desire for Vaseline and isotonic beverages.

I consulted the map. "Well I guess we won't make it another 15 miles to the State Park, but there's a YMCA campground at somewhere called Lost Lake, about two miles yonder."

"Great. We can sit around the campfire, sing kumba-fucking-ya and pray this madness ends soon."

At the YMCA, the path was blocked by a chained gate, a 'Closed' sign and another saying 'No Trespassers', which had a sieve-like appearance, suggesting it had been used for pistol target practice. But even law breaking was preferable to further ass agony and we lifted our bikes over the gate in an orgy of exhalation. Lost Lake's nature could not be separated from its name. The last vestiges of Summer Camp were a few miserable black logs located in fire pits beside a table tennis table, and a display of flaccid balloons. It looked like the last village in Chernobyl to be abandoned but even that would have been a welcome sight right then.

As I started to merrily prepare some tuna rolls, Killer went off to find water, only to return minutes later, ashen-faced, hurriedly reassembling his belongings onto his bike.

"We must leave, Bone. Now," he said.

I looked behind him and saw a man, seven foot tall if he was an inch, emerging from the sort of hut associated with the opening scenes of a horror film, wearing a butcher's apron and holding a cleaver. He wiped his nose against the back of his fist as he watched us. Oh. Shitpants. He started walking towards us and we ran with our bikes like little girls, heroic little girls though, to the gate.

"What did you do to make him so angry?" I asked Killer when we had rejoined the main road.

"Nothing! I just said we needed to camp for the night and he said 'I can't let you do that' then he smiled and picked up his fucking axe. Bone, it had *blood* on it. What the hell is this place?"

Well at least we knew where the Summer Camp kids were. Our legs started rotating in autopilot. We had drained our energy reserves and were desperate. After we had hit 50 miles for the day, an extraordinary feat, we pulled over to buy sustenance and pray for rescue. As we moved on again I suggested to Killer that what we really needed now was for some friendly local to insist on us staying at their house for the night. Anything less would be an affront by the gods, I declared. I slammed my fist against the handlebar to summon some damned divine intervention.

"I heard from the lady who runs the store back there you guys need a place to stay." A man had pulled up in his truck and appeared to be speaking to us. I looked at Killer and then up to the heavens, suspiciously. The man was slight, had a neat goatee and a cheeky grin. He had a baseball cap that said 'I'm the bass' on it, with a picture of a fish wearing a tie. It took all of, oh, ten milliseconds to agree to his suggestion to camp up by his trailer home on the banks of the nearby Lake Star.

"The place is *full* of rednecks," he joked, "but at least I know them all, so you'll be safe enough."

He was Mark and this was his getaway home; a place to go fishing and hunting. It was a small trailer, almost dwarfed by the stars and stripes that billowed above it. We pitched our tents on his lawn, by the lake shore. We cooked some soup on the burner and made tea. Fishermen stood on jetties or in boats, the low sun lit darting insects on the surface of the water, before the golden ball slipped behind the mountains, pulling a palette of colours with it and then disappearing, allowing the stars to reveal themselves brighter than they had for some years.

Mark wandered down and gave us both a beer.

"This is quite a place," I said and Mark nodded thoughtfully.

"It's nice to escape here." And then he said something I hadn't expected. "It's nice to get away from all that *Bush* crap."

I had assumed that all the patriots with high flying flags were fully on board with the programme but Mark's sentiment was typical of a number of people we met that first week. America was the 'best place in the fucking world' but 'fuck the government' and 'fuck the taxes' was the common line, even amongst those who openly adored Bush, or at least what he stood for. For Mark, it went even further - it was also that America was assuming too much power in the world. He seemed to be getting more angry with every new thought when his friend turned up to go hunting. The friend introduced himself as Yarborough, presumably a surname, and asked us hopefully if it was an English name. We both instantly said it was a good English name and he was pleased. It seemed the best way to find out who people really were was to agree with them, even when they were being mildly racist.

"You ain't bad for a couple of Brits. At least you ain't French," joked Mark.

"You try living next to them," I quipped - keen to see what else this might open up in him - and Mark smiled, encouraged. His daughter had gone on her honeymoon to France. "Why not England," Mark had told her. "At least they already speak the language there." She hadn't enjoyed France. Mark knew she wouldn't.

By the time they went off hunting, they had already had a few beers and Yarborough couldn't control the volume of his voice. "You're just going to leave them there at your friggin' house?"

"Why not - they're Brits, not foreigners."

They drove off on a small four-wheeler, rifles over their shoulders, and we heard them crash into a tree and laugh.

And so it was that characters started to enter and leave The Limey Project. They'd drop in, add to the colour of the adventure, and then we'd be gone, down the road like the Littlest Hobo. Every one of these personalities helped to gradually build up the picture of America (as seen by a couple of naive, young, half-men). And we appreciated every piece they left us with - whilst we joked about our encounters and sometimes did impressions of the way they spoke, this was out of excitement for the exotic and never (well, almost never) meant mockingly. We loved the richness of life that they represented.

The first encounters were particularly noteworthy - as they are with any trip - and so it is hard not to convey the story of The Limey Project without going into the details of those first days. But particularly deserving of close examination is the town of Aberdeen and the man we met there, who seemingly wanted to murder us.

We got there via an altogether different environment. Having left Mark, we continued through woods, which occasionally cleared to farmland and large red barns, before we turned off and descended to the pine-soaked valley of Lake Sylvia State Park. I crashed out and slept before dinner, exhausted. We lazed around for most of the next morning too, reclining waterside, daring to imagine that the whole of our journey might be filled with pleasant weather, wide views, good cycling, and welcoming people…

It only took another ten miles to burst that dream. Approaching Aberdeen, we moved off the quiet back roads onto the

Olympic Highway. The road was thick with cars and haulage trucks. The small mirrors on our handlebars were quickly turning into the most prized possessions of the expedition and revealed huge leviathans bearing down on us. We watched them approach - all metal grills and headlights - and then felt them consume us whole. As they passed, inches from us, a bow wave swept us up. I just held on and rode it, invariably letting out a yelp from adrenaline-pumped fear, as my bike was slingshotted ahead.

Arriving in town, the sky thickened and the heavens opened with ferocious force and we took refuge at the Travelure Motel. Ah the motel, a mainstay on the 'to do in USA' ticklist. The rooms were in a single-story building, arranged around a central car park like a three-sided bungalow with a concrete garden. The proprietor was Korean and keenly told us he had just one more year to wait to get his citizenship. He displayed proud plaques and certificates of his progress to that goal and emphatically declared that he loved America, repeating it as if we might be undercover immigration officials. We noticed a guitar and he urged us to play, saying he had been playing for as long as he could remember. It was out of tune. How did he come to be in Aberdeen? He turned away and said it was a long story.

In fact, how had anyone come to be in Aberdeen? Maybe the angry clouds and the hard ride had greyed my mood, but the whole place had an air not just of hardship but also of misery. 100 years before we arrived, Aberdeen had become home to scores of saloons, whorehouses, and gambling dens as the port grew. It was nicknamed 'The Hellhole of the Pacific', and then 'The Port of Missing Men' due to its extraordinarily high murder rate. This was largely thanks to Billy Gohl, a union worker who used his position to covertly rob and dispose of passing sailors and workers over several years in the early 1900s. He may have killed more than 100 people before he was eventually found out. The town later enjoyed a more buoyant economy as the timber business boomed, but by the late 1970s most of that resource had been logged and the town collapsed. By our arrival in 2003, a quarter of the people lived below the poverty line. Industry was replaced by homelessness, alcohol and drugs. Meth and heroin seemed to be the preferred stimulants, and it once again felt like a hellhole town where people, or at least their potential, went missing.

We wandered for a mile or two - past car lots, cranes and quaysides - to find a place to eat but merely encountered drive-thru after drive-thru. We settled on Taco Bell, a sort of Mexican McDonald's, but I couldn't even finish my meal. I was longing for the park and the trees and lakes. Aberdeen was the worst of my fears of what America might be and I didn't like encountering the reality so vividly and so early on in our journey. Under a flickering neon sign, we entered a beer-soaked saloon. We sat at the bar and watched baseball. The players seemed to run, throw and swing at random, accruing points beyond any system I could fathom. Not even this made sense. I turned to the guy next to me and asked him to explain the rules. That was, in hindsight, a mistake.

Tom Toseland looked like he had stepped from the pages of an illustrated guide to axe murderers - deep set eyes that bled cold fire. His face framed in a wiry ginger beard, his neck as thick as pine, and his lean frame sinewy; the muscles of his forearms exploded like Popeye underneath his rolled-up tartan lumberjack shirt. His trucker's cap hung low over his brow and he tipped it up with one finger to get a better look at the varmint that had just addressed him.

"You. Are. Fucking. Shitting me!" he said, his fighting fist clenched tight on his beer. "You ain't ever watched baseball – you don't know the rules... I mean..." He half smiled and looked around to see if anyone else had heard this. Was this some cruel joke? He dropped his smile and stared at me again with a mix of confusion and hatred as if I had just announced I was door-knocking for Al Qaeda.

I tried to reassure him: "I love baseball. It's a great sport played by proud men but sadly we don't get to watch it in England much so just a quick recap on some of the rules would be great."

This, and the mention of England specifically, seemed to calm him a little and he proceeded to explain the 'outs', when teams switch, and even touched a little on tactics. It sounded stupidly complicated. It's just not cricket. After a while Toseland had started to cautiously tolerate us. He told us about his kid, how he'd go to the woods to shoot 'any shit that moves', fish for salmon or ski in the winter, and he listed the various wooden constructions he had crafted from his bare hands over the years – cabins, furniture and a curiously extensive number of gun racks.

As he carried on drinking and explaining why he liked killing things so much, I noticed a mini photo shrine on the wall to Kurt Cobain. As the frontman for Nirvana, Cobain had reinvented American rock music, selling millions of albums and becoming one of the most influential musicians of his generation before in 1994 – at the age of just 27 - he penned his final line, 'Love, peace, empathy' and took his shotgun.

Killer's obsession with grunge rock had brought us to Seattle and it was by pure chance that our improvised route from there to the coast then took us through this small town, where the music revolution all began. Aberdeen was Cobain's birthplace and in its empty timber yards and stagnant backstreets I also saw his desperate teenage years and the shadows of his darker lyrics. Was it not the drugs, the weight of his genius and desperate self-delusion that killed him but perhaps also this town that he was never able to shake off? Indeed, in a recording made by Cobain called 'Aberdeen' he reveals how he never fitted in with a 'community that stresses macho male sexual stories as a highlight of all conversation'. And he explains that it was here - amongst these dark, satanic wood mills - that he first turned to drugs to escape his daily reality, and how as a teenager that felt excluded and unaccepted, he tried to end his life. He put large blocks of concrete on his chest and legs and laid down on the railway track. "The train came closer and closer but it went on the next track beside me." It would catch up with him later though and he'd become another statistic in America's swelling suicide crisis. Amongst US adults it's the tenth leading cause of death. But it's even more for men, especially in economically depressed rural places like Aberdeen.

I pointed to one of the photos and asked Toseland if he liked Nirvana.

"Oh sure," he said. "That there's Kurt Cobain.... I know him."

Toseland returned to his beer while Killer and I stole a confused look at each other.

"You...*know* him?" I asked, stressing the use of the present tense.

"Uh huh. He comes from Aberdeen."

I decided to move on and to try and draw him into our world instead.

"You ever been to England?"

"Why would I? Anyway, I couldn't if I wanted to. Not allowed to leave the country for a few years, on account of me being a felon and all."

I didn't so much as ask for clarification on that last point as drop my jaw.

"That's right," he said. "I got into one small bar fight. The guy ends up injured [I imagine he killed the man] and I get locked up and now I can't leave the country. And all I did was poke him in the chest."

Toseland then decided to demonstrate the force of the assault, with a series of sharp prods of his hammer-like fingers upon my soft sternum.

"Does that seem fair to you?" he said, pushing me half way back to Bremerton.

"It does not," I said through watering eyes, my torso now resembling swiss cheese.

"America is the best fucking country in the world but if anyone tells you it's free they are fuckin' lying. They lock you up for farting here."

I exchanged another nervous glance with Killer.

"It's all nice freeing people from dictators and all, from like Saddam - wherever the fuck he's hiding - but at the end of the day I'm the cunt that has to pay for it. Everything costs too much, taxes are too high and you have to work your ass off."

In many ways Toseland was like Mark, just a psychotic version of him. For Toseland hard work meant hauling timber from 4am until midnight some days. He used to cut the wood but too many trees had fallen on top of him so now he drove it. He proudly showed us the scars of his labours.

Toseland was an enigma. He would by turns insult us, then flatter us, buy us beers, then rage at us. He swore he'd kill anyone who insulted the USA but lamented its injustices. It was hard to keep up. Above it all, he had a deep hatred for cyclists.

"Yeah cyclists are cock-suckers. You need to see America but you're going too slow. Ditch the bikes, get a truck and see all the national monuments like Mount Rushmore along the way."

I considered saying something like, "Well, actually Thomas, we want to fully throw ourselves into the experience of America and only the openness and pace of a bicycle will reveal the shade and nuance of this cocktailed continent to us, and hopefully we'll learn something of ourselves in the process," but instead I laughed and agreed with him.

"When I'm hauling timber, I'm hauling ass and I don't stop," he continued. "If I see you faggots on the road then I ain't pulling over. You better watch out." He added that he was on the road early the next morning, as if to underline his threat. We decided to leave before it escalated.

Killer and I agreed that, after camping, sliding under real bed sheets was akin to being covered in warm honey and then having it licked off by Christina Aguilera. But we went to sleep with the image of Toseland's furious face still engrained on our minds. For this reason Killer wasn't surprised when he awoke at around 1am thinking he heard Toseland's voice in the back of his consciousness. But when he heard a roar from the parking lot, the sound of something no smaller than a truck being wrestled with, and the blood-curdling declaration: "I'm going to fucking kill someone!" it really hit home.

"Booooone!" he whispered. "Booooone! Toseland's outside… He's found us!"

I sat bolt upright: "WHAT?"

The racket in the car park was getting worse as Toseland remonstrated with the one brave fool who'd told him to keep his voice down. Toseland was audibly much drunker now. We didn't even pause to wonder *why* he might have wanted to find us. As far as we were concerned, he was intent on Limecide.

"What do we do, Killer?! HOW has he found us? We didn't tell him what motel we're in!"

"We're in Aber*deen*," spat Killer. "This is probably the only motel in a 20 mile radius!"

"We didn't even tell him we were staying in a motel!" I said.

Killer's eyes widened. Had Toseland *smelled* us out?

"He's come to kill us Bone."

"He'll just kill you. He liked me. I asked him about dodgeball."

"Baseball."

"Oh yes…"

"It'll be a bloodbath Bone."

Then suddenly there was the thump of a car door, a screech of tyres, and silence. After 10 minutes I worked up the nerve to go to the window and peer out, fully expecting to draw back the curtain to see Toseland's fire-breathing nostrils. He was gone, but something told us it wasn't entirely over.

We feasted and fueled at Denny's the next morning, getting confused over the myriad ways by which you can cook toast and eggs, and at the cheerfulness of the waitresses. "It's so good to see you. I hope you have a *fantastic* day."

"Let's get the hell out of this mad town," Killer said.

The first hill to the south rose up like a mountain. We lowered our heads and churned the pedals, slowly pushing on. And then, there he was. A truck rounded the bend ahead of us and charged down the hill towards us, sped by the weight of two dozen shaved conifers. It let out a mighty blast of its horn and at the last minute veered violently towards us across the highway before moving back. As it passed, we saw the distinctive form of Toseland laughing maniacally behind the wheel before we heard a loud shout of 'faaaaaaaaaaaggottttttttttts'. And with that both he and Aberdeen were, thank fuckily, behind us.

This close escape was also the moment we joined Highway 101, an iconic piece of American infrastructure that we would dance on and off for long stretches of our southerly passage. And with it we had found the first hills of the trip. They were still just preludes in scale for what was to come but they were enough for now. Whilst some of these hills were thick with trees, there were many, many that were clear-cut or stump-covered pastures. The view from the top of each of these extended unnaturally for miles. The loggers had been busy. We laboured up and on the descent temporarily discovered that bringing your feet back over your panniers to stretch out your body gave you the sensation of almost flying like Superman. That was until our bikes started to veer wildly under the lack of control.

We descended into Raymond, sorry, I mean the City of Raymond. Many small settlements are called cities – wide streets, prefab store fronts, trucks piling through the centre – there's even a sign saying city limits and a building called City Hall but all were the size of English villages or small towns. Raymond had a population of less than 3,000. We stopped for a 'frappuccino' served by another

Korean, a woman who had married a serviceman after the war. After I mentioned we had just been in Aberdeen, she proudly told us her city had 17 churches and very little crime.

We camped at Bruceport, overlooking the wide bay. Our evening routine was now becoming well-rehearsed. If there was a fire pit, we'd lay out some logs and start it going with the help of a little secret squirt of meths, always accompanied by a raised finger pressed against the lips, 'shhhh'; promising we'd get better at this camping lark eventually. Then we'd sit on the picnic bench and play endless rounds of Shithead, a card game of simple but perennial enjoyment. The pleasure was intensified by our cards having celebrity faces on each one. We came to know them so well, we no longer spoke in numbers and Kings or Queens but in Brad Pitts, Damon Albarns and Beyonces. The most versatile card in the game was Jude Law and therefore its every deployment was delivered with a triumphal declaration of 'laying down the Law'. And bizarrely (actually, not bizarrely as you will understand when you have learned more about us), we never tired of the joke over the next four months...

The conversations in camp (and on the bikes) then didn't go too deep. Not at the start. I knew Killer better than most but even to me he remained intensely private. His preferred medium of communication was film quotes and impressions, for which he had a freaky ability for both recall and pin-point delivery. A few selected words would bring anyone from Arnie to Homer Simpson to life, joining us around the fire.

Killer had once explained his enthusiasm for these utterances by remarking, 'Why should I try and say in my own words what somebody else has so eloquently expressed?' but this hid a greater truth: if I needed the adventure to control my thoughts, Killer needed it to free his. He struggled with emotional connection so kept the possibility buried. I hoped that by getting out into the world, he would learn how to let it in. Meanwhile, I had learnt to gauge his mood and relay my own by joining in with well-chosen lines. And I was far from protesting this language; being quite partial myself to deflecting sincerity with sarcasm, and finding endless bellyaching enjoyment in Killer's repertoire.

Over the days and weeks, we added to the film and TV quotes lines from the people we encountered on the road - many miles and evening hours were whiled away perfecting the precise way Toseland said 'cocksuckers' or trying to say 'Yarborough' in increasingly convolutedly British ways, until yet more, madder characters entered our lives. It was like it was not just us on the trip, but a growing menagerie, an invisible community that was becoming increasingly real in our heads and which made us very happy (but which would very soon grow beyond our control).

If there was no fire to cook our dinner we'd use the Trangia, a meths-burning cooker renowned the world over for its lightweight ingenuity, where all the parts and pots are stored within each other like a Russian doll but which, in our hands, became a machine seemingly designed primarily for the creation and distribution of soot. It left its mark on most of our possessions, as well as over our hands and faces. We'd cook pasta and then stir in a tin of soup with a stick and maybe eat some bread. Some days we just ate the remains of whatever we had for lunch. We had very little understanding of nutrition or what might constitute a handy meal plan for the road. We had stocked up on expensive bags of 'Trail Mix' at REI, lured by the images of athletic outdoorsmen on the packet and ignoring the voices in our heads that said 'this sure does look a lot like a bag of pricey peanuts' but these only lasted a couple of days, and we indulged in Snickers bars and bottles of Gatorade when we passed a store.

The mornings did little to nudge us towards our five a day - we smeared peanut butter onto bread rolls and washed it down with black instant coffee, adding sugar and cream if we'd stayed at - and raided - a motel recently. This was usually followed by a couple of ibuprofen. My already-thin inflatable sleeping mat was punctured in several places and, despite trying to fix it with bicycle tyre patches, I invariably woke in the night with my back pressed against the freezing ground. But the next morning at Bruceport, the rude awakening was even more severe.

"Some DICKHEAD has stolen our food!" shouted Killer angrily. His fondness for swearing was growing with each new Limey challenge.

I got up and looked around. There were no other campers. Examining closely, we saw scraps of bread on the ground, leading away into the trees. In the revelry of a Law-laying marathon, we had left our food out overnight and this wasn't just stupid, it was dangerous. Signs warned us to seal food away or use the bear-proof cupboards provided in the campgrounds. And James had warned that when you ignored the basic rules, bears can open your tent like a chocolate bar. There were also scratches on Killer's pannier that had been left on the picnic table, as if something was trying to get inside. It might not have been a bear of course, it could have been racoons, but in our minds it was an army of ten trained bears at least, and we weren't going to take such a chance a second time. And the result was that we had just one tin of tuna between us to last to the next town. We ate it hungrily like vagrants.

It was a two and a half hour, 25 mile ride until we finally spied a roadside cafe. We almost wept into our burgers, before ordering a second round. We had cycled through thick, cold fog. Our breath clouded in front of us and we wiped moisture from our fish-juice-infused beards as we cycled, passing through corridors of trees dripping in lichen. It was beautiful but we could barely raise our heads to notice. Crossing 'Bone River' was a temporary spirit lifter but by this time my knee had also developed considerable - and concerning - pain, which demanded all my anxious attention.

Before we left the UK, we had attempted a small marketing push. However, there were really only two media outlets to share our story with and Killer worked for one of them. Regardless, we wrote up a press release and sent it to the other, a large regional weekly newspaper called the Western Gazette. They bit. They called me for more info. I was pretty naive back then, unaware that everything I said was being considered as fodder for the story, and I mentioned in passing that I had crashed a moped in Thailand a few months before. At the time it was pretty scary - I went flying off the road into a drainage ditch, the front of the moped caved in and I had to go to hospital for stitches on my knee. But after a few days of limping I wasn't aware of any lasting damage. I didn't even remember mentioning it to the journalist beyond it being a small inconsequence. The story came out - the opening of the story read:

'A cyclist who regained his fitness after injuring his knee in a motorbike crash has decided to take a 5,000-mile journey by bicycle in aid of a cause close to his heart.'

It wasn't until then that I had even considered the accident might come back to haunt me on the trip. And it wasn't accurate to say I had 'regained my fitness' as it never really existed. Even so, I had been taking more exercise than Killer; something else I must have mentioned.

'I'm not too worried about my fitness. It is Nick I am most worried about.'

After another 15 miles we spied the mighty Columbia River and with it the border between Washington and Oregon. Connecting the two was the extraordinary Astoria Bridge, three miles long and one further feat of tear-inducing endurance. The fog was now so thick that half way along we couldn't see any land on either side; as though cycling in the middle of the ocean. Dead birds - all of them black - that had been smacked down by trucks in the fog, littered the hard shoulder like a Biblical plague. And swerving to avoid them was virtual suicide. The road was so narrow that the traffic that passed us at speed - possibly not even noticing us - would have happily taken off a leg (which I momentarily contemplated as a form of pain relief). I was riding behind Killer and would often see his frame shake as he went over another corvid corpse, signifying my own need to brace for impact. Killer moved further ahead and I saw him a mile in the distance rise up into the sky as the impossible road curved over, like the arc of a roller coaster, to let ships underneath. I followed him, squashing beaks and wings, cursing loudly into the wind and then, finally, descended freely into the City of Astoria. Killer was waiting for me by the Oregon sign and - in a ceremony we would repeat with every new boundary - clapped me into the new state. It felt nothing short of earned. We had covered 200 miles in six days. It was less than the average we had hoped for, and I was in far more pain than I had anticipated, but we were one state down. So far, so not dead.

3. The wild Oregon coast

Do you want to know who you are? Don't ask. Act!
Thomas Jefferson

Almost 200 years to the day before we rolled our bikes out of Seattle, another couple of dashing young men were just beginning training for their own trans-American expedition. Meriwether Lewis and William Clark had been challenged by President Thomas Jefferson to cross the continent until they found the mouth of the river we had just crossed. This was no small undertaking. In 1803 this was Phileas Foggean in its fantasy. Jefferson wanted to know more about the new lands America had just acquired from France, and to claim new territories further west, sticking his flag in the ground before the pesky Limeys could get there (never mind the fact these territories were already occupied by native Americans). Jefferson was hoping they would discover a navigable route from the Missouri to the west coast to take trade by water, but such was the unknown mystery of the frontier, he fully expected them to encounter mammoths.

Jefferson believed that it was impossible for any animal to go extinct, and so he was convinced that every animal that had ever disappeared was just hiding somewhere in the uncharted parts of America, waiting to jump up from behind a Jub Jub tree. They needed to keep an eye out for any woolly proboscideans that might be prowling about. They were to expect them to be about 'six times the size of an elephant'. Oh, and ten-foot-tall lions might also pose a problem, Jefferson added.

Sadly these beasts eluded them - early man had already seen off most of the North American megafauna. But they did find dogs (as we would later, in legion). And as they ran out of food and money to trade with, partly because they spent much of it on bartering for marathon sex sessions with local women, they ended up eating more than 200 dogs. Suddenly our Limey Project diet didn't seem so bad. If I summarised the trip by saying they would freeze, starve, get sick and lost along the way, you might say Lewis and Clark were the Killer and Bone of their day... but in truth they were exceptional. They did encounter those difficulties but they also carried on (well, having the name 'Meriwether' in their ranks must surely have been a daily pick-me-up in itself), and they mapped all number of creatures and plants; plotted mountains (including naming one phallus-like peak, 'Cock Rock') and recorded the native Americans. One tribe they encountered told the expedition that they had already picked up some English from fur traders. Asked what he knew, one tribesman said, with a proud smile on his face, "Son of a bitch!"

When they finally found the ocean near Astoria, their relief was palpable. But by that I mean in a mildly-expressed 19th Century manner of course. Clark noted, "Ocean in view. O! The joy!" in his diary. I think our arrival into Astoria came with a few more expletives. And they didn't have a motel and a hot bath waiting for them, with 100+ cable channels, a fax machine (still a draw in 2003 apparently) and a burger joint next door. Indeed, they had to camp out the winter, stitch their own shoes to survive and then journey home overland in the spring. They would become the most famous explorers in American history. How tragic then that after all this surviving, Clark would take his own life three years later. He had seemingly never been able to settle back into unadventurising. I thought of a sketch by the comedian Stewart Lee; he imagines friends of Neil Armstrong asking him to go for a pint, only for the first man on the moon to point out their trivial ales now hold but few rewards for him. I started to wonder, how would The Limey Project change *us*?

Lewis and Clark's journey is celebrated along the northern Oregon coastline in the form of statues, historic walking routes, visitor attractions, curiously named cafes and kitsch memorabilia. In all these places, it is the Disney-washed triumph of the epic journey that is marked, and not the fact they nearly all contracted syphilis and often seemed to behave like they were on a stag weekend. We were being quite boring in comparison. But at least we banked on the Americans we encountered taking more favourably to us, because of their regard for such adventures.

"Do you think they'll build a statue of us if we survive this trip?" I asked Killer.

"I expect they're working away at the marble as we speak Bone."

Whilst Lewis and Clark had a few months to prepare for their trip, being tutored in botany, astronomy, zoology and meteorology… essentially everything but how to ride a bike, we by contrast were vastly unprepared. One week in and our limbs were aching and our bikes were groaning emphatically under the weight. The pain in my knee continued as we headed south but it became manageable enough for me to hope that I could 'ride it out'. The expedition weight situation, however, had to be addressed immediately. We hosted a ceremonial burning the first night past Astoria to jettison some ballast. We made camp at a place called Circle Creek, which sounded like a romantic Lewisandclarkian folly but was merely a slither of land by the main road, with a long dribble of water circling behind. We needed to get better at planning good places to stop at. I bought wood and a firelighter from the camp store. The label for the firelighter warned in large letters, 'Caution! Flammable!'

"Oh dear. Do you have any that are non-flammable?" I asked the manager.

"Huh? You need them to be flammable! How do you think you… I mean do you… Hell!"

The firelighter even came with instructions. 'Open wrapper and light edge'.

"It's too complicated, I can't fathom it out," I told Killer.

"That's a shame. As I have very little meths to spare, I'm afraid."

On to the fire we cast excess socks, shirts, books and bottles and all the pages from the Lonely Planet guide to the USA that covered the states we would not encounter, shaving pounds where we could. Between these objects and the items left in the hostel in Seattle, we could have probably stocked a whole new Jefferson-style hunt. We also discarded the first ACA map, having victoriously completed it upon arriving at Astoria. I looked into the fire for some time after Killer had retired, defeated by my Shithead skills. I let my mind wander, to gauge where I was at, wanting to see if it veered to dark thoughts before I would have to pull it back into focus. We were a week in. There was still so far to go. We might not find real mammoths but what mysteries and beasts lay ahead of us. And what of the people we had left behind? I shook myself back from that thought and turned in.

We hadn't stayed long in Astoria but it had been enough to stir a feeling of familiarity. There was something about the ramshackle wooden homes next to this huge breath of fresh air from the wild ocean. I'd seen this place before. Cycling south, the feeling intensified when I saw a bay in thick mist and ghostly sea stacks and I let out a cry, "Hey youuuuuuuuu guyyyyysssssssssss." 1980s cult film *The Goonies* was made here. Their house - it turns out - was near our motel and the final scene (spoiler alert) where the pirate ship emerges into a misty bay was the very misty bay we were looking at. The film centres on some youngsters who undertake a mission that many say is impossible and maybe even deadly. They have the chance to turn around many times but they press on. Give up, the young hero Mikey says, and lose everything but keep trying and there's a chance of winning. "Goonies never say die."

One scene involves a car race along a wide stretch of rock-fringed beach. That was Cannon Beach, one of the most photographed places along the coast. The town might have even been a movie set. Sweet shops with multi-coloured facades displayed fantastic machines pulling and stretching sweets, and toy stores with fairy lights illuminating hand-made wooden trikes and toy figures jostled on the main street with bijou eateries blasting the delicious smell of fresh pastries, cinnamon and coffee into the cool morning air, wafting past art galleries and surf shops.

It was one of a number of small towns, like Seaside before it, that gave you the clear impression Oregon was emphatically awesome. Welcoming, relaxed and beautiful. And above all, great for cycling. The coast road had wide, generous shoulders to ride on and it was well signed. There was even a free map distributed by the state authorities to cycling the Oregon coast. Cyclists weren't just accepted, they were encouraged.

The most striking thing about Oregon is its rugged, brutal beauty, and this was appreciated all the more for pedaling through it, at a pace that gave it the attention it deserved. The sea charges in uncontested and smashes against the masonry of millennia. Every bay seems to have a scattering of proud rock-hewn apostles and the cliffs can carry you high up. At times the fog descends like a carpet but then it moves off, through the marine architecture like a spirit and leaves behind it something always unexpectedly magical. Amongst the many things I had been unprepared for on this trip, the majesty of the views and the enjoyability of cycling in Oregon was definitely one of them. Cursed harvest vegetables was another...

The Neahkahnie viewpoint provides an 800 ft high view, down to a bay that sweeps away to the south as if to infinity. It is magnificent. A sign read, 'If sight of sand and sky and sea has given respite from your daily cares, then pause to thank Oswald West'. I was kind of hoping it would rhyme but still, I gave Mr West a hearty cheer. As Governor of Oregon just before the First World War broke out, he'd had the foresight to conserve this natural landscape. From the Columbia River to the California border, 400 miles of shoreline was protected for public use and saved from later development. It was as I contemplated this a truck pulled in, a colossal orange orb balanced on its back. It looked like a house-sized pumpkin. I went to inspect and as I got closer, I realised it was, in fact, a house-sized pumpkin.

"We're taking it to the show," said a small girl.

"The show?" I asked, immediately regretting it.

"The giant pumpkin show."

"Ah. How much does it weigh?"

"Six hundred and sixty six pounds."

I roughly converted that to be around 300 kg, which is equivalent to approximately four well-fed Bones, a massive Pumpkin weight in any language. But there was something oddly familiar about the number she said. What was it? Oh yes, it was the same as that of the fucking antichrist.

"You mean, it weighs…?"

"Yes, 6 - 6 - 6…pounds", the child cackled.

It was the number of the beast and I was soon to feel its evil powers. Killer had set off before me, tired of my insistence on digesting every information display board, of which there were many (flora, fauna, Lewis, Clark, fellow Englander Francis Drake, sunken galleons, buried treasure… oh this was quite the stop). When I eventually followed him, the road descended sharply and I gathered speed. And when the accident came, it came without warning, just a massive explosion of colossal, unnatural, mechanical system failures.

Kafuckbangwallop

I was moving at around 35 mph when the front baggage rack came loose and got caught in the wheel, ripping through several spokes as if they were dried spaghetti and throwing the panniers into the road. Two cars swerved to avoid them and me. I wrestled with the handlebar and brakes to bring the bike to a stop, by now on the wrong side of the road, fully expecting some oncoming traffic to add to the fun. I pulled myself and the bike to the verge and took a long, heavy breath as I looked over the edge of the cliff. The adrenaline was flushed out in a mighty, nervous and exhilarated laugh. Goonies never say die.

I inspected the damage. The loss of spokes had caused the wheel to buckle like a pringle and the hard metal rack had wrapped itself around the front axle like a snake. The only way to ride the fiend again was to wrench the rack off. No easy task. I yanked and pulled, bending the bastard back a few millimeters at time until after half an hour it was free. I then tied the front panniers to the back of my bike to shift the load. I took another breath and then started to roll, wobbly and slowly, down the rest of the hill.

"I was just writing a letter to your parents in my head, announcing your tragic demise," said Killer who'd been waiting a few miles ahead. "It was easier than cycling back up that frickin hill to find you. What happened?"

"I was touched by the fate of the devil's pumpkin, Killer. And I'm afraid I might need your help carrying some of my bags…"

Killer considered the prospect of his burden as I strapped my front panniers to his bike. "Hmmm, maybe I will need to write that letter after all."

The ACA maps suggested there was a bike shop at Manzanita, a few more miles ahead. After crossing another mighty mountain we arrived at said shop to find a cheery note on the door that simply said: "Closed for the Fall and Winter. See ya!"

Whilst Killer contemplated 666 ways in which he would like to cause death to the shop owner, I surveyed the maps. The next shop was in Tillamook, 28 more miles down the road. We could do that, but there was no way to make it that day so we set off for a campsite at Rockaway, halfway between the two. The route curled around the Nehalem Bay, then continued to undulate. At the Cape Arch Tunnel, we hit a large button to activate flashing lights that go on for a short period to tell other road users there are cyclists in the barely-lit passage. I hoped the timer had accounted for people on two wheels travelling as fast as if they were on two feet.

Arriving into Tillamook reminded me of Aberdeen. It had that 'let's stick a few shitty houses either side of the highway and call it a city' feel - but it was still a welcome sight. At the bike store, the wheel was righted, spokes fitted and it only cost me $19. They had no front rack to attach. It looked like that would have to wait another 85 miles until we reached Newport, but at least I was roadworthy again.

"Thank you, thank you!" I said.

We checked into a motel and searched out a beer, chancing what looked like the sort of place Toseland would turn his nose up at for being too gritty.

The owner was an old walrus called Gordon. His moustache curled out like cellos and he had arms like anvils. His patriotism was worn in the flags and mottos behind the bar and his knowledge of the existence of life outside his homeland seemed to be fairly typical of the region.

"Can we get a couple of Buds."

"You got any ID?"

We pulled out our passports and he looked at them in puzzlement.

"Errrr, you got any *US* ID?

It took a while to explain why our British passports indicated that such a possibility was sadly precluded and he eventually gave in, begrudgingly putting down two beers and a bowl of popcorn.

His voice was like gravel stirred into toffee; deep, slow and purposeful. In part we engaged in conversation just so we could hear how low his register could descend and to consume lines for our daily impressions. And he did not disappoint.

"You know the Point Reyes lighthouse? My grandfather built that. He lost an arm. Then he built another lighthouse. He built lighthouses. He only had one arm."

We were unsure where the arm-losing took place in the sequence but the message seemed to be his grandfather was tough, and so therefore was he.

On the TV, it was baseball. The World Series. We asked Gordon to help build on the foundational knowledge that was poked into us in Aberdeen. Despite the name that suggests some sort of involvement beyond the borders, the World Series is competed for exclusively by North American teams, with the winner of the championship then referred to as 'the world champions of baseball'. Naturally, there's not even a whiff of irony. If anything reflected America's view of itself it was this megalomoniker. And this year was extra special, having been contested for 100 years, since 1903. That night, it was the Red Sox vs the Athletics. I tried to determine what was happening but it all still just looked like a field of people in pyjamas under attack from an invisible swarm of bees.

Gordon sensed our confusion at his attempt to enlighten us and put down two fresh beers and a new bowl of popcorn before resigning to stand at the far end of the bar. A man beside us with a black hat and silver-topped cane then leaned in. How had we not noticed him before? "These teams suck anyways. Just enjoy the music," he said, nodding to the stage where a band was setting up. "You're in luck - it's Bill Hagen tonight."

Bill was the singer and lead guitarist. He had shabby jeans, a shirt that had a button missing over his belly and he wore big grubby white sneakers. He was joined on stage by a drummer and a bassist, both with alluring knitted vests.

"Oh goodo," said Killer. "It's the science department of Tillamook High School."

But in reality, they were goddamn bonafide, eye-meltingly brilliant, musical geniuses.

The songs ranged from Muddy Waters to Hendrix to the Stones. Bill would come forward to the table, almost thrusting his guitar in our faces, to demonstrate incredible fingerwork. People have woven silk with less intricacy. And he continued the trick one handed while chugging on his pint before using the glass as a slide to bend his notes. He played behind his back, he pouted like Jagger and did the duck walk. All the while he was smiling and infecting us with an immense enthusiasm.

Our neighbour introduced himself as a friend of the band. He said his name was John.

"You look a lot like the musician Dr John," said Killer.

The man who we then actually started calling Dr John nodded. Perhaps he got this a lot. But he wasn't... was he? He then took us over to the band and I thanked Bill for entertaining us. Bill looked me dead in the eye, hung a hand on my shoulder and said, "Thanks man, that means a lot." He introduced us to his new wife, even pulling photos from his pocket of their recent wedding day. In the photo, Bill wore a suit, hair slicked back, his wife wore a low cut top that showed off a chest the size of two deviled pumpkins.

"Just look at that rack," cheered Bill, and his wife laughed. "Oh Billy."

Killer joined in, trying to emulate the vernacular, "They look like a pair of parked cadillacs."

I waited for the expected punch to the face but Bill and his wife roared and slapped him on the back. Badly-dressed-Bill could not have been happier with his life. We bought the happy couple a beer, settled in to some 'hanging with the band' and decided the next day would be a 'rest day'. Whilst Killer got into a long discussion with Bill over how the bejeezus he played so dexterously, I played pool with Dr John.

"What do you want to get out of this trip?" he asked.

It was a new question to me and the directness caught me off guard, forcing a surprising honesty.

"I'd like to remove some barriers."

Dr John nodded at this. "Sometimes you have to get past the obstacles everyone can see to remove the ones that only you can see."

"Yeah, I guess so," I replied, "And there seems to be a lot that is unseen."

"Indeed. But you are not alone. We all like to think we are uniquely lost in thought but each of our minds is like a constellation and in any one room," he gestured across the bar, "there will be whole galaxies of ideas, hopes, fears and fantasies. It is quite dizzying to try and comprehend the scale of it."

It was a strangely philosophical and lucid exchange for two drunk men in a dive bar.

We set our sights next on Cape Lookout State Park, a densely wooded beachside campground. It was only 12 miles and it was stunning cycling so we continued to take a slow pace; Route 101 having turned inland we had the less direct coast road to ourselves. We passed a toothless guy, tash past his chin, sleeveless leather jacket, astride a kids' bicycle seemingly from the 1950s, complete with handlebar tassels. He gave us the bull sign with his fingers and shouted, "You're doing awesome, fucking awesome!" It was encouraging. I decided to look past the fact he was obviously insane.

At the park, we scrambled down a path through the thick pines and walked on the beach until the sun set. The waves were for once gentle, the sky was cobalt and the sun like a ruby. I skimmed stones into the ocean. Back at camp we started a fire and set up our nests, before we were joined by a cheery ding of a bicycle bell and a volley of "Well hello there" as a fellow cycle tourer approached.

He seemed to be riding some sort of armchair on wheels, low to the ground, sloped back with his hands steering the front wheel from under his knees. With nowhere to hang a pannier, all his kit was piled up like an angry mushroom on a trailer towed behind.

"What even is that?" I asked.

"It's a recumbent, a sit down bicycle," he said proudly.

"It looks bloody ridiculous," whispered Killer.

"It looks bloody comfortable," I said loudly. "How's it on the hills?"

"Well, not so easy. But hey ho."

This guy was blisteringly easy and friendly. Unnaturally so, even by the very welcoming people we had met so far. There was only one explanation.

"Are you from Canada?" I asked.

"Yes, what gave it away?" he laughed, and pointed at the small Canadian flag that hung dutifully from his trailer. I nodded as if that had been my clue and pointed in return to the Union Jacks on our panniers. We hadn't applied them as a force of patriotism but merely to see if it bought us some credit along the way with Anglophiles, of which there seemed to be a plethora.

"You're the first cyclist we've really met since we set off from Seattle ten days ago. I guess it really is the off season," I said.

"Seattle? Ten days? That's… I mean, are you taking it leisurely?"

"Er, yes. That and trying to work out what the hell we are doing."

He came and sat down at our picnic bench, extending a gloved hand of friendship. "I'm Greg. Tell me - how are you getting on?"

And with that, Greg entered The Limey Project roll call. Not the wackiest character we had met. In fact, refreshingly the opposite, but the one we needed to meet. He told us about the route ahead and how to tackle the hills. He told us about these magic energy gels called Gu that act like rocket fuel and gave us two for the next day's ride. And he passed on the secret of a guidebook that cyclists carried along like Bibles. 'Bicycling the Pacific Coast: a complete route guide.' I flicked through his copy in awe - it had long prose passages about the route and what to see, outlines for daily itineraries, elevation profiles, and suggestions for the most scenic camping spots. If the ACA showed the way, this book held your hand as you travelled along it. And, from what I could see, the authors seemed to have a penchant for extending each day's ride with enumerate suggestions for 'side trips', as if cycling the entire seaboard was a little pedestrian for some. This included Greg who had taken such a trip that day, stopping at the, apparently, famous Tillamook Cheese Factory. He laid out a bag of cheese blocks and shared them with us. I put the pan on the fire to boil water while he enlightened us further. All we could offer in return was tea and the rules to the greatest card game ever invented, ever.

Greg was 28, studying for a Masters and while he had a few weeks free, he decided to just cycle south, solo, and then make his way back on the train. He was covering twice the distance we were each day and had all the right kit. I decided very quickly I needed to be 'more Greg' even though he didn't even have a name for his expedition.

"What is the 'Limey Project'?" he asked, spotting the words inked onto Killer's panniers.

"It's this," said Killer, gesturing to the wet tents, the bench overflowing with cooking equipment and food packets.

I stepped in. "So, apparently, the Brits used to get scurvy from the long boat trips over here, so they'd suck on limes to get the Vitamin C. So they got known by the Americans as *Limeys*. And this is our *project*. So…"

Killer gestured again to the bench and tents. "Like I said."

Greg nodded, still confused.

I later discussed his reaction with Killer.

"I wonder if the word limey is not perhaps as mainstream as we may have anticipated."

"Yes, isn't that part of the beauty of it, Bone!"

As we wrote our diaries by the fire, Greg started to pen a letter to his girlfriend, Jessica[1]. "She's the most beautiful girl in the world," he told us dreamily, as if rehearsing a role for a Disney musical. He must have been telling her about the weather we'd been experiencing as it stirred a thought.

"Oh, have you heard about the storm coming?"

"Um, sorry, say what now? Storm?"

---

[1] Dear reader, you'll need to remember all these names for later.

We had assumed these misty, rainy and cold days were just standard bad weather in Oregon but when we'd complained to the good, granite-hewn folk of Tillamook they had laughed.

"You're lucky," Gordon had growled. "Normally by now we have rain so hard it bounces back off the street and hits you square in the face and knocks you over. Why do you think the trees are so fuckin' tall. Huh?"

He spoke as if indignant with the feebleness of the current weather. I later looked this up and found that Tillamook receives around 88 inches of rain a year but on some coastal slopes in Oregon it can reach as much as 200 inches. To put that in perspective, London's pathetic pitter-patter is a mere 23 inches. They don't even know what rain is. And now Oregon's rains weren't just beginning, they were coming in hard.

"Yes, there's a storm moving in," said Greg. "So you had better get ahead of it as you can't really cycle through it. Gonna be a bitch!" Greg looked around as if the Mounties might be about to arrest him for public indecency. When Greg said 'bitch' you knew it was serious.

We waved Greg off. He was going considerably faster than us but something told us we'd see him again. Having purchased the cyclist's Bible at the first shop we saw, we stopped for lunch at one of its recommendations - a wild, wide beach. It was spectacular, and we could easily have passed it by without our new guide. We surveyed the book's pages for what else lay ahead, pausing excitedly on the photos of the scenery we would pass. The book was by a husband and wife team, Tom Kirkendall and Vicky Spring, but the focus of our attention - and affection - was directed mainly at the guy. The sentiment was so great that 'Kirkendall' soon became shorthand for everything that emanated from the book, regardless of who had written it (Sorry Spring!). The first reason for this was the simple pleasure of the sound of it, *Kirkendall.* Just say it now, out loud - it is incredibly satisfying; the contrast of the aggressive first 'K' and the soft, long ending. I thought people with names like that existed only in Jules Verne novels, travelling the globe in 80 days or journeying to the centre of the world. Kirkendall, I suspect, could have achieved both these feats with a skip and a whistle. The second, main, reason was that he appeared every few pages in photos (that presumably Spring was busy taking) that aimed to show the simple daily pleasures of cycle touring but had the added effect of making Kirkendall look heroic, at least in our eyes, and causing him to become the ultimate cycling role model we had been searching for. He strolled amongst the waves after a long day's ride, inspected historic monuments and enjoyed friendly laughs with other cyclists by the side of the road. All of this whilst displaying glorious, granite-hewn calves.

Such effortless ease was a far cry from our start, especially in one regard: Kirkendall seemed to love hills. The book described their approach like a chef listing the specials. Leaving Cape Lookout, it announced, we had two wonderful 900 ft climbs back to back. We prepared our minds and bodies, arming ourselves with Greg's Gu after overly-lengthy discussions as to the optimal time to consume the highly sugared snacks. I favoured three miles before the start of the ascent to give it time to set in, Killer favoured one. It was finger in the air territory. On that day we were also impeded by two things - the first was a coastal fog as translucent as a duvet, which moved in as we passed the alarmingly aptly named Cape Foulweather (I had long given up trying to explain the bizarre coincidences and ironies of this adventure). The second was RVs.

Far from the humble, wobbly caravan of home, in America these 'Recreational Vehicles' have been supersized into total entertainment complexes, with satellite dishes, boats, bikes, and even smaller cars either strapped about them or towed behind. And they all seemed to be heading south, following the sunshine, or perhaps chasing us down. At least we were in agreement with Kirkendall on that one. He wrote: 'Many of these vehicles are rental units, and drivers of these "camping" machines may lack experience in handling them. Ride defensively and try and anticipate the problems these drivers will have when they pass. Most of all, pray…'

We pressed on and made it a little over 40 miles into Lincoln City, hoping for more from the day but it was like someone had turned the lights off. It happened just as we passed a sign indicating the 45th parallel, halfway between the Equator and the North Pole. This otherwise insignificant latitude marker showed we were now on a line with Bordeaux and Venice, and that we still had so much further south to go. The sky shifted from grey to black and with a loud crack the rain came down. Gordon was right, it was quite a thing. We were either reliant on the 'word on the street' for our weather warnings or taken completely by surprise. And most frequently it was very much the latter. As we took shelter in the city library, a similarly-soaked 12 year old boy rushed past me and, seeing the bikes, said loudly, "Man, I do not envy you guys!"

"Where did that come from?" I asked him, pointing to the street-shaped water slide we'd emerged from.

"That's Oregon for you dude."

I was only just getting used to the open, and vocal adults, and now the bloody kids were breaking past my British defences. What was with this robust self-confidence? Earlier that day a girl, perhaps the same age, had complimented me loudly when she saw I had selected her favourite flavour of Gatorade at the store. Message to children: do not speak to strange men with beards who hang out in gas stations and wear lycra to libraries!

With zero communications technology on our person - no phones or computers - libraries were our main connection to back home. Remember this was 2003. At that exact same time, in a Yale dorm room, a young Mark Zuckerberg was writing the code that would change how we communicated forever. But here, on The Limey Project, we kept paper diaries, tried to email home once a fortnight to tell them of the extraordinary number of miles we had achieved (!) and uploaded 50KB (yes, KB!) photos once a month to our ugly website, that as many as a dozen or more of our family and friends were checking. There was no social media and unless we stopped at a motel or chanced on a newspaper, there was very little of any media.

All of this meant conversation was much more abundant between strangers and all ages were actively volleying comments our way. And the 'Where are you headed?" question had now been replaced by a series of more specific questions, to which the answer was always yes. *You heading south? Bit late in the season ain't ya? Have you heard it rains so hard here in Oregon that...* Yes! Yes! Yes!

Anyway, they were all saying 'Oregon' wrong. Idiots. As the Americans had taken it upon themselves to pronounce the herb oregano with the emphasis on the second syllable, we took this as an invitation to apply the same tonal logic to the state name. orEgon. We applied this whenever possible in conversation, simply to see how people would react. And we immediately decided to engineer similar stress shifts for all ensuing state names. Most people just assumed it was a quirk of our limeyness; an ongoing attraction for our hosts.

When we found a motel, the owner delighted in learning of our provenance and called out jubilantly to his wife in the back office.

"Hear that Margey? British!"

His wife came jogging to reception, beaming. "Hey, do you fellows want a cup of tea? I just knew if we got some tea in some British folk would turn up sooner or later and, well, here you are. I mean, that's just great. Let's all drink tea!"

"What a welcome we're getting in orEgon," I chimed.

"You mean Oregon?"

"Yes that's what I said. orEgon."

"How funny. You hear that Margey? Let's see if we have some cake too."

We found ourselves slipping comfortably into catching up with our new favourite cable shows but it was two too many motels in a week. We vowed to camp at Newport the next day no matter the weather. It was 32 miles to the campground but we took it slowly, distracted frequently by the scenery. We occasionally had to stop and just sit by the beach watching the mesmerising ferocity of waves. One such stop - which we would have passed by unknowingly but for Kirkendall - was the Devil's Punchbowl. Killer was not convinced by my eagerness for these extensions to the route but the fact this one had 'devil' in the name won him over. And it was worth it. Imagine a blowhole in a cliff but extend it by a hundred feet, carved out over aeons, then imagine waves smashing into the bowl through a small arch and churning around inside it violently, foaming madly like Satan's cauldron. At high tide, you note your expanding insignificance in the face of mother nature's fury. At low tide, you walk inside the bowl and hope to beelzebub that you have the tide times right.

We eventually made it to Newport. The rain had eased off but apparently it was just a first barrage, the actual storm was right behind it. We had managed just 140 miles in our week in Oregon. Accidents and weather hadn't helped but we needed to get better at this cycling thing, and fast. And even with such little progress we felt exhausted.

The bike shop owner looked and sounded like bartender Gordon. And it turned out his name *was* Gordon. So for ever more, we decided Gordon would just be the name of all gruff but helpful people we would meet on the trip. And there would be a few. To qualify for the sobriquet, all Gordons needed to provide some service to The Limey Project and here in Newport a new front rack was being soldered into place with a low growl.

"What the hell kind of rack was that you had on before? Nah. Piece of crap. I'll fix you up."

It was a thing of beauty and mightily needed. On seeing it, Killer decided not to take any more chances with his own wheel-chopping timebomb and to also switch to the Gordon method. But we'd have to wait until the next day so he could get the part delivered. More delays.

As I waited in the campground for Killer the next day, I saw it as the perfect chance to try and be 'more Greg'. I took a spare stretch of bike chain and tried to open and close the connections with my multi-tool, in anticipation of needing to fix a chain at some point on some lonely stretch of desert. It was impossible. I later told Killer that breaking a chain on the expedition was simply no longer an option. After a campfire and Shithead, two raccoons came and seemingly wanted to dance on their tiptoes beside us. We joined them, the four of us performing a comic dance as if in some sort of Marypoppian montage.

"Did you put some LSD in my tea Killer?"

"No, just some raccoon pheromones."

Eventually the fuzzy foxtrotters got bored and moved off to find people with food. Killer and I then entertained ourselves by jumping up and down to see how high we could leap.

"Do you think maybe we are already cracking, less than two weeks in?" asked Killer.

"Oh, indubitably Killer. Positively absotively."

In truth it was also a distraction from the conversation we needed to have. The night had once again seen a lashing of oceanic rain on to the tents and there was more and bigger to come. The delays due to the accident and rack repairs meant we were now too late to get ahead of the storm and we faced a very simple choice; either sit it out or get a bus a little down the coast. Killer was very clear - we had to get a bus as we couldn't afford to wait. I knew he was right but I hated the idea that less than two weeks into our cross-continental cycle and we would have to get some assistance. It would not be a long bus but the idea clawed at me. Would Lewis and Clark have got a bus? Well they had horses so they were already cheating, right? Those dirty dog-munchers. Were buses really so bad? Or were we failing already in our mammoth mission?

4. California dreamin'

Newport, OR to Fort Bragg, CA

Strength does not come from winning.
Your struggles develop your strengths.
Arnold Schwarzenegger

You meet a very different type of person on the bus than any other form of transport. Our collection of curios as we headed south from Newport resembled the day trip from *One Flew Over the Cuckoo's Nest*; equally odd and loveable. One old man near me was sick on himself in his sleep. He awoke momentarily, looked at the mess on his chest and nodded to himself as if he had been expecting it, then closed his eyes again. Another took it upon himself to point and laugh at random things outside the bus; hilarious observations like a parked car or a traffic light. Behind Killer was an excited, wild haired man with a pencil behind his ear and a notepad in his hand. Sometimes he would note something down and then look at it, highly satisfied. "Oh, that's great, just great!" he'd declare. He saw in Killer an obedient, or rather captured, audience for his life story. He would lean forward occasionally and rest his head beside Killer's, slinging his arm over the seat back and starting every new chapter with an urgent whisper, "Listen man…" When he learnt of our Limey status, he verbally orgasmed and informed Killer he had once sent some of his poetry to a website based in Gloucestershire. Had we been there, he wanted to know. "To the website or the county?", replied Killer, confused. The would-be bard had not heard back from his submission so desperately pressed his scribbled email address into Killer's hand, suggesting a closer geographical presence might help his cause. "You *do* mean closer to the website?" Killer suggested. The man nodded as if to say, 'well obviously'. Killer promised to 'see what he could do' and then pretended to sleep.

The journey was around three hours, covering 150 miles (which would have taken several months by bike at the recent rate of travel). We passed a menu of enticingly named destinations - Humbug Mountain, Sea Gulch, Whisky Run, Face Rock, Devil's Elbow… and a number of other destinations that provided even more than just marvellous monikers: the much photographed Heceta Lighthouse; the elevator-accessed Sea Lion Caves; and the vast expanse of sand dunes at Jessie M Honeyman State Park. As if I even needed being told, Kirkendall confirmed it in the guide book… 'This section of the coast includes some of the best scenery.'

I was really struggling with the decision to take a bus but Kirkendall had other, more comforting words too. 'Cyclists on the Oregon coast should carry waterproof gear for protection against long, rainy days.…' and at this time of year 'expect heavy rains… and strong winds…' And that was on good days - any lingering remorse was flushed away when the sky turned black and fat waves of rain lapped at the bus windows creating the feeling of travelling in a submarine forty fathoms down. The impeccable driver, bow-tied and hatted as if driving Miss Daisy, and desperate for conversation, then started providing a regular running commentary through the speaker system on the weather we were getting ahead of. He informed us that the waves on the coast had built to 20 ft, with twisters spotted near Newport. "Good job you're all shootin' south," he said, as if answering the demons in my head.

We made camp at Gold Beach where, the next morning, we awoke to the coldest morning yet. Winter was on its way. But there was to be no warming coffee until we spotted a gas station, as we were out of cooking fuel.

"I'm surprised we lasted this long, to be honest," said Killer, with no sense of guilt.

As we cycled on, we discovered the wonders of the Oregon coast that we thought we had passed were still in full abundance. In fact, even more so; if I had read ahead a little, I would have seen that Kirkendall preludes this section of Oregon by saying 'Saving the best for last…', picking out details of the 'breathtaking scenery'. And he was right. Coves and wide beaches, graceful arches, sheer cliffs, and the sea peppered with defiant stacks as the huge Pacific waves rolled through. And this could all of course be enjoyed simply from the road, which occasionally rose and twisted, adding new perspectives and vantage points.

We squeezed the last juices from Oregon but our sights were firmly set on California, approximately 45 miles down the road. California then; the third largest of the states and the most populated. The scent of its industry and enterprise was already creeping into our nostrils and pulling us ahead. It is the home of lush vineyards, wide beaches, cosmopological cities, ancient forests and, importantly, our hero Arnold Schwarzenegger, who had coincidentally become the State Governor - or 'The Governator' as the media had it - just the day before. He had already started to manifest himself in our daily impressions, and now these became more animated as we got closer to his kingdom. His call to urge us on took the form of a bastardised version of the final scene from *Predator*. "Come onnnnnnn, do it, do it. I'm here Governating. Come on Bone & Killer. Do itttttttttttttttttttt."

But at times it felt like even this close border would elude us, as we stopped regularly to take in the wild beauty. At Pistol River, we almost exploded with excitement when we recognised two large rock stacks in the bay beside us as being precisely the same as backdropping a photo of Kirkendall in the guidebook. I scrambled up a steep verge to locate the exact same view and then snapped Killer as he rode past.

"Send it to Kirkendallllllll," roared Killer.

Kirkendall was by now legend to us, and his wise words were read aloud at night by the fire. He gave the scenery and sites a heroic soundtrack and if ever there was a question as to what lay ahead - even with the excellent ACA maps on display in my handlebar bag - we would declare in a confident west coast accent, "Let's see Kirkendall's rowt", before reaching for 'the book'. And the success of Pistol River had us flicking ahead to images from Santa Barbara, Los Angeles and more, and we excitedly plotted a full series recreating the iconic imagery of Kirkendall.

"We'll gather all our homages into a leather-bound compendium and then send it to him, to honour him," suggested Killer.

We stopped for a lunch break at the book's next recommendation, Natural Bridges, where the tide rushed under an impossibly perched rock arch. We took turns to pose for photos, standing on a hidden promontory, to make it look like we were grasping at the long grass at the top of the cliff, pulling ourselves away from the long fall below. It soon became apparent we were being watched - an old woman with a lipstick stained cigarette holder in a gloved hand was taking in the spectacle, leaning on the side of her vintage Buick. She called over to us, "Where are you guys from? France?"

France? FRANCE? Why did people find it so hard? Were the French noted for their fake-cliff-climbing-photo sensitivities? Or - like Mark felt - did they typify a European less aligned to the American values than the English-speaking English? Either way, you would have thought that speaking good English, and with strong English accents, that more people would guess we were, indeed, English. But it never seemed to be people's first guess. Australian, Kiwi, South African, German... but rarely English. When I told her our real patrimony, she, like all the others, became discombobulatingly buoyant.

"Well I must congratulate you on Prince William - he's just great."

"Oh, not another loon, please," said Killer, barely lowering his volume.

She went on. Apparently half of her lineage had been beheaded French aristocrats. And the other half? But of course...

"My ancestors on the other side actually came over on the Mayflower..." To hear this was like getting a full house at American Bullshit Bingo. It was shorthand for saying you're as American as John Bundy (don't worry, we'll get there...), and to hear someone utter this with genuine intent, claiming their ancestor just happened to be one of the intrepid 102 passengers that made the famed 1620 crossing (minus the 32 that died on the trip), was just delicious. I said 'wow' a few times, which she took to me being impressed by her story, but was actually an appreciation for her telling it.

"I heard most of the Mayflower passengers were pimps and gangsters," offered Killer.

The woman replaced her cigarette and returned to her car.

"What is it about us that causes these people to migrate into our personal space, Bone?" Killer then asked.

"We're British, for God's sake," I said. "We are the most unwelcoming nation on the planet. We've imposed ourselves on countless peoples since the invention of the invasion. Why is everyone so anxious to spend time with us?"

Well, being British seemed to be a big part of it. The enthusiasm for the UK - like this woman and Yarborough before her - was a frequent conversation point with the Americans. Even Toseland had emphasised his surname to evidence a British ancestry. "Apparently there's a town with my name on it somewhere over there," he'd said wistfully, before returning to the subject of guns. And the day before, inside a supermarket (in the ass-chafe-cream aisle to be precise), a man approached us, with his wife nervously in tow. He'd seen the small flags stuck to our panniers on the bikes outside.

"Hey, are you guys the British cyclists? Well I'll be... My name is Guthrie. My family comes from Aberdeen in Scotland. What do you say to that?"

Killer and I looked at each other and stuttered for a while. Not getting the response he'd hoped for, he tried a different tack, pulling his wife into the frame.

"Her name's Bowman. What do you say about that?" He was now drooling in hope. "*Bowman.* I mean, they must have been archers for the Queen's army or something, right?"

His eyes pleaded now and I gave in.

"Yes, no doubt about it," I said. "It's not a common name 'Bowman' and from what I know that name does indeed come from the royal archers."

He slapped me on the shoulder. "I knew it. KNEW it!" His wife was also smiling and they walked away as he kept repeating Bowman to himself in a British accent, making himself sound more like Mr Bean on every attempt.

That same day, outside Subway, (really, if you ever needed us it was a safe bet we'd be in a supermarket, Subway or gas station) a man in his late 20s asked us how he could say 'I love you' in English.

"In English??" I replied, looking even more sabotaged by insanity than Toseland did when I asked him to explain a 'home run'.

"Yeah you know, *old* English. I know it in other languages but I am going to England soon and want to know how to say it when I meet women, like, *authentically.*"

We stood there in confused silence while he slathered in anticipation.

"Well that *is* how you say 'I love you' in English," I offered eventually.

He nodded, but that wasn't the answer he'd been hoping for. "You mean I don't need to say, like, *thee* or *thou*?"

I shook my head slowly. We all looked at each other awkwardly and started to back away simultaneously.

"I guess it's just the same language, just with a different accent," he said, trying to conclude proceedings.

"Yeah, try that…"

But perhaps it was also the historical connection that the Britishisms represented that they were reaching for. When they asked us of England, it set off the same far-off, romantic gaze that befalls me if I try to contemplate the age of a mountain. The landscape we cycled through was impressively hewn over millennia but the people - the ones that lived here now - had only been here for a few centuries. Even an oak tree lives longer than most towns have existed on the west coast. The historical sites and the official, signposted 'historical districts' of the towns we passed through were obviously revered and well maintained, but they betrayed an exclusive interest in their recent history, detailing their discovery by white explorers and settlers, and those that followed them. Everything else - the traditional, native culture - was left in the past, indeed it was someone else's past. When people we met tried to look further than Lewis and Clark, they looked beyond their shores to an English boat or a French guillotine, as if being American meant being from somewhere else, and bringing the best of that together to create a new land, afresh. I wondered, then, when did the drawbridge go up to more outsiders. When did they start to say, 'We are American enough now'?

Killer roused me from my mind-wandering. "In fairness to that old bat, you do look French, it must be the tricolor beard."

I shrugged in gallic resignation.

A few more miles and we hit Harris Beach. In warm sunshine we poked in rock pools and strolled amongst the expansive sands. We stopped next at Brookings, a hip little timber clad town where the air smelt of artisan coffee and middle class muffins and people seemed at ease. It felt like a teaser for what lay ahead and after just a few more miles we were there - the Californian state line.

I went ahead and took my turn to clap Killer in.

"Come onnnnnnn, do it, do ittttttttt."

"I'm coming, Arnie. I'm bloody doing it!!"

We jumped across the state line backward and forward excitedly and we carved our names amongst the many others on to the back of the wooden sign. 'And then Bone & Killer entered California'. It felt like a mental boundary had been crossed also. We *were* doing it. It was another 15 miles to Crescent City. Could we do that too? Could we make our first 60-mile day? "DO ITTTTTTTTT," shouted Arnie. A feat that had at one time felt impossible, suddenly felt like the start of something. We made it, and to treat ourselves, we feasted at Pizza Hut before warm baths and bed in a motel.

"Mmmm, warm honey," cooed Killer.

As we rolled out the next day, we passed fleets of old Mustangs and Chevrolets, and even a familiar-looking Buick, in town for a classic car rally. We paused after a few miles to take on some strategically-timed sugary snacks then headed up into the Crescent City Hills - three mahoosive peaks in succession, with the largest being 1,200 ft.

Some wise words from Kirkendall on this: 'When loaded with another 20 to 30 pounds, a lightweight bike behaves like a lopsided tortoise on level ground, and what it does on the uphills defies description.' Well, let me at least try to define it for you. Cycling uphill with a bike the weight of a small horse is not easy. In the early days, we'd sometimes shift down to what we thought were a couple of gears above the lowest, to give us some room to retreat to when desperation struck, only to find we were already as low as we could go when the gradient got even tougher. The discovery was always accompanied by a sad little whine and we'd then have to swerve across the width of the road in 'switchbacks' to try and reduce the angle of assent, even if by just a couple of degrees. As we laboured, time seemed to slow, and the mind would unconsciously count every pedal stroke like it was a day in solitary. After a while you'd hear yourself saying, '576, 577, 578...'. Or you'd just look desperately at your cycle computer or the mileage markers beside the road and will the tenths of miles to tick along, wondering for the love of God

WHY has it NOT clicked over for HOURS. At least, that was our early experience.

Whilst the physical exertion took place, a mental one was also playing out; you push with your legs and you pull with your head. As you do, both get fitter. Overcoming the physical challenge was making the mind stronger, and this in turn was making the physical journey easier. A stronger mind is also a clearer one, a mind that is easier to navigate. This is helpful because as you journey down the road you spend a lot of time travelling *inside* your mind; reflecting on the past, considering the future. For the time being, it was enjoyable to take this inner exploration. In fact, I was drawn to it. I wanted to know what was really in there, and with every hill I felt I was getting closer to discovering it.

So we pushed and we pulled and we reached the top of the third Crescent City peak, the burn and breathlessness of the ardour surprising me in its happy endorphinising. The view from the last summit was sensational, and was even carpeted in forest, and from there we were able to roll down for miles, all the way to the Trees of Mystery and the start of California's slatheringly anticipated Redwood forests.

How to describe the Trees of Mystery? To say it is the world's largest collection of redwood carvings doesn't quite do justice to the infinite bizarreness of some of the shapes and creations that scatter this visitor attraction. But impressive it is - most notably because giant (and I mean GIANT - almost 50 ft tall) fully-painted carvings of American folk hero / lumberjack Paul Bunyan and his blue ox, Babe, greet you as you approach on US 101. Beyond their current role as parking lot MCs, the original duo were known for their legendary superhuman labours, which grew in grandness (as did their reported size) every time their mythic tales were passed around the American loggers. Their strength and size are credited with the creation of several American landscapes, landmarks and natural wonders, with one tale suggesting the 10,000 lakes of Minnesota were formed by their footprints.

So we gave Paul and Babe a respectful wave but paused only for a coffee, knowing the very best of the still-living trees lay a few miles ahead. Once back in the saddle, though, any further progress for the day was impeded by Killer's flagrant disregard for the rules of sod's law.

"Well Bone, it looks like we definitely got ahead of that weather…" he beamed, putting his sunglasses on.

I shook my head. "Don't you know never to say that out loud. Bugger HQ is now on the case and the clouds are being rerouted as we speak."

Killer scoffed but I could almost see the wispy white tendrils in the blue sky put a finger to their ear as if receiving an urgent radio command.

"Come in Cumuli. Please divert immediately to Klamath. It seems we have a case of a young man with an overconfident meteorological observation we need to set straight. Use full force, repeat, full force."

"On our way chief."

In my head, the clouds then made a sort of World War Two fighter plane noise as they banked to come round and gather in formation. Sure enough, within 20 minutes, the squadron was overhead, and the payload delivered.

It felt like every millimetre of the annual allocation of precipitation was pouring down on us. We couldn't see the road ahead and the water was even seeping through our coats. "Sure, you don't let air through but for rain the doors are wide open. Twat," I cursed the jacket aloud. We tried to press on but Killer pointed out that there was, in fact, no point. Despite my protests, I knew he was right, and after just two more miles - a weasley total of 20 for the day - we pulled in at the next campsite.

We sheltered in the games room and played table tennis with a bouncy ball and no bats and then, to kill further time, we took the opportunity to recraft our faces - shaving off parts of our beards to leave goatees, to try and cheer ourselves and to try and look more

'American'. They looked rubbish but that only added to our enjoyment. When the rain finally paused, we pitched up. We lit a fire, warmed some beans and then retired to bed. We would try again the next day.

And yet the day was far from through... What happens next kickstarted an exponentially increasingly surreal nature to our exploits. As if doing impressions of people we'd met or recreating famous lines from our heroes (we love you Arnie) wasn't enough to conjure up a Limey caravan, at Klamath a completely new character appeared; a companion that would allow us to bring the full luxury of our overactive imaginations into our daily realities. Subconsciously, we must have known that we needed a third friend to share our adventure with.

It started with a rustle outside the tents.

"Hello, who's there?" I asked.

A deep, friendly and booming voice replied calmly, "Oh hello. Not to worry, it's just me - Brian the Bear."

Coincidentally, or perhaps due to a limited imagination, he sounded a lot like the barrelous, bearded actor Brian Blessed.

"Don't worry, not going to eat you - just out for a shit in the woods, passing by."

I can't recall who started the voice but to know that would be to insultingly remove some of Brian's reality. And indeed that is the last time I will suggest in this book that he was anything other than what he truly is, a real talking bear. The California state mascot - that we'd seen standing proud on the state flag - was now *our* mascot. Yes, he only spoke to us (initially...) while we were tucked away in our separate tents and we never actually saw him (initially...), but he was very quickly one of the most important, comforting constants of our trip. That first night we learnt he was actually from a little further north but was 'on a little trip' south to get away as he was having a few domestic issues that he didn't want to bore us with. He also told us how thrilled he was about our trip, which he strangely seemed to know all the details about, without ever having been told.

"The great danger in life is to not take the adventure," he said, dancing happily between flatulent commentary and philosophy. "That's something I am only just learning."

We spoke just briefly that night but we felt an instant connection to our new friend, and he had lit up a grey day. And of course, we did not realise then that he would be visiting us again regularly for the next 4,000 miles (and the next 16 years).

The rain awoke the scent of the forests. A cool, sweet smell of pine needles and bark enveloped us as we de-tented in the morning. As was typical by now, we started out in fleeces and long trousers and gradually removed layers as the day warmed. Most days would see one of us declare 'shirtage' at some point, and we'd pull over to remove our jackets and fleeces. On the rare day (until we got further south), we'd also experience a shout of 'shortage' and the bottom of our trousers would be zipped off.

The route took us off the main highway and along a short winding parallel road, into the Prairie Creek Redwoods State Park and we were soon riding through the most spectacular scenery. We cycled slowly and just gazed in awe at the towering trees, with sunlight breaking through their branches.

A VW campervan parked up beside one tree gave a sense of the scale, looking like a matchbox toy car under a Christmas tree. They were not only frickin massive but they also filled you with an immense feeling of calm. There wasn't a sound but for a faint breeze whistling in our wheels. Naturally, this did not last long though. Killer leant in his saddle, broke wind and a clutch of birds broke from cover to take flight.

"Extraordinary," said Killer.

We stopped to walk on a suggested route to the appropriately named 'Big Tree', which measured an almighty 304 ft tall, 21.6 ft wide, and 68 feet around the trunk. The story continues underground where the roots reach out for around 100 ft. And its age was colossal, estimated at 1,500 years. It had been around for the fall of the Roman empire, the entirety of the reign of the Aztecs and was already a thousand years old when America was 'discovered'. Few living things have experienced more than the redwood. Most remarkably, Big Tree was just the 15th biggest of its kind, the largest being over 370 ft tall. And all of this from a cone the size of an olive. The scale of it all was breathtaking, and they extended in every direction.

The smaller pines, that were assembled between the redwoods, were dripping with mosses and lichens; a testament to the purity of the air and the extent of rain and fog this area receives. Every cloud eh... And the forest floor was carpeted in lush, fat ferns, taller than any man (apart perhaps Bunyan). They very wisely call this part of California 'The Redwood Kingdom'.

But these trees only survive through the protection of these parks, like lions in the Serengeti. Prior to the arrival of Europeans, about one half of the United States land area was forest. Then 300 million acres were cleared for farm and living land, making places like Aberdeen rich in the process. The American naturalist John Muir said that 100 years before we had passed through, the Redwood range had extended from Oregon to Santa Cruz, in a band some ten miles wide and that 'between every two pine trees there is a door to a new way of life'. It is true, being amongst trees changes the mind. We walked off the path and got swallowed up by nature. I felt my spirit being cleansed, but also chastened. I was both in awe of what was around me and in mourning for what was no more.

At Orick we'd expected to find a town but instead found endless yards selling redwood carvings, and shockingly bad ones at that. Some you actually had to squint at to work out what they were.

"I think this one is called 'chainsaw accident'," I remarked to Killer.

We did find one restaurant and inside met a family who had come together to remember a loved one who had died recently of cancer and who had loved these trees. They were appreciative of our fundraising efforts and we felt humbled.

It was here also, over a bowl of warming soup, that we met Dr John again, only in a slightly different physical form. To keep track of all the colourful characters we were meeting, it was clear we needed some sort of system to categorise the curiosities according to their key characteristics. And so it was we created the Limepedia. The first entry was, of course, Gordon; the name given to every angry but kindly older man that performed essential services for the benefit of the expedition. And now here we had Dr John, named after the first incarnation as the sage of Tillamook, and now applied to all men who came briefly into our lives, imparted some key useful information like a prescription, then pissed off without us even knowing their real names. To our minds, they were all the same person, like every new Dr Who. As well as Gordon and Dr John, other categories of Americans would reveal themselves along the road. And to record them all accurately in the Limepedia, every appearance took on, as a surname, the name of the town where we had met them.

Dr John Orick stood proud, bulging in his tight cycling shorts. It seemed so alien to us to be so on show, but he looked so liberated. Hands on hips, groin thrust forward, it was clear he did not give one shit about people's thoughts. He was a tall, middle aged man and his bike looked lived in. He was headed south to San Diego, the same way as us. But there was one part of the route he said we had to either taxi or bus. Just for the love of god, whatever we do, no matter the circumstances, he said, please do not cycle in Los Angeles.

"You wanna die? Listen guys, I gone and done me 4,000 miles on that there bike but I'll be *damned* if I'm going to cycle through LA. Forget gangs and guns, it's the cars that'll get you."

It was still around 900 miles down the road and already we were being warned of Los Angeles. Fast, frantic freeways and a

100% guaranteed road death awaited us, apparently. And as it turns out, he was right to warn us.

We learnt John had built up a biotech company then sold it. His bike ride was to help him think about what to do next and there is nothing quite like a bike ride to let the mind run free, I was discovering. John said he liked the sound of Killer's job as a writer. I told him I did too. I had also been thinking about what happens next.

We found him again - or rather he found us - the next day at Acata, as we enjoyed tuna sandwiches in the square. Acata is a quaint university town with some attractive Victorian buildings, and a population of around 25,000 but according to Dr John Orick all you really need to know is that it's the 'dope growing capital of California'. He waved his arm across the sweep of the park, as if in demonstration as he took a long, happy inhalation through his nostrils. By the central fountain old and young hippies were growing their hair, juggling and playing the didgeridoo and bongos like it was 1969. "Damn good hash," John concluded.

An old man approached us, with a noticeable limp, to enquire about our journeys. The man was enthusiastic but significantly struggling over each word. The left side of his face was almost immobile. It was clear what he had suffered - there was no need to ask. Or at least we thought so. For John, it was obvious that we should *actually* all discuss it very loudly.

"What is that - a STROKE?" he shouted at the man.

The man tried to talk but no words came out this time. He held up four fingers.

"Four? FOUR strokes? Ok, yeah, my uncle had one of those."

We were dumbfounded but the old man seemed strangely comforted by the interest and happy to go on, and so the two men chatted away in half shouts, half stumbled whispers and sign language. John even pointed at the smoking students with a chuckle.

"I think I know a guy who can help with the pain," he bellowed.

The old man laughed too.

So this was just Americans being American then, talking loudly about personal things to strangers. If everyone was following the same rulebook, I was learning, then there was nothing odd at all. In fact, the odd thing was that us finding this all odd was now odd itself. Odd! I was starting to see Americans as they understood themselves, and the lesson from Dr John was clear: say whatever the fuck you want, wherever you want, to whoever you want. Is that what it meant to be the land of the free?

It was Columbus Day, a national holiday to celebrate someone sailing to the Bahamas 500 years ago. The American search for history was able to even bridge this into a patriotic fervor. And, appropriately, we had camped the night before at a State Park called Patriot's Point. Many families were taking advantage of the day off so the campsite was busy but it was also beautiful, with an elevated view from a 350 ft sandstone cliff through pine trees to a stretch of golden bay below. We lit a fire, cooked noodles and then settled in for the games. Normally, little could detract us from our enjoyment of the simple pleasure of a multitude of rounds of Shithead. But to mark the national holiday, and in honour of our location, we decided to divert our attention momentarily into inventing a new game called, wait for it, Patriot Points.

The rules were not simple. You start by asking your opponent a question about American history. The other player (of the only two people who have ever played this) then has to - having first thanked his opponent for the question - give a considered and intelligent answer, the sort a true patriot might give. The first player then gives a detailed critique of the response, based not just on factual accuracy but also delivery and passion for America, before finally assigning a score out of five. A large amount of the pleasure came from consuming time - of which we had a surplus - in the extensive rounds of answering and answer-critiquing. Oh, but this was just half the game… These points can then be traded in for Patriot missiles (heroes of the American war broadcasting at that time) to help the patriotic search for Saddam Hussein. Now, you weren't expecting that were you. In this second phase of the game, the assembled mess on the campsite picnic table becomes the battered ruins of Baghdad and Basra. You must send your missiles into the rubble to seek out the deposed dictator. Here, again, is time to indulge.

"Well, I am sending my first strike into the area of dirty pans. It was well known Saddam never enjoyed doing the washing up so it is likely he would have hidden himself away there."

An air strike is then mimed and it is revealed whether or not the strike was successful, Battleships-style. The game concludes when the first strike finds its target.

"This is goddamn brilliant, Bone. It's going to make us millions."

"Yes, any patriot worth his spangles is going to want this playful and intriguingly complicated nonsense in their lives," I agreed.

"Well, I think it's fucking genius," shouted Brian the bear, taking us by sweary surprise. I hadn't noticed him in the darkness but it was very comforting to hear him again. He also visited us again the next night at a campsite in Eureka and, well, many many nights after that. I tried to determine if there was a pattern to his popping up; was it in moments of us experiencing extreme, happy delirium or a need for comfort? But there was no rule. He spoke when he wanted to speak. At Patriot's Point he told us the truth of his relationship problems with his wife - he told us he had finally admitted that he was gay. He said he had been nervous about coming out to the traditionally conservative bear community, but felt utterly liberated from sharing his truth with us. We told him not to worry about the old bears, he's in California now.

"Well I decided that if I couldn't come out to two gay men then who could I?"

Killer looked across at me as if to ask if we should correct him. I shook my head.

"Just leave it," I whispered. "If it helps him."

Brian said he was looking forward to letting his fur down when we got to San Francisco but for now, he seemed to be content to search for food scraps in the campsites we stopped in. He was having a tough time finding said food though as you are constantly reminded in these remote campsites to lock your food way in bear cupboards and remain in your tents if you hear bears approaching in case they should choose to eat you. Thankfully, we didn't need to worry about that. When your best friend is a bear, there's very little chance of being attacked by one. But there was one thing still niggling at me.

"Is it a bit weird that Brian, who has lived all his life in the USA, has a British RADA-tinted accent?" I asked Killer.

"Hmm, I think it's best not to question things too much Bone. If you pull at that thread, the whole thing could unravel."

From Eureka, the path found a couple of diversions away from the now heavily trafficked US 101, with a long stretch taking us through flat, open farmlands, with just a few rolling hills. We passed run down shacks and cow sheds that looked for all the world like the farms of our home in Dorset. Then onto quiet winding lanes where an eagle flew just six feet away from me. We camped beside more Redwoods at the 'Avenue of the Giants', gazing at night at the giant black shadows. Then onwards, pressing against the wind and some twisted tricks of perspective. There were times when it looked like we were going downhill only for us to come to an abrupt halt if we didn't pedal hard.

The days were finally displaying the famous California sunshine but winter was taking hold, so nights and mornings were now, excuse me, fucking freezing. Between the weather and hills we could never take in enough bodily fuel. We gorged on granola bars, Snickers, Baby Ruth chocolates (in honour of the Goonies), Subways and burgers - anything we could find at the trusty gas station - but it seemed not even that could match the calorie burning going on. We made it to a campsite just past Garberville, a giant G marking our location on the side of the hill, and collapsed onto the trusty picnic bench. We'd covered almost 250 miles since leaving Newport around a week before, plus the bus, making it over 400 actual miles and yet, somehow, someone else we knew had covered the whole distance in the same time without any assistance.

A guy with a thick moustache and a silver sweep of hair rolled up to the next camping spot on his fully laden touring bike, before strolling over to us. He spoke slowly, with a Californian coolness and sashayed in the shortest of pink shorts. He seemed to know instantly who we were, addressing us by our names. We were excited. Had our fame already reached the retired pornstar community? But no, even better than that.

"Hi, I'm with the guy that gave you the Gu," he offered meaningfully.

The happiness of our reaction surprised even ourselves. "What? You're with Greg? Greg's here? WHERE?"

We didn't even pause to consider what sort of mocking conversation about our naivety of Gu must have been exchanged for this man to use that as evidence of his having heard about us. We were too thrilled to see the trusty (ridiculous-looking) recumbent slide into sight. With a ding of his bell, Greg pitched in.

"Gentlemen. Well, we meet again."

We had already decided that if we were to see Greg we wouldn't mention the bus but it was almost impossible that we could have leapfrogged him so athletically.

He smiled, "You're making good time. Or did you, perhaps, maybe..."

"Yes, yes, a small bus assisted us" I confessed, and then tried to limit our embarrassment. "But only around 100 miles."

"Yes, just 100," echoed Killer quickly.

We appeared to have made an impression on Greg as when he got closer he saw our shaped goatee beards and forlornly stroked his own stubbly face, untouched since we last saw him.

"Oh, you, you, er, shaved?"

Or perhaps he was trying to emulate the man behind the moustache, Steve, who was heading home to Santa Cruz. They'd met along the road and formed a team. Steve spoke deliberately, often taking long pauses through his sentences, which had the effect of infusing each word with a sense of philosophy. As we relaxed into the evening, he looked meditatively at his steaming mug of tea, then turned to me.

"You know, they do say... the second harvest... of Darjeeling... is the best."

He then took a sip and nodded to himself, satisfied with the taste of his wisdom. He went on to tell us of the mysterious Green Flash. "A wonderful, magical, mystical thing that - do you know what [grabs my arm meaningfully] - just happens to be true." The conditions have to be just right, he said, and you have to be looking at just the right time. Blink and you'll miss it. But just before the sun goes down below the horizon, a shot of green flashes out. He'd only seen it once, but he just wanted us to know it was there. He nodded again.

I had hoped for more sagacity but it seemed Steve had used up his quota.

"I always wanted to go to England," he remarked. "I've got a cousin in France."

Greg and Steve did a convincing impression of an old married couple, as they passed and chopped vegetables to cook together.

"Where's the kale, Greg?"

"Oh yes, here's the kale, Steve."

"What the fuck is kale?" Killer asked loudly, wondering how they were surviving on so little instant noodleage.

In fact, Greg and Steve seemed to operate as if one being, so we started to refer to them, in private, simply as one word too, Greve. And we very much liked Greve. We agreed to meet up again with them / him / it the next night.

"See you on the other side, gentlemen," said Greve setting off the next morning, with a ring of his bell in punctuation. *Ding ding.*

The 'other side' referred to crossing the infamously, bastardly, dastardly, rascally Leggett Hill; the highest point on the entire west coast cycle. We'd seen its devilish 2,000 ft profile approaching in the book and each sighting brought with it a fit of nervous giggles.

I prepared with a cocktail of Gatorade and PowerBars, Killer laced himself with chocolates and No Fear energy drinks, such was our immense confidence in our abilities. Kirkendall advised us to dismiss the rumours that cyclists' gravestones and discarded panniers line the hill, and whilst we didn't trust such guarantees from demi-gods, unfathomably, he was right. Helped by a warm sun and chatting, singing and quoting the characters we had met (including Greve, 'You know, [pant] they do say [wheeze] the second harvest [strange, pained sound I have never even heard before] of Darjeeling…'), we reached the top. Without even stopping. I felt like Rocky at the top of the steps of the Philadelphia Monument and raised both fists as if I had pugiled my way there. Little did we know we would have many, many much harder rides to come, but ticking this one off gave us another boost of confidence. We were no longer totally faking it.

Before Leggett, we had turned off US 101 and on to famed Highway 1. The traffic was lighter but the road was also narrower, with little or no shoulder in places so switchbacking was no longer an option, as traffic could approach from any side at any time. But coming down, this wasn't a problem. Fully laden bikes are like hauling bricks going up but take off like rockets coming down. We sped through narrow, winding roads until it levelled out at the base of another climb. We paused to enjoy our sandwiches - tuna and avocado, and seasoned with 'Krazy Mixed-up Salt' (an American way of saying salt with herbs).

Ding ding. "Gentlemen!" We momentarily rejoiced in the thought we had overtaken Greve but the suggestion was just met with laughter. They had simply stopped to refuel much earlier than the hill and they weren't stopping again.

"Let's go Steve, my legs are warm."

As I watched Greg start to ascend the hill, I was mesmerised by his apparent anti-gravity armchair. How could he wheel himself up these hills when sitting back? And yet there he went, on his Gu-powered pedalo. It then dawned on me that actual cyclists would not have sat down for a heavy lunch right at the bottom of a large hill. Still some work to do then, I thought as I reached for another sandwich. Indeed, I later discovered that cyclists call Leggett Hill 'Killer Mountain', not just because of a general unwelcoming attitude but precisely because of the false sense of victory you feel before the punch of realisation hits when you see there is another, steeper peak to climb.

We dug in and chipped away. Over the top and we were back on the coast, with a deep blue ocean rolling through sea stacks, which poked out of the water like dragon's teeth. At Westport, we found our friends, sitting with cold beers ready for us. But after the brief pause, there was still another 12 miles to go, and that actually *was* tough. The road dipped in and out of coves, a thick fog rolled in and it grew dark as Greve slipped out of sight, but we made it, albeit utterly exhausted, eventually to MacKerricher State Park.

After we ate together, Greg went in search of beer and returned almost an hour later, drunk. *Ding ding.* He crashed his recumbent into a tree and rolled out.

"Gentlemen, I got distracted BUT I bring treats. Sopapillas!"

He had found a bar, got talking, then got drinking and left with a bag of sweet Mexican donuts and a business card of a stripper. It seemed that being 'more Greg' was taking a very different tack. We played cards and made fun of each other like old friends. A

German cycling couple - Mikhail and Anke - camping nearby joined in too. It was like a night out at the local pub but all within the staggering beauty of the national park. Behind the dunes, waves pounded a black sand beach where, on the right day, there were seals and whales to see. There was a lake, set back from the beach, wetlands and forest to explore. And by virtue of arriving on a bicycle - you only had to pay $2 to camp here. Well done California, well done.

We waved off our friends the next day. And I mean friends. You form fast but lasting bonds when cycling. We had our own sights set on staying another night and just nipping the next day to the nearby town of Fort Bragg to re-stock and re-lax before the final push to San Francisco. And as we were in Arnie-land, the destination felt appropriate: a scene in *Predator* sees our hero getting incensed when he finds the skinned bodies of some Special Ops men in the jungle of Mexico. "I knew these men - green berets out of Fort Bragg. Now what the HELL were they doing HERE?" (I write the words as they are spelt, but of course in Arnie language they sounded more like 'Wad de heyalllll were zay doing heyerrrrrrr,' (of course, with a huge amount of Austrian-flavoured emphasis on 'heyalll'). In the film, Arnie almost spits out the line in animated anger. We, of course, had tried to do his performance justice with our own imitations whenever we saw the mileage sign for Fort Bragg beside the road, volleying it back and forth in increasing hysteria. The fact that the Fort Bragg he referred to was another place entirely, in North Carolina, mattered not to us. If there was a chance to shout out Arnie lines, we took them.

Another reason for the pause here was to patch ourselves - and the expeditionary equipment - up. Both my knees were crying for a break - the initial delirious agony as we crossed into Oregon had subsided, leaving a rumbling pain that pulsed periodically, as if warning further trouble was ahead. A day of ease was called for. In addition, our clothes reeked and, coming as no surprise to me, I had the shits. This was possibly related to the fact we rarely cleaned our cooking pans with more than a wet finger and because our water was sourced, without inquisition, from any tap we could find - from public bathrooms, besides outbuildings and from random faucets beside the road. It is also quite possible - in hindsight - that I needed more kale in my diet.

The irony was that I was almost too filthy to wash - when I tried to use the toilet in the campground, a parent from a group of visiting school kids stopped me.

"Oh I'm sorry sir, we don't like strange men using the restroom while the children are in there." Great, there goes another pair of boxers.

In town we laundried, internetted and groceried. I also purchased a new sleeping mat. Damn this trip was getting expensive. In a hardware store we nearly purchased a camping lantern to extend our Shithead playing hours but were put off by the advertised 'romantic atmosphere' it generated. However, we did spy a much needed battery charger. The store worker was a girl of about our age, not particularly attractive but she didn't need to be. The sight of lipstick and makeup had us as giddy as sailors on shore leave. Hormones racing. She tapped her fake nails suggestively on the charger while she checked the price. I felt drops of sweat form on my brow.

"Remember, it's not far to San Francisco, my Bone," whispered Killer, reading my mind. We were looking forward to some bars, some nightlife, and perhaps meeting some people other than sweaty, lycra-clad, bearded cyclists.

Back at the campground, I walked along the beach. The surf was strong, the sun low. It was a warm Friday evening and families were walking their dogs, kids playing in the waves. As the sun went down, they gradually all peeled away and left just me. I sat there, watching the seabirds and the colours of the sunset swim over the Pacific. It was peaceful. It was perfect. And we really had come a long way since the bus. I had one of those moments, those rare and precious moments where you have a big smile on your face and you feel total contentment. If everything went to shit when we started heading into the desert, I thought, at least right then I felt total happiness. And just as the sun dipped below the horizon, I thought I saw something, a line, a flash, something green perhaps, and then it was gone.

5. Going to San Francisco

Every time I see an adult on a bicycle,
I no longer fear for the future of the human race.
H G Wells

People often asked me what the 'garth' bit referred to in our band name, Stonegarth. "Not Garth Brooks, right? That's weird." No, no. In fact, the 'Stone' bit didn't even refer to me. The name was just a happy accident, like (and these are genuine examples we discovered in America) Sgt Paul Paulos who worked for St Paul's Police department, the TV meteorologist Storm Field and the Nascar driver Scott Speed. Stonegarth was actually the first house Killer had lived in in Sherborne, and the band was formed by him and his brother. Given my omnipresence at Killer's abode, I was at first given the honorary title of 'manager', designing a logo, making T-shirts, whipping up some local buzz amongst our half dozen friends... and then imposed myself further on the 'group' when I started making up lyrics for some of Killer's melodies. It was the night that I improvised the lyrics to 'The Utah Light Blues' that cemented my status as leading a new wave of songwriting mastery. The opening line was thus, 'I knew this chick up in *U*-tah, she had this thing about the *gui*-tar...' Beyond my obvious abilities, Killer was a bonafide, raw and unquestionable talent. One night, I watched as he listened to a whole Pearl Jam album, then nod to himself and play it back on the guitar, having just learned it in his head with one listen. Acting, writing, music, being grumpy to strangers... just four of the things Killer excelled at. And it was my genuine hope that this trip would help give him the focus to take at least one of those to an extraordinary height. I was particularly hoping he would choose the last talent.

The debut Stonegarth album was called 'Travels through UTville' (and you can listen to the whole thing on Spotify). The 'Ut' part of the title referring to the simple noise Killer, his brother and I would make many dozen times a day. With varied tone and stress, it could be whispered, barked or chewed over to mean anything from, 'Another pint?' to 'Let's go' or even 'I forgot to apply my Vaseline today and my ass is frickin killing me.' It can mean the start of something, or even the end of something. A line in the song 'What Ut Means' explains it simply: 'It can mean anything you please.'

And this meaning was both actual and emotional. Killer felt he was successfully managing to keep all his emotions deeply buried inside himself, but when you knew him well, you might find that his subtly nuanced delivery of a single 'Ut' would betray more meaning than any sonata or Sinatra could in a whole hour.

Stonegarth was of course loaded onto both of our MP3 players. Forget iPods, our expedition was powered by rechargeable AA batteries, and our music machines took four each. The Archos Jukebox looked and weighed like a small house brick. In fact, it might have served better in that role. It had a small grey digital display with fat, raised buttons to navigate what was stored within it. Given how long the charge was and how infrequently we passed powerpoints, listening to music was always reserved for the days when riding was tough; for the hills, the long desert days or just the days when you needed to distract the body from pain and exhaustion. On the lighter days, I tuned in to Jack Johnson, Tenacious D and Gomez but when my knee was in full blazing fury, only the grunge and metal that Killer had introduced me to would do; Alter Bridge, Creed and Mastodon.

The bricks would reside in the back pocket of our cycling shirts and over the weeks we would become so accustomed to the finding of our tunes that we could locate the right song on the right album by the right artist just by memorising the blind sequence of buttons, applied with one hand behind our backs. Often I would just let the music come on at random though, and it often appeared like a soundtrack. As I cycled south from Fort Bragg, I heard Tears for Fears tell me 'Everybody wants to rule the world.'

It was now just around 200 miles further to San Francisco. We decided to take the journey easily, spread over five days, so we could arrive just ahead of the weekend and enjoy some of that famous San Fran flower-powered fun. But even with shorter distances, they would still prove to be long, hard days in the saddle. Indeed, we soon discovered this was to be the most physically challenging section of the Pacific coast, seriously testing our tired limbs and aching joints, but continuing to pay us back in further unforgettable scenery.

The cliffs were high and fringed again with sea stacks, which seemed to be alive, shifting under the weight of thousands of birds. The sea shimmered in the bright sunshine. Every few miles were inlets, river valleys or just sudden, deep gulches that required hard pedaling to climb out of. These appeared to gain in frequency and steepness as the miles went on. It was a constant cycle of flicking from near top gear to come down them to first gear to go up, again and again and again, up and down, up and down in exhaustive Sisyphean repetition.

On some ascents, where the road was carved into near 500 ft cliffs, I would occasionally hear Killer shout out, "Damn you Kirkendaaaaaaaall," his voice trailing off into the wind like Ahab crying at the white whale, as if our hero had personally chiselled this coast with his monstrous hands just so its contours could add colour to his guide book. But even the man-mountain confessed to this section being tough, saying in the book this ride is 'long and demanding'. Up one ascent, we saw a sign warning, 'Narrow, winding road for next 21 miles'. When the road is twisting and cars are speeding, narrow is not a comforting width and 21 miles is an extremely long way. We put our heads down, gritted our teeth.

But for every demanding climb there was another outstanding view. We passed Russian Gulch, Jughandle and Van Damme State Park. In our excitement, we hoped the latter had been named after the kickboxing 'muscles from Brussels', but alas it was after the 'ferry-man of San Fran', a rich businessman who'd bought up this vast tract of Eden before it became part of the expansive and brilliant California State Park network (more on that anon). Within it, you can find a pygmy forest, where poor soil has created a marshy ecosystem of stunted cypress and pine trees and rhododendrons. A natural bonsai garden, where trees a century old stand at waist height and you can walk about growling like a giant Paul Bunyan. Or, at least, some people can.

Route 1 is certainly quieter than 101 but with no shoulders to the road, the trusty mirror was getting constant and often panicked, or rather sweary, use. The first day out of Fort Bragg was particularly expletified as hundreds of people returned, nay raced, south to the cities of the Bay Area after a weekend in the country. The cars themselves had changed too. The four wheel drive pickups of Oregon were now family saloons and sports cars; their windows open, tunes blasting out, California dreamin'. One car had two bikes strapped to the roof, the bikes had their saddles removed.

"Look, Bone, some savages have stolen their seats," cried Killer.

"Or, perhaps," I replied, "maybe they just don't have asses."

Most cars rolled by but at Jenner, as we paused before another monstrous gulch to admire the view across the wide Russian River valley, a car approaching uphill slowed as it neared. The passenger wound the window down. It looked like he had something important to say. We craned our ears to the expected wind-borne wisdom.

"NICE COCK!" came the shout, and they drove on.

Killer and I looked at each other. 'Did he just…?' Yes, we nodded to each other. We looked down to check ourselves, that nothing had somehow fallen out. Nope. "I guess we'll just have to take it as a compliment," I suggested. We tried to imagine the conversation that must have taken place in the car in the preceding moments.

"Slow down, I'm going to shout something at these losers on bikes."

"Oh yeah, cool, what are you going to say?"

"I dunno, something great is going to come to me, I just know it."

…

"I'll drop you at the bus stop."

Without the 101 rolling through, the towns also became more distinct and had more character. Old, wooden-slatted buildings, artisan coffee houses, organic food markets. At Mendocino, a quaint New England style town perched on the cliffs, we stopped for coffee and muffins. And at Elk, we were approached by a wild-eyed local who lived part of the year in Thailand, growing and selling marijuana, and who insisted on giving us detailed directions to his beach hut on Koh Samui, "in case we ever decided to pop by."

Between the two towns, the scenery shifted to the pastoral; rich grazing lands, flocks of sheep and herds of cattle, and the occasional wide cattle grid, that required lining up precisely and hitting confidently at speed. A sense of our southerly progression was also confirmed in the dry, brown grass that spilled over these hills. And as the days heated up, vultures wheeled hopefully above our heads.

We made it to Manchester State Beach the first night south of Fort Bragg though, where we found five miles of gentle sandy shore. There was no energy left to explore but the sun was warm and we stretched out our mattresses in the long grass and lay there on our backs.

"Is there anything fluffier than a cloud?" asked Killer, demonstrating his feeling of utter relaxation by quoting a favourite scene from *Scrubs*.

"If there is," I returned on cue, "I don't want to know about it."

There was always a feeling of contentment arriving at the day's destination; cycling round, spotting a quiet site and then making camp. Within minutes of the tents going up, or the mats being laid out, any strange patch of earth, any wilderness, anywhere, could feel like home.

The only other campers we saw were two American guys, slightly younger than us, cycling as far as San Fran, having taken their bikes north up to the state border on the bus to start. Instead of panniers, they towed small trailers behind them.

"It's convenient to throw all your SHIT in, but they are sons of BITCHES to drag behind you when you are trying to get your ASS out of these valleys."

Greve, they were not. However, they did share one piece of useful information with us. They were churning out 70 mile days, inhaling energy bars throughout the day. And apparently this was where we were going wrong.

"You dudes are really hauling ass," I said, trying to speak in words they would appreciate.

"Yeah," one replied poetically.

"What do you do for lunch each day?"

He looked at me angrily. "LUNCH?"

I nodded, a little embarrassed.

"Listen buddy - lunch is everything that you shove into your mouth from breakfast to dinner. It's all lunch. Everything is lunch. Lunch is everything. THERE IS NO LUNCH."

"Maybe he's onto something there," I said to Killer later from my tent, when I had recovered.

"You mean, there's a better way to get more miles in each day than stopping for a leisurely, perfectly seasoned, tuna sandwich atop a viewpoint when the sun is at its zenith?" he replied.

"He may be right", chipped in Brian, known for his species' grazing dietary habits, and adding a valuable third perspective, "but just remember - they do seem a liiiiiiittle weird."

We all agreed to take their advice with a pinch of Krazy Salt but to revisit our refuelling approach when past San Fran, when we'd have longer warmer days and would need to increase our southerly speed to make up for our dwindling purses.

We camped next at Stillwater Cove Beach and then it was on to Bodega Dunes State Park. As we approached the park, the swirling wind blew through the vents in my helmet, creating a breathy whistle that sounded for all the world like the song 'The long and winding road'. The irony was too heavy but I found that if I changed the angle of my head I could control the pitch of the sound. And so it was that I took on the wind on my terms, twitching my head from side to side to change notes, playing out the theme to Baywatch. *Some people stand in the darkness, Afraid to step into the light.*

We sat shirtless in the warmth of the park camp and, over lunch, wrote up the adventures of the past few weeks for the magazine article. There was still lunch. Then we headed into the town of Bodega Bay. We found an office that offered internet access - at $20 for an hour it was extortion but we had no choice if we were to meet the print deadline. We sat together, me reading out our story aloud as Killer typed it up and sent it. The road was still battling with us but already we felt so much stronger than our laughable early efforts. Flicking back in our diaries to prepare the piece, we had read and laughed at the 'sheer tortuous hell' of the early climbs, which were like hillocks compared to the current terrain, and would look like mere speed bumps when lined up against what was to come.

As we went to pay, the ladies in the office said they had heard us mention we were raising money for cancer research and so waived the fee. Further fortune awaited us outside. The owner of a nearby shop had seen our bikes and came to say hello. He pressed a firm hand into ours.

"David Love," he stated.

It sounded like a command to worship Hasselhoff (already on board, buddy), but he pointed at his name badge.

"What a great name", I told him, unable to hide my joy. He shrugged casually and held his hands up as if he got told that everyday. He was tall and athletic, with a big bouffant of luxurious hair that he combed back with spread fingers to emphasise key parts of his speech. He spoke loudly and confidently, his hips were thrust forward, accentuating the shortness of his tennis shorts.

He told us his shop was called 'Candy & Kites' - it sold candy, and kites. Most importantly, it sold a type of candy named salt water taffy. He presented us with a paper bag of the soft multi-coloured sweets and told us the story of how, many years ago, a taffy maker (what the hell is taffy, is it toffee? If it's toffee then just call it toffee, whoever heard of taffy, I mean…), sorry, a taffy maker was making her delicious taffy, when a big wave splashed up and covered her lovely delicious special taffy. She cried out because they were ruined, but a kindly man passing by tasted one and told her they were delicious, asking her the recipe for this new magical salty taffy. It was a nice story but the taffy tasted a little crappy. We waited until the next grand comb of his hair, then spat them into our hands and dropped them by our feet.

All the talk of our adventure got David Love reminiscing about his own.

"Oh yes, the open road. I used to cycle tour, back in the day. Just throw some stuff together on to the bike. Take off." He gestured down the road we'd just come from then let out a small chuckle. "Well huh, there was one time I met this…"

He tilted his eyes to the heavens as if a picture of his youth was marked upon it, and laughed again before returning his gaze to us.

"Well you don't need to know about her. Anyway…"

I instantly imagined a series of cycling related porno films, every one of them beginning with David Love - possibly also involving fellow short shorts fan, Steve - getting an unfortunate flat tyre outside a bored housewife's secluded bungalow. "Excuse me, I need a pump." Hmmm, maybe it was more *Carry On Cycling*.

He pressed more taffies into our hands and waved us off. Huge generalisation, I know, but we really liked these Californians. We'd recently been passing trucks with canoes tied to the roof, cars with bikes strapped to the back (most of which did have saddles). These Californians, at least in the north and central parts of the state, seemed to lead a fairly active and healthy outdoor life. And everyone we met was genuine, helpful, open and kind. They seemed cool, cultured and connected to nature. We were quickly coming to very much like, dare I say, *love*, these Americans.

"Thank you David Love!" we both said in unison, as if he was their elected representative. If only.

One reason for the proclivity of outdoorsitude here is the abundance of protected nature areas to explore. The California State Parks system boasts more than 290 State Parks, Beaches, Recreation areas and Reserves, ranging from just a few acres to the 586,000 acre Anza-Borrego State Park in the Colorado Desert. (We hoped to pass through that behemoth in a month's time, all going well). To find a cheap spot to pitch a tent, eat and wash, every day, and in such idyllic locations, is one of the highlights of cycling the US coast. And all the wonders were appreciated even more fully for the slower pace and quiet peace that cycling affords. I read in 'the book' that Kirkendall and Spring had started to write their guides to share their knowledge and inspire more people to get out and explore nature. And when people are more connected, they said, 'then more people can help protect these sacred places from exploitation'. Amen to that.

But this also required funding and the incredible parks system was under threat from a lack of sufficient state backing. It was clear they needed to be supported, at all costs. This included the next park in our sights, Samuel P Taylor State Park, the last public camp before San Francisco. Its 2,700 acres of redwood and grassland was bought up by the eponymous gold rush industrialist and is now free for anyone to enjoy. To get there, we had to pass the two large bays that cut deeply into the coastline. The route turned inland to bypass Estro Americano Bay, then skirted along Tomales Bay, where the expansive views of nature offered a display of thousands of birds, as well as seals. Oh, the views. There were fewer hills but those we did find sapped the energy due to the heat of the day. The climate can vary by as much as 20 degrees from the coast to just a few miles inland.

We moved at speed. We enjoyed the hard push to Point Reyes at 33 miles, where we took a break to admire Gordon's grandfather's handiwork on the lighthouse.

"It looks wonky," offered Killer.

It was here - near this very bay - that in 1579, during his three-year circumnavigation of the world, the English sailor, Sir Francis Drake - later also famed for his role in defeating the Spanish Armada - had landed and claimed California for the Crown. That was back in the good ol' days when all you had to do was step ashore in any place they had worse guns than you and say, "Yeah, lovely, I'll take it." So much has changed. Drake was more than just an explorer or sailor though - he was also known as a privateer and a pirate. They were all much the same thing back then, on the lawless high seas. The English saw it as their right - perhaps even obligation - to establish some order, and to do so by any means.

Drake was not alone in all this, of course. He was a contemporary of Sherborne local Sir Walter Raleigh. No doubt, the two men discussed the charms of our small Dorset market town - and ways to get rich - whilst smoking Raleigh's tobacco and enjoying some light pillaging. Four years after Drake completed his circumnavigation, Queen Elizabeth granted Raleigh a Royal Charter, authorising him to explore, colonise and rule any 'remote, heathen and barbarous lands, countries and territories, not actually possessed of any Christian Prince or inhabited by Christian People', in return for one-fifth of all the gold and silver that might be mined there. This led him to establish a colony in what is now North Carolina (which is ironically now over 70% Christian). In fact, whilst Drake landed first - near Point Reyes - it was Raleigh's work on the east coast that set the course for the English colonisation of North America.

In all of this, Drake and Raleigh's expeditions made them incredibly wealthy. Drake himself captured so much gold and silver - mainly by seizing Spanish ships - that he could never carry all of it home, and his exploits gave birth to the very legend of buried treasure. People still follow Drake's clues to try and find some of his haul near the spot we were standing on. But despite fame and fortune, both men met unfortunate ends - Drake died of dysentery while attempting to seize Puerto Rico, and Raleigh was beheaded by Queen Elizabeth's successor, James I. It is said that Raleigh called out to his executioner - in standard Sherbornular gusto - to get the job done, saying, "Strike, man, strike!" His wife then carried his embalmed head around with her in a velvet bag, until her own death 29 years later.

Remarkably, all this juicy history was untold by the displays at the Point Reyes Information Centre. Also missing there or anywhere you found the Drake or Raleigh names was their connecton to the slave trade. Both men had been on slaving expeditions and Raleigh even kept slaves amongst his household servants, according to an extraordinary 'fashion' made popular by his wife. Only in 2020 did Raleigh's role in the history of slavery start to be truly scrutinised more publicly, and only now have I learned about it myself. The global shift in understanding modern day oppression (and we were to witness open, racist discrimintion further down the Limey road) that was instigated by Black Lives Matter even reached sleepy Sherborne, where some people voiced their anger at Raleigh's statue outside the Abbey. It is said history is written by the victors, but that doesn't mean we can't write a new future, inspired by those voices that have not yet been heard.

The Information Centre at Point Reyes did, however, provide a feast of facts on the flora and fauna we had been seeing at a distance, and I learned the area around us was home to several hundred different species of birds, including stilts and sandpipers, woodpeckers and wood warblers, waxwings and wagtails.

We also learnt about the unique geology of this place, astride the San Andreas Fault. But I wanted to know more. Naturally, Kirkendall had a suggested 'side trip' for this stop, on both bike and foot. 'If the scenery weren't enough of a distraction here then there are plenty of trails to lure you off your bike.' "How are you doing all this?" we had previously cried out, but now I felt strong and I insisted to Killer that we take inspiration from our fellow Englanders and explore. I wanted to see the history that predates even the Mayflower or the Golden Hind. Killer's initial reaction was to suggest he'd quite like to carry *my* head around in a velvet bag, but we set off. We took a quiet bike path that led us closer to the coast, where you could see the actual fault line and its tectonic elements exposed. We peered into a motionless crack in the earth, somehow expecting something to happen. Was it too much to ask for an eerie creek and a puff of smoke? It was strange to come face to face with the thing that Californians live in fear of and that has already caused so much devastation. It was strange that it was so calm there, just the light chorus of birdsong. It was quite moving. That is, until another sound bellowed out.

"Come on Bone. Let's go. The fault's not working today."

Having followed Sir Francis Drake Boulevard, we set up at Samuel P Taylor, camping one last time in the shade of the glorious giant redwoods. One tree behind us had a large gap you could walk through so we set up the camera and took photos of ourselves pretending to pull each other out of the trunk. To us, with little but Shithead and conversations with our ursine imaginations to entertain us each evening, it was hilarious. As we did this, a curious young man approached us to enquire of our activity.

"Are you birding?" he asked.

"Sorry?"

"Birding. Bird watching…?"

"Yes," said Killer, still enveloped in tree. "I thought I saw a parrot in the tree so went to investigate. Turns out it was just a peacock."

I went to shake the guy's hand by means of offering an apology. He introduced himself as Diony. He had binoculars slung around his neck, a keen smile and thick glasses like jam jars. He was short, wore oddly mismatched clothes and twitched like a nervous robin. He'd cycled over from Oakland, on the other side of San Francisco Bay, to see the birds we had been reading about at Point Reyes. His bike was held together with tape and he had old buckets tied on to the back instead of panniers. He was the sort of guy you imagine got picked on in school, because no one understood what a precious soul he was. Indeed, he was the sort of wonderfully unique quirky treasure to whom you just wanted to say, "Sit down and tell me eeeeverything." He asked us to do two things. "Please go and eat burritos in the Mission District when you're in San Francisco. And also - please have a most wonderful time on your journey." Sadly he had to get exploring before the sun went down. With a click of his heels, he looked at us brightly and simply stated, "OK, I'm going to go birding now." And off he flew.

We were left forcing ourselves to appreciate the unique flavours of David Love's salt water taffy, until Killer turned the package around and looked at the label with some alarm.

"Bone, it says here the taffies are no longer made with accidental splashes of sea water, but with deliberately salted mineral water. What is this fakery? I don't know how to proceed."

We headed out the next morning, first along a wooded cycle path and then back on to Highway 1 as it snaked through small towns; Lagunitas, Fairfax, Larkspur, Sausalito and Marin City. Along the way we saw one thing in abundance - cyclists. It felt like a homecoming, finding our 'people'. They drifted to the shops on their bikes or headed out as team day-trippers; enjoying the countless possibilities of marked cycle routes. Some rode in file in matching team jerseys, some sat casually outside quaint coffee shops, waving at us as we passed. It was a place where carefree happiness - and, yeah, perhaps the well off - lived. It was a place I wanted to live.

Another reason for all the cyclists was that we were in Marin County, home to many of the people and places that shaped the sport of mountain biking since the first informal, and now-legendary, races down Mt Tamalpais, which lay just a few miles from our path. In the 70s and 80s, as the races became more popular, entrepreneurs and bike makers collaborated to innovate the perfect frame until the modern mountain bike was forged. Amidst this explosion of new businesses, Marin Bikes - which made our own bikes, the Marin Muirwoods - was founded in 1986. Our bikes took their names from a glorious pocket of protected woodland we were passing through, named after John Muir. And being here, after nearly 1,000 miles of use, it was a chance to reflect on the bikes we had selected for this expedition. We liked them, sure, and it was energising to consider they were named after one of the greatest environmental philosophers - 'on a mission to save the American soul from the total surrender to materialism' - but were they the best choice?

Every bike has its purpose, and small changes in design can reorientate its practicality entirely. From speedy racers, to upright shoppers, foldables and cargo pullers, there are a myriad of bike designs, all based on very specific intentions. And the form of each of my previous bikes had fitted their function. My first bike was an Apple. I got it for my fifth birthday. Bright red with matching cream-coloured chain guard, saddle and handlebars. It was my one new possession in a youth of hand-me-downs. I sat on it proudly with my big mop of primary school hair in clothes not yet my size. After that I had my brother's old Grifter. Bolder, as I was now older, with a chunky frame in black and blue. It had three gears, coloured for their difficulty, not numbered. "You never got all the way up the hill in red gear?" my brother asked. "I did," I replied. I didn't. The local mechanic, Mike the Bike, would fix our bikes and Mum would pay him in cakes. One summer holiday we cycled as the whole family around the marshes by my grandmother's house in Kent and we sang loudly when it rained. Some of my happiest memories have been on a bike. When I was 13 I got a mountain bike. I invited everyone to come and see it. We'd head out after school and fly down the grass hills.

The Muirwood came next. And it had not been sketched out with any cross-continental desires. In our naivety we had gone along with the first bikes recommended to us in the shop - a bike shop that sold mainly mountain bikes. They had never catered for tourers but were eager to help out. Muirwoods were a kind of modified compact mountain bike frame marketed to urban commuters (we later learned). They were sturdy and comfortable, yes, but have smaller wheels (meaning you pedal more for each mile covered), and smaller frames (hence our occasional heel clipping of the panniers) than specialised touring bikes. And they have straight handlebars, rather than the dropped bars, which would allow for many more possible hand placement options, ensuring you can vary your muscle use and don't get numb fingers (which we did on occasion). They are also more upright, meaning you do get to enjoy more of the view, but you travel slower as your torso pushes against the wind. With hundreds of bicycle geometries for every occasion it seemed extraordinary that we had ended up with bikes for couriers.

I turned to Killer. "Do you think anyone else has ever attempted to cycle across a continent on such a contraption?"

Killer laughed. Then he laughed some more.

But at least they were somewhat more practical than used on earlier challenges. I had read in my trusty 130-years-out-of-date cycling book that the first ride to John o' Groats (leaving from London not Land's End) took place in 1873, with riders racing the 800 mile route on Penny Farthings. They tumbled over hedges and flipped over cart tracks, and yet they covered the distance in 14 days, considerably quicker than our current progress. Although, I reminded myself, we didn't set off on a race, but an adventure.

The idea for such an adventure had not just come from famed explorers like Slavomir but also from family. I grew up surrounded by incredible stories, and felt encouraged to add my own to the canon. In the 1960s my dad had spent a short time in the Merchant Navy, and at the same time my mum had travelled overland from the UK to India with University friends - they were shot at by the Khyber Pass but survived to dance on stage for Indira Gandhi (actually, Mum fell through the stage but that's for another book...). My two grandfathers were decorated for bravery in the Second World War; in the air for the Battle of Britain and on the ground for being the very first Allied soldier in to liberate Belgium. My grandmother was brought up in India when it was the jewel of the British Empire, going to school on an elephant and playing with Princes of the Raj. Her father had - one hundred years before The Limey Project - travelled around southern India in a Rolls Royce with a Maharaja, writing up his discoveries in a book called *In Kerala*. There's a copy of the book in the British Library. There's another copy in my parents' glass-fronted bookcase; the one where the special books live, to be revered, untroubled by the dust of time. For years, the book sat there twinkling at me, almost staring. 'One day my own adventure will sit on that shelf', I resolved.

After around 30 miles, including several wrong turns as we navigated the Marin headlands, we arrived at the Golden Gate Bridge lookout. Or at least, we thought we had arrived there. For days, the usual thick coastal fogs had been ominously absent, but we seemed to have found them all hiding in the one place we had hoped for good weather. In front of us was a wall of swirling white. Bugger.

"Are you sure this is it?" queried Killer.

"Er...."

"The guide book promised me a majestic view across the world's most wonderful bridge to the city beyond. A once in a lifetime unforgettable experience, it said. And this looks a lot like *cloud*."

"But I thought you liked clouds," I offered.

"Just the fluffy ones, Bone."

But then, it started to peak out; first the very tops of the red towers appeared in a break in the swirling fog, then a whole tower, before it was once again consumed. It was short lived but we saw it, calling us. Perhaps it was dangerous not to wait but we were too excited to get to the city. And we'd learnt well by now that sometimes mental barriers - like passing our first 1,000 miles - can take on physical forms. If we could make it through the clouds, we would celebrate in America's most liberal city, liberally. Very liberally.

***

In 1906, an earthquake and fire destroyed three quarters of San Francisco. More than 3,000 people died and 300,000 people were made homeless. That little crack in the earth we cycled past had ripped the city apart like a rag doll. Shaking was felt from Oregon to LA and out to Nevada. Remarkably the city was rebuilt in just nine years, such is the spirit of progress here. As the rich eyed up where to put their new houses, they looked beyond the rubble to a previously untouched area south east of the iconic Golden Gate Bridge called Pacific Heights. They covered it in neat wooden-clad homes and mansions, perhaps hoping that one day the houses would be split up into flats, and that people would move there to show their friends they were successful because they lived in Pacific Heights and that these people would also speak funny and eat weird food, but that they would also be conveniently located for a couple of passing travellers to drop by as they headed south. I guess what I'm saying is, if there had been no major earthquake 100 years ago, I might never have tasted 'Extra sour traditional English sourdough muffins' and thereby learned a new way of using the word 'traditional'.

Our host was Sebastian Harrison, a fellow Englander but now turned native.

"What even is sourdough?" I asked him.

"I don't know. Perhaps it's just... *sour... dough.*"

Harrison was a stock analyst and subscribed to Trout Monthly. He lived with this girlfriend and they ate artichokes together. And muffins.

He was a few years ahead of us at school. Killer had got a few addresses of former pupils who now resided in the States and who were eminently more successful and embracing of adulthood than we were, and Harrison had returned Killer's inquiry with an invitation to stay. I had never met him and Killer only vaguely remembered him but Harrison had recognised the call of the 'old boys network'. If only the call had been met by another fellow pupil, a year older than us, Chris Martin of Coldplay. It seemed that band was doing slightly better than Stonegarth. On Harrison's wall there was a long school photo of about 600 boys. It was strange to see myself there, on this stranger's wall in this strange city, like I had been here all along. I was 13 and looked apprehensive. Killer was standing immediately in front of Chris Martin in the photo. As if they'd just been shown a future vision of their musical careers, Martin has a huge smile on his face, Killer looks thoroughly pissed off.

"Hey, do you guys like PBR?" asked Harrison, pointing at the TV excitedly. As he spoke, his voice would break halfway through each sentence as he continued his assimilation into his adopted country, moving from a King George accent to that of George Bush. PBR turned out to be Pro Bull Riding. It was Harrison's new addiction, he said, explaining the rules. You have to stay on the bull for eight seconds as it bounces and bucks, whilst keeping one hand in the air. If you manage it, you get rich with prize money and sponsorship, if you don't you might snap your back, or get a horn in your eyeball (I know this as I will introduce you to such a broken American further along the road). The sight of these strong men being thrown around like wet pasta was strangely captivating. The TV shows a close-up of their muscular, sinewy arms strapping one hand to the rope around the animal's chest and then, as the gate is opened and the bull is free, the camera pans out to reveal the lolloping linguine.

After that it was baseball and Harrison added further to our knowledge. The Miami Marlins were up against the New York Yankees in the final of the World Series. The Marlins had had a 'shitty season', finishing next to bottom in the league. They then fired their coach and brought in 72-year old Jack McKeon to replace him, before incredibly then securing a wildcard entry to the World Series. The next few nights would decide it. If the Marlins could win against one of the most successful teams of all time, it would be the sporting story of the decade.

"If you like TV and sports then America is great," said Harrison. He seemed happy with his relocation and told us about the city's extensive bike routes (as well as its recent multimillion dollar investment in extending these), its cultural variety and openness. "You'll find it's quite different from Bush's America." But we couldn't really drink it all in from his flat, or his TV. He had said we could stay a couple of nights but we decided to make it just that one, opting to move to a hostel closer to the action. But before we left, we needed a deep cleanse and refuel. Harrison had said we could help ourselves to what we needed. He left at 6am to enjoy his happy life looking at all that stock. We snoozed on but once up, we didn't hold back on accepting his offer. As well as a thorough personal scrubbing (with multiple differently scented shower gels), we boiled our water bottles to clean and sterilize them, noticing for the first time the ring of black mould that was gathering menacingly inside.

Then, as well as more of the curious muffins, we ate sandwiches and pizzas and drank tea and smoothies. We packed our bags and left a thank you note, signing off, 'You need more groceries.'

We had seen the promise of this city open up to us as we had neared the end of the Golden Gate Bridge the day before and we were hungry to explore. If you had to compile a list of the most iconic man-made structures in the world, surely this incredible architectural wonder would place strongly. To then cycle along it, along its 1.7 mile span, watching ships pass 700 ft below when the fog billowed clear… was just epic. It seemed a fitting, triumphal arch to frame the amazing city ahead and to mark 1,000 miles on the bikes. It seemed to almost come with its own angelic chorus of 'ta daaaaa'.

We stopped for a coffee and discovered our waiter was also a limey. He had a gruff tough northern bastard English accent. He had a face like a punch and a frown that suggested his whippet had just slipped its string.

"Do you like it here then?" I asked.

"Well, it beats the fook out of Rochdale."

He said little so we assumed he hated us and our posh southern accents but he brought a bag of cakes for us as we left. "For on the road," he said. He then started to clear a table only to drop his tray. As he tidied the mess he turned to me and smiled, "Well she were nice though, weren't she." He nodded to a girl that had just sashayed past, indicating he hadn't been entirely concentrating on his craft. Indeed, and not to sound too much like teenage boys discovering their hormones for the first time, it was pleasant to be mixing with beautiful women again after a month on the road.

That phrase then, repeated by the waiter, 'on the road'. We heard it a few times in San Francisco. It didn't seem to be deliberately placed, just slipped in, part of the lingo, such was the pervasive influence of the iconic novel by Jack Kerouac. People didn't ask 'how's the trip?', they wanted to know 'What's it like on the road?' And it wasn't just Kerouac, the legacy of all the Beats was quite apparent in the city. They had centred on the North Beach area where we found the City Lights Bookstore still thriving. Here, Kerouac, Keesey, Burroughs and others had brought out groundbreaking, often contentious works. They had shaken up the conservatives and paved the way for a new direction of liberalism for the city.

In Kerouac's novel, they cross the country, they break free from what they know and what has been expected of them, and they discover something of themselves. I picked up a copy of the book in the store and turned to Killer.

"Remind you of anyone?"

"What, an aspiring writer travelling across America with his smelly friend, meeting oddballs and living off strange scraps of food. Nope. Sounds dull. And there aren't even any whales in it."

I read a passage, '...*the only people for me are the mad ones, the ones who are mad to live, mad to talk, mad to be saved, desirous of everything at the same time, the ones who never yawn or say a commonplace thing, but burn, burn, burn like fabulous yellow roman candles exploding like spiders across the stars.*' It seemed fairly accurate of the people we had already met, and would prove highly portentous of some of the yet madder out-of-Earth-orbiters we would encounter in the coming weeks.

We drank the Beats in (or at least I did), then walked back along Columbus, ducking into bars like Vesuvios - once a strong Beatnik hangout - and took turns to smoke cigarettes on the street with friendly strangers, feeling like Sal Paradise and Dean Moriarty, collar pulled up, one shoe against the wall. In one bar we played pool, in another we just listened to John Coltrane and Miles Davis, and in one more we watched baseball. The city had a mad jazz rhythm and it carried us along like a dancing high hat.

With so much time on our hands, we had got used to expanding every small action into a laboured ritual. And so it continued here. The first beer in a bar was now always marked by the 'Limey toast'. The beer purchaser would propose a toast with an encouraging raised glass. The other would take this as a cue to taste the beer, running it around his mouth a while as if a fine claret and then ponder the enjoyment meaningfully before letting the frown of concentration break slowly into a satisfied, knowing nod. We would both then drink, with a cheery, questioning "And ut?", followed by a confirmatory, "And ut!" This ritual was an addition to the already-established 'Limey salute' - in a counter cultural gesture to the

American habit of hugely flamboyant gestures, when Killer and I greeted each other after any time apart or set off on the bikes after a break, it was not with a whoop, a high five or a fist bump, we simply extended the index fingers of our right hands and pressed the tips together softly and silently. And ut.

We Limey toasted our way along, bar-hopping in the direction of the hostel. In an Irish bar, Killer slipped into a strong Irish accent and a fellow countryman offered to take us sailing at the weekend.

"Anytin fur a fellow Oirish," said the man.

"Well oil be," declared Killer merrily, even though he had no intention of going. The man's American girlfriend was drunk, lipstick smeared on her face and she sided up to me.

"I can tell you're a bullshitter cos your legs are so skinny," she whisper-stumbled. "Ain't no way you're cycling to Miami. Don't worry, I won't tell anyone. Hey, it's a great story and good luck to you. But I bet your French accent is even fake."

She then took a shot of Tequila, slammed the glass on the table and said loudly 'Cheers to Miami', then winked at me before falling off her chair.

I liked this city, people all around us were happily exploding like spiders, whatever that means. At the Warfield, a famous live music venue, Beth Gibbons was headlining the next evening. She was the haunting voice of Portishead, a band very close to my home both geographically (formed near Bristol) and emotionally (because my first ever girlfriend had played their song Glory Box on loop when we 'made out'). The chance that Gibbons would just happen to be playing the one night we sought out a concert… it was starting to feel like the script had been written for us as we made our journey through this country.

In the Warfield queue we met Freddie, all long cotton dress and a flower in her wild hair. She was a local girl and sang in a band about love and happiness. But she also loooooooved to drink. We got a table and were soon joined by her two friends - one a mournful looking, bedraggled brunette, the other a more detailed blonde.

The music was exceptional. On occasion, the large band filled the width of the stage and created a wall of sound that just hung there, then reverberated and grew. I was spellbound. Organ, drums, guitars, Gibbons' vocals. It just kept hitting me, pressing at my chest until I could hardly breathe. It was like a scream that asked 'are you fucking alive?' and I almost cried out 'yes I'm fucking alive'. I sat there, mouth open, a tear was even on my cheek. What had just happened to me? And it all ended too soon. Gibbons then proved the rebellious San Francisco spirit was infecting even her as she sparked up a cigarette and took a long puff. Indoors! In California!

The girls wanted to take us to explore more of the city. All night, the bedraggled had been a fairly mute companion but behind the wheel of her battered 1980s Volvo estate she came alive. She took on the city's famous hills like she was recreating the movie Bullitt. She was Steve McQueen and this family car was a Ford Mustang. Cross junctions in the city are made so that no one has the right of way, you just approach slowly and give way to whoever was there first. Bedraggled's approach was to take each one at speed and hope for the best. As the road then took a sharp decline after the short flat of the junction, the car would launch into the air and come down hard on its rear, letting out a scrape of sparks and a cheer from the mad driver who would then pull the car sharply round the bend and laugh again as we flew into each other in the back seat, screaming.

We pulled up, remarkably still with our undergarments unsoiled, at the Mission District. It was known as a dodgy neighbourhood but was being discovered by a new generation of cool white kids who wanted to feel 'edgy' and get '*the* best burritos in town'. It was also where our "I'm going to go birding now" friend had recommended, so I suspected not a huge crime den any longer. The hipsters were moving in. We feasted and then slipped into a dimly lit bar called Amnesia, filled with cool young things. We played pool and listened to the Violent Femmes. The bedraggled discussed rock bands with Killer, the blonde chatted Beats to me. They wanted to keep the evening going but we needed sleep. We dropped the blonde at her house and she asked if I wanted to continue the tour inside and I gave her a weird excuse about not being able to leave Killer, confused what to say when I realised I had not once mentioned my girl 'back home', asking myself why not.

Our new home in the city then was the Hostel International by Fisherman's Wharf. We stayed three nights, which seems highly excessive given our intention of eventually completing this cycle across this continent, but we planned to get to Alcatraz and had to wait for tickets. I'd said rather miserably, "Not sure what the attraction is of seeing where a bunch of twats did time." But for Killer, this was the main draw of the town. The boats heading over to the island were stuffed with people, all excitedly drawn to 'the Rock'. To me it was still just a prison and I was not interested in revelling in it. Besides, behind the tough inescapable image of the place, I read many criminals had asked to be transferred *to* Alcatraz, as they valued the safety of their own cell, and because this prison reportedly had the best food. And the Birdman of Alcatraz was never even allowed to keep birds! Just like the stories of circling sharks to put off escapees, much of the place was mere fable. And, for me, that was the most interesting point, that it wasn't what it was. America liked big myths and this was one of the best. But this also served as a distraction. Thousands of tourists a day listened to the stories as if prison was some historic American adventure, ignoring the fact that elsewhere the country was being incarcerated still at a greater rate than any other country in the western world. One in four of the world's prisoners are in the US. And behind this number stands an even more troubling statistic around systemic racism and racial inequality: while 1 in 17 white men are likely to go to jail at some point in their lives in America, the figure is 1 in 3 for black men.

But I did enjoy one thing very much - we created a series of photos of Killer seemingly escaping his cell, breaking out of the building then running past the guard hut to flee the island. We completed the series later down by the water's edge on the mainland where, island and bridge in cinematic background, Killer climbed over a sea wall and spat a jet of water into the air as if arriving from a long, shark-infested swim to freedom. Waiting the extra day to make the trip had suddenly been worth it.

The other days in San Francisco were spent lazily walking around and enjoying the curiously named neighbourhoods. The city was founded by the Spanish in 1776, was under Mexican control for some time and became part of the United States in 1846. The neighbourhoods are a glorious cocktail of all these times. Alcatraz itself comes from an old Spanish word for 'Pelicans' who had set up their own fortress there. In 1827, a French Captain noted it was '...covered with a countless number of these birds. A gun fired over the feathered legions caused them to fly up in a great cloud and with a noise like a hurricane.' Oh I'd have liked to have seen that much more than prison cells. Other neighbourhoods are named after Gold Rush captains of industry or named for their modern uses, like Harrison's second home, the 'Financial District'. But there are others that are much more interesting. Dogpatch is apparently named after the packs of dogs that roamed the streets, lured by the scent of the area's countless slaughterhouses. Cow Hollow was named for the lands occupied by the cows before they were taken to Dogpatch. Then there was Tenderloin, presumably named for the best cuts of said dog-patched cow-hollowed cows but often claimed to represent its history as a 'soft underbelly' of vice and corruption. One of the best was Nob Hill, which came from the slang given to describe rich people, originally British, profiteering on other people's misfortune. Now of course nobs are any sort of dick. But my favourite, of course, was a small area between the two aforementioned neighbourhoods, and that was Tendernob.

Another great name is Polk Gulch, named after a US President. It was once the centre of the gay community and it would be conspicuous by its absence not to mention the city's inclusive approach to the LGBT community. Along with the Beats, this community has done much to define San Francisco's open-to-all atmosphere, as well as to challenge LGBT stigma around the world. Brian said he felt proud. "But I can't wait for it to be so normal we don't need to celebrate it," he added.

Sailors dishonorably discharged for homosexual activities from the US Navy in the Second World War were left in San Francisco, and soon formed their own force for change. And with that the city was open to so many other forms of progressive thinking. This even extended to the welcome cyclists feel here. The willingness to see a different type of social progress brought with it a celebration of the bicycle and the understanding of how orientating a city more around the bike can shift the entire psychology of a place, to be more human-centric.

I saw a woman in her 60s dancing in a bikini in Union Square outside Saks. A little further on, chess tables had been laid up and homeless men played each other, and one tried to sell me a poem to raise a little money. A little further and I felt I had crossed the tracks. A huge mean looking mofo staggered menacingly and then spat on the ground, but when he noticed an old woman nearby he removed his hat and said, "Oh I'm sorry about that ma'am." Yes, I liked this city.

At Pier 39, sea lions lazed on floating platforms, watching the boats come in and occasionally barked like a pack of dogs when another ball of blubber rocked the deck to try and pull themselves onto a slice of space. Here I enjoyed the local speciality Clam Chowder in a bowl of a carved out loaf of sourdough. Still none the wiser. And there were galleries. In one, a photographer showed off the landmarks of the coast and forests we had just passed and those that lay ahead, on the road. Whilst my efforts to record the passing vistas were laughable, these images finally said something of the majesty and emotional power of the place. I bought a dozen postcards and sent them home to friends and family so they could see what I felt here. Yes, I really did like California and felt nothing but the bike could have given me such an intimate access.

It was then with a feeling of being entirely sated that we headed back to Vesuvio's on our last night for a final Limey toast and to watch the crucial final game in the World Series. We'd bought a copy of the San Francisco Chronicle. On the front, Arnie appeared with a raised fist, bedecked with giant gold ring, and a promise of 'Action, Action, Action' in the headline. The story started, 'Schwarzenegger to address host of hot-button issues'. Beside it, another story was headlined 'Rumsfeld Dubious Terror War Being Won'. And the last one, 'All Tied Up: Marlins even series with dramatic HR'. I assumed this meant 'home run', and not an over enthusiastic human resources manager.

The Marlins had - against all expectations - taken the games on the previous two nights to set up a once unimaginable decider. The bar was full, people moved tables and chairs to get a glimpse of what was happening. These were teams from two cities on the other side of the country, which would otherwise have been of passing interest, but here - with a new mythology in the making - people wanted to be part of it. And so it was. At the fortress of Yankee Stadium, the Marlins took the game, and with it the series. They were the baseball champions of the world. We all cheered heartily. This was indeed quite something. I felt again the strange knot inside as if the fates were drawing this all to my attention for some reason; that there was some lesson in here for me as we ourselves celebrated already going further than had once felt possible. The Marlins were proving you should never dream too big.

6. Big smiles at Big Sur

Nothing compares to the simple pleasure of riding a bike.
John F Kennedy

We needed a new goal, a new place to aim for whilst we continued to contemplate the enormity of the full task that still lay ahead to Miami. Looking at the whole map of the USA was too overwhelming, so we had to set our sights a little closer. Los Angeles was almost exactly 500 miles so that would do. La la land. Tinseltown. Where the promise of a stay at a Hollywood mansion awaited. *No doubt we'll be snapped up and cast in some exotic action adventure movie*, I told Killer before we even left England. *No doubt we'll die*, he replied.

As we climbed back on the bikes, they felt alien, unbalanced, and our legs felt weak. It was like starting all over again. We continued south. Ocean Beach was teeming with people; swimming, sunbathing, playing volleyball. It was fringed with a wide cyclepath and we rolled happily along. A guy on a racing bike and thigh-hugging lycra zipped past us and rang his bell in a cheery 'hello'. The way he breezed away stirred my own limbs and I took off in pursuit.

"I'll show him what The Limey Project is made of," I shouted back to Killer.

"Do ittttttt," he encouraged.

My legs were burning as I caught up with the cyclist, then overtook him on my mule. I continued racing a few more metres to an imaginary finish line then punched the air in victory. As I slowed to allow Killer to catch up, the man cycled past again, chuckling.

The day was marked by sunshine and surfers but darkness descended whilst still a few miles from our destination. We were riding with lights on for the first time. We fumbled with the attachments, flicked the switches and the narrow beams carried us nervously along Highway 1 - now called the Cabrillo Highway - and around Half Moon Bay. A few expletives were offered to the near-passing cars, and then gusto was added to the shouts when we discovered our intended campsite was closed, forcing us to press on further into the dark. Whilst night-cycling on a busy highway was another item that got added to the list of exciting new 'firsts', it was not one we enjoyed.

We made it to a private RV Park at Pelican Point. I had high hopes for the stop, having marvelled at the eponymous birds earlier that day. They flew over our heads and then dove sharply into the bay, marking a much more pleasing first. I nearly crashed into a parked car just south of Ocean Beach as I followed their path, spellbound. Their huge frontal loads seemed to defy the laws of flight and an old limerick got stuck in my head.

A wondrous bird is the Pelican
It's beak holds more food that its belly can
It can store in its beak
Enough food for a week
But I don't know how the hell he can.

It was a shame, then, to have such a good name wasted on such a disappointing stop. The facilities were all geared to the colossal recreational buses, with every 'camping' spot offering the same footprint as that of a small family home, and consisting of connections to electricity, water and sewage. The only price advertised was a flat $20 fee, even though all we wanted was a small slither of earth to unfurl our stitches of nylon. We'd hoped to argue our case for paying less - given our significantly smaller demands on resources and the environment - but as the office was already closed, we decided immediately to shun the use of anything but their basic toilet facilities and just get back on the road at dawn without paying, leaving no trace.

Pelican Point was at risk of being spitefully ignored in my diary if it wasn't for the life-changing thing that happened there at our evening meal. For this was the day we invented 'choodle'.

Having experimented with soup stirred into pasta, and bread dunked into beans, we had finally discovered the dish that would fuel our expedition for the next three months. A tin of chili, a packet of instant noodles, a love of portmanteaus... Choodle. It may not have been the most nutritious - no kale was harmed in its making - but it was available everywhere, easy and quick to cook, and had a punch of flavour (perhaps assisted by juuuuust a few artificial ingredients…). You'll hear more about choodle later, as the happiness it brought into our daily lives started to affect new cultural rituals, but for now let me just say... don't judge us until you have tried it.

That night's choodle was also an opportunity to make first use of the EXCELLENT mini gas burner we had bought in San Fran. Our hands no longer sooted, the pans no longer caked in black evil, we had left the Trangia behind, deciding that a little technical support was what might turn us into seasoned campers. We'd made the purchase at a veritable warehouse of things we never knew we needed, called Sports Basement. In what felt like a deja-do of Seattle's REI, we picked up small gadgets and treats and contemplated the many ways they might enhance our expedition, only to return them to the shelves when we assessed their cost and weight. That is, almost inexplicably, except for one small pair of foldable binoculars. I am not sure what came over me - perhaps it was Diony's walking advert for birding or the promise of wildlife further along the journey that I didn't want to miss - but they found their way into my bag, accompanied by a loud chortle from Killer.

"Oh, these little things are going to come in veeeeeery handy," I assured him in reply, totally unconvinced myself.

Zipped back up inside the tent was womb-like in its reassurance, with just the rhythms of nature outside. In the hostel we'd shared a dorm with around 20 others, including a world champion snorer. I had thrown pillows at his face and kicked his bed but he was on autopilot to annoy until morning when I wept at the receptionist's desk, pleading with her to let us move rooms. It was in such a sleep-deprived state that Killer and I had formed a new coded language to keep track of our 'movements'. Living in such close proximity, it was hard not to be aware of the progress of each other's bowels as we cycled along, especially when we wanted to share the burden of concern - or just plain consternation - for a growing gas abundance. But discussing such issues was not - apparently - publicly acceptable.

And so it was we developed an abbreviated code to capture the progress of each bathroom visit and pass on the essential information in a way that bypassed any public indecency or, indeed, nuisance. Just the essential words 'gas', 'piss', 'shit' were blended at first - listed in the order in which the motions occurred but congealed into one homologous mass, wasteful consonants or vowels abandoned. A *gissit* or *pitas* was a standard and unconcerning rest stop. But soon we extended the code beyond pure utility to include all bathroom reference terminology - 'shower', 'wash', 'shave', 'brush' and more. A standard morning when camping was generally just a *pissush* but a motel day started in luxury with a *pissitashushowerave*. Naturally, this quickly escalated, and we soon enjoyed extending our bathroom visits for the sole purpose of creating virtual triple word scores in our coded scrabble.

"Everything alright today Killer?"

"Yes, splendid, although somewhat surprising. It was a gissitasissitas."

"No wash at the end."

"No. I wanted to but just didn't like the idea of finishing with a 'sh' sound. Anyway, nothing to consult with Brian over. How's Bone doing?"

"Oh, splendid."

"Splendid."

"Um. Is this getting weird yet?"

"A liiiiittle bit, yeah."

However, there were no words yet to describe the strange feelings inside Killer's core the morning of our dawn escape from Pelican Point. We were on the road at 7am and away. Killer had a nervous look on his face and I assumed he was, as I had been, picturing the troupe of trained Pelicans that would surely soon be charging after us, beaks flapping, demanding payment and apologies. I was then convinced this had been his concern when, after two miles, he raised a weak arm in surrender. But he had more basic concerns.

"Um. Bone, I think I might actually soil myself. It's like the Battle of Sedgemoor in there. How far is it to the next toilet?"

"Sedgemoor? The last battle to be fought on English soil?"

"Bone..."

"Oh you mean, it's like the last battle in your bottom also, because this feeling is like the end of all things? Well that was obscure if that is what you meant."

"Booooone!"

"Or did you mean it is like battles in general and you just used Sedgemoor as it was reportedly quite 'messy'?"

"BONE!"

I consulted the map. "Er, eight more miles. But flat and fast."

He groaned.

"It's either that or head back to Pelican Point and confess to our crimes, or we find a dune and pray you don't get mauled by an elephant seal. In fact, I'd like to see what happens with that last option."

Killer weighed it up. "And ut," he confirmed, nodding to the road ahead.

We progressed, me staying tactically in front of Killer.

After being on the run for a whole ten miles we stopped at Pomponio State Beach. Killer raced in to use the pit toilet, shouting to the heavens for just a few more seconds grace, while I prepared a breakfast of peanut butter on squashed bread rolls. In alarming visual synchronicity, it reminded me of something. Killer returned some minutes later and rummaged in his pannier for his spare cycling shorts.

The route was skirting beautiful stretches of sand and dunes. The beaches heaved with tourists in the summer weekends but today Pomponio was all ours, apart from one sole woman. Perhaps in her 50s, she had parked up, walked on to the sand and then thrown herself into the waves, splashing and rolling about in a shriek of orgasm with every ebb and tumble. She'd get knocked over and giggle with delight then get up and thrust herself into the sea once more. She was a large woman but there was something oddly beautiful and compelling about watching her. After 20 minutes she returned to her car and drove off, tooting her horn, happy with life.

At Santa Cruz, the route ducked off the busy highway and turned on to a bike path that skirted the bay. The paths were alive with all sorts of cyclists, just getting about, some even with surfboards hooked on to the side of their bikes or under their arm as they headed off to find the best breaks.

Santa Cruz is known for its socially liberal leanings. Like San Francisco and, it seemed, much of California, it felt like the antithesis of the Bush rhetoric we'd become used to coming out of much of the American media. Perhaps no surprise that when we passed through it had just become the first city in the US to denounce the Iraq War. On one newspaper vending machine, I saw someone had daubed 'Bush sucks Dick Cheney' and on another 'Laura Bush is a ugly whore'. But the aggressive anti-establishment rhetoric seemed to be quite contained. Mostly folk were content to lead by example, and it looked to be a pretty fine place to live. In every laid back smile we saw, our favourite Santa Cruz resident - Steve Darjeeling - beamed back at us.

We would have stayed longer but we were expected further down the road the next day. After 60 miles we hit Sunset Beach, precisely at sunset. But it was closed so we pressed on, again with our lights shining. They say the biggest danger to cyclists along this coast is the dense fog that appears from nowhere and swallows you whole. Whilst we had been lucky to only meet that challenge over the Golden Gate Bridge, so far, the clocks going back while we were in San Francisco meant darkness now became our regular hazard, creeping up on us with a similar deadly stealth. But we survived the next ten miles to the campsite and celebrated our first 70 mile day. The flatter terrain, the warmer days… 70 miles was doable, for sure. It just takes time, a full day of up at dawn and riding until dusk or beyond. But we needed to dig yet deeper if we were to sustain and even pass it. I lay back on the picnic bench and watched a rich soup of shooting stars above, making wishes for the miles ahead, and thinking, still too much thinking.

Whilst the days were shorter, the Californian sunshine was noticeably stronger, resulting in absurdly comical tan lines. A growing golden brown hue extended over our forearms and faces but our chests and upper arms were ghostly white. As we wore fingerless gloves our hands were also white but for the very tips, which made it look like we must smoke ten cigarettes at a time. The overall effect was accentuated by the cleanness of the division between light and dark due to the tightness of our costumery. On our heads we had a small white band at the top of the forehead from the shade of the helmet, lines beside the ears from the helmet straps, and white ovals on our eyes from our sunglasses to complete the look. If the cycling didn't work out, we could have always tried the circus. But this two-toneular transformation had gone largely unnoticed by us until we approached Monterey the next day.

We first passed endless fields of vegetables at Castroville, where a sign proudly announced it to be the 'Artichoke capital of the world'; presumably the destination for many a romantic mini break for Harrison and his artichokiphile girlfriend. It was just one of a string of California towns claiming world capital status - drift through the state and you could get the self-declared plantery's finest abundance of grapes, dates, apricots, and almonds, and much more. Up in Washington we had also passed the oyster and apple global capitals. No wonder Americans felt so bloody important, they just kept appointing themselves world champions, whether it was baseball or broccoli. I imagined the meeting that must have taken place in the town of Gilroy, California…

"Ok guys, we need to get one of these bloody world capital things. Any ideas?"

"Pear?"

"Taken."

"Raisin."

"Obviously taken."

"Garlic?"

"Oh, curveball. Yes, yes I like it! That will pull the tourists in! Everyone likes to get their kids in the car and drive up to the garlic patch for a good ol' picnic. Done! What's your name, kid? You'll go far."

"Van Helsing, sir."

As we neared Monterey the route moved onto a long and wide cycle path that cut through the dunes of Monterey Bay. We took the opportunity of the delicious warmth to slip off our shirts and helmets, and on seeing our bodies for the first time, we laughed loudly.

"You look like a goddamn penguin, Killer!"

As we continued to inspect each other and laugh, our bikes collided and I tumbled off into some bushes, emerging with some cuts and grazes but still laughing. I was still composing myself when an old woman cycled past on a recumbent. She stopped for what we thought was to offer assistance - which was strange as she looked as old and mobile as Leggett Hill - but instead just said what was on her mind.

"Hell boys, your white chests look like my upper thighs!" She rang her bell and rode off chuckling. Killer and I looked at each other.

"Get this image of that woman's thighs out of my head," pleaded Killer desperately.

In Monterey, we had an email from Greg saying he had been in town a few days before us and had 'torn up the bars, got drunk and got punched in the face'. He sounded delighted by this.

"Er, is this Steve's influence?" I pondered to Killer. But we couldn't linger ourselves as were due that night in Carmel, which is officially and more romantically named as Carmel-by-the-Sea. We'd never heard of the place but, as it turns out, it is a very special place indeed, offering all the chewy, sweet indulgence of the sweety treat that almost bore its name. We got to the entry gate of the approaching toll road (having an entry gate should tell you all you need to know) and were just let through by security as it was, again, getting dark. We cycled through cool woodlands and beside world renowned golf courses, then past exclusive homes, each with perfectly manicured lawns and driveways that were like cat walks for bespoke sports cars. On the pavements beautiful people jogged without sweating and people walked dogs that no doubt never pooped. We eventually hit the beach road; a narrow, winding lane with the vastly understated name of 'Scenic Drive'. We passed one breathtaking home after another. Until we arrived. And there, standing in a large bay window, enjoying their millionaire view of the Pacific, were Bill and Patsy.

"Welcome, welcome, come on in. You found it OK?"

Bill - much like his namesake, musician Billy in Tillamook - was immediately warm and welcoming to us, even though we had never met before. He ushered us inside. Patsy was hurrying around in the background, tidying up like the Queen was coming, but she stopped when she saw us. She beamed and gave us a hug. They were two of the most splendid septuagenarians the world has ever known.

"Well this is just such a treat," Patsy declared, as if mistaking host and guest.

On a street where every house could have been a Grand Designs season special, Bill and Patsy's stood out for its understated elegance. It was a low, timber home, painted in a cool grey, fronted by large windows that framed a view that carried you through twisting Monterey Cypresses to the ocean, where the last of the sunset was still rippling on the water.

"You have a wonderful home," I said, feeling embarrassed for the inadequacy of my words, and already nervously contemplating the inappropriate baseness of my first washisitowerave. "It is so kind of you to let us stay."

"Nonsense, nonsense," said Bill. "In fact, I know you said you only needed a night but we think you should stay for two - there's just too much to see."

"Yes, We'd love to show you around," added Patsy.

We had absolutely zero inclination of turning them down.

"If you really insist."

Bill was the cousin of Killer's boss, who'd fixed up our visit. He had neatly pressed cream trousers pulled high, a white short sleeve shirt tucked in. He was deliberate and sincere in his manner. He opened the garage to let our bikes in and a vintage convertible Mercedes shone in the half light. It was like the garage in Ferris Bueller's Day Off, with a vehicle of such precise polish that it must exist mainly for the driveway, not often the highway. It was ice blue with cream leather seats.

"That is a very beautiful car. You obviously look after it well, Bill," I said, again words failing me.

Bill thrust his hands into his pockets and leaned back. You could sense his pride.

124

"Well, yes, yes," he started to lose himself in a dream. "But it doesn't get so much use now."

He then stepped forward and patted the side of the car as if a horse in the stables.

"Why don't I insure you on it and you boys can drive it around tomorrow, head inland, see the vineyards. It could do with a runaround."

A few minutes into our visit and I felt like Jean Valjean again. Convicts on the run, now furnished with more good favour than we perhaps deserved. We drew the line at such kindness, partly as we were convinced we would crash his joy, and refused. Bill held up his hands as if to say 'OK, I won't push it but the offer's there.'

So instead *he* drove us, in his more practical sedan, out to dinner nearby and then, the next day, into the countryside. That second day, we passed vineyards that had grown fat and lush in the Pacific fog that blows in. And at an antiques and reclamation store by our luxurious lunch spot we found British red telephone boxes being sold for $5,000 each.

Over lunch, Bill and Patsy kept asking questions on the journey so far and they would just shake their heads with happiness. Bill called over the waitress to share his joy.

"Young lady, I just thought you should know we are dining today with two wonderful young men who are cycling all the way to Miami whilst raising money for charity."

Bill spread his arms out and rested a hand on mine and Killer's shoulders. He then slightly went on a tangent to explain to the girl why Caesar salad - pointing at the menu - is called *Caesar* salad[2], before then ordering the fish. The waitress left and Patsy leant over to me.

"I think that young lady might be falling in love with you," she laughed. "It was written all over her face."

---

[2] Named after a man called 'Caesar' remarkably.

The waitress returned at the end of our meal with a bag of scones to give us "energy for the road", and Patsy elbowed me in the ribs. She had a glint in her eyes, delighting in small mischiefs despite being in poor health. At the house, we'd observed her occasionally pause to plug into oxygen pipes to top herself up, with Bill dutifully walking behind, ensuring all was as it should be and that no one would trip over the cables. It was the small gestures of a long and loving marriage.

After lunch, we headed back to Carmel and Killer and I took our bearings on a stroll. The whole town has strict planning rules, ensuring every construction is stylish, considered, in keeping. It took two years to get Bill and Patsy's planning application approved for their simple home. Even the Shell gas station in Carmel was elegant - an art deco wonder with a forecourt that resembled a supercar showroom. There's no mail boxes on the street and house names have to be painted subtly on to each home, as if a whisper.

The strict rules extend to a ban on chain restaurants, and there is even a law that prohibits anyone wearing heels longer than two inches, a hangover of 1920s lawsuits from falls caused by pavements cracked by tree roots. The laws were so extensive they even motivated one resident, actor and director Clint Eastwood, to run for Mayor on a ticket that included overturning the ban on ice cream parlours. Bill told us Clint had been popular, for a while, until some punk in planning refused to make his day and let him add another storey to a restaurant he owned, so he sacked the entire planning commission. I like to think Clint did it with a two-fingered gun and then blew the imaginary smoke off afterwards.

Unsurprisingly, given the glorious backdrops, a number of films and TV shows have been set here, from Vertigo to Basic Instinct. But we felt there was still potential for more. Based on our observations of absurdly crafted coiffures and chiseled chins on the American soaps, we imagined a new show, set in Carmel's elite elysium, simply called… *Carmel*. We even made up a theme tune.

As the opening music plays, beautiful young people jog, swim, play golf, walk dogs, drive fast cars on twisty mountain passes, laughing. Then... drama.

- *Hey Rex, I saw you with Cindy at the beach club last night. What the hell's going on?*
- *[long pause] Listen Dick, I got some news for you and you need to deal with it - Cindy and I are in love.*
- *[cold stare] Oh yeah, well what about Summer?*
- *[Slow smile, evil laugh] Ha ha. Summer doesn't need to know. Besides, she still thinks I'm dead.*
- *[camera pans back] Hi Rex*
- *[slow shock, confused eyebrow] Summer!*
- *[knowing nod] So you didn't drown in that freak yachting accident that helped settle your business debts after all. Well, if no one knows you're alive, I guess no one will mind if you... DIE."*
- *[multiple shocked-faced-long-paused sequence that for no good reason ends on a dog]*
- *[end credit theme tune plays in harmony]*
  You can walk through the trees, drink coffee or tea, in Carmel by the seaaaaaaaaa
  They'll love you there, if you're a millionaire.
  It's Carmel by the Sea
  Caaaaaaaarmel. Caaaaaaarmeeeeeeeeeeeeel.

I was still contemplating the millions this new show would net us when Bill's sister Barbara arrived for dinner. Bill had thought it was just her joining but Patsy reminded him their friend Roxy would also be coming, and he busied himself about the living room in preparation. "What, Roxy's coming over? Oh my."

Roxy was of the same age but wore a red chiffon blouse and her face seemed to have been assisted a little by the antigravity of a cosmetic consultant. She moved confidently and spoke closely, throwing her head back occasionally to laugh in a Mae Westish way. I imagined in her younger days she must have been quite the seductress. I'll have to pen her in to *Carmel*, I thought. We drank wine like civilised citizens (how easily we drifted between tent and town) and spoke more of the journey.

We loved the polite American formality of our hosts. Questions were always prefixed with a clear indication of the purpose of the refrain. "Ok, so now I'm going to ask you how old you are what you do for a living." This formality would later find its way into how Killer and I would occasionally speak to each other. "Ok, so now I'm going to ask Bone if he'd like a beer and if his bowels are all in good order."

The TV news had been flashing softly in the background. It wasn't particularly happy stuff. In Iraq, more than 40 people had been killed and over 200 injured in a wave of coordinated bomb attacks on a Red Cross compound and on several local police stations in Baghdad. Bush said it was a sign of 'desperation' by the insurgents. The search for Saddam goes on, he vowed. Then the news of the Californian wildfires caused us all to focus our attention a little more closely. The worst wildfires in the state's history were quickly devastating huge swathes of the south. Hundreds of homes had already been destroyed, thousands of people evacuated, and it was still far from being under control. The fires stretched from LA to San Diego and inland as far as the desert. It was unprecedented and our trip was due to head straight through it. If we got held up or had to abandon because of this, then it would be the smallest inconsequence compared to the tragedy that was playing out in the images of families devoid of everything that mattered to them.

"You boys need to keep an eye on this, and take care of yourselves," said Bill.

The severity of the situation needed no inflation and yet Fox News was doing its best to try. I was not used to seeing such garish graphics, such loud swooshy spacey noises every time a headline popped up, such white teeth, such emotional newscasters, such exaggerated opinions disguising themselves as 'news'.

"It's quite different to the British news," I offered, not wanting to offend.

"Yes, we normally do watch the BBC just to find out what is really happening in the world. I think that's quite a California thing to do that," said Patsy. "You often can't get an ounce of truth or perspective in the US news."

Commenting on the emergency was the new Governator, at a family shelter.

"Oh, I can't stand him," said Patsy. Bill agreed.

"Oh... really?" I asked, feeling emotionally torn.

"Schwarzenegger is a Republican like Bush. He may not be *like* Bush but he's one of them all the same. But this state really is quite different to others you are going to pass through. I don't think you'd be having this conversation, questioning the position of the President, in Texas or Louisiana, for example."

"Wild things happen in Louisiana," Roxy added dreamily.

"Yes, you boys need to take care of yourselves down there," concluded Bill, ever mindful of our safety.

The evening concluded with Barbara asking us to visit her at her other place in Colorado, which is approximately 1,000 miles off course, and Bill embarrassing us with words of profound kindness as we talked more about our trip and our motivations for its success. I even told them about Penny.

My godmother, Penny, was one of those rare lights that not only illuminated the room, but also your soul. When she was a small girl, she'd fled from East Germany to West as the Iron Curtain was being raised. Her mother held her face and looked into her eyes and said, "We are going to run now. If you hear guns and one of us falls, you keep running until you reach safety." Penny made it. Her cousin remained trapped in the East. In 1989 when the wall came down, Penny went back and walked back over the same land, hand in hand with the one who had been left behind. There was never anger, just love. She gave me a piece of that wall in a way that suggested I could overcome any obstacle. But even though she fought and she fought and she fought, she could not beat breast cancer and she died, aged 52. Whenever I think of her now, it is with a growing sense of injustice but also with a growing appreciation for love.

"I think I speak for us all when I say I wish more young people had your initiative and were as conscientious," said Bill, standing so he could place a hand on each of our shoulders. "We're going to make a $500 donation to your charity, to support Cancer research."

As I contemplated forming some new language that might possess words potent enough to express our gratitude for their welcome, Bill signed off by saying, "And now we'd like to thank you for visiting us and honouring us as our guests."

Him saying this to us made it feel like the world was upside down but I wanted to live inside this kindness forever. When we left in the morning it was with the most genuine of thank yous.

The coastline south of Carmel, extending around 100 miles to San Simeon and known for much of this distance as Big Sur, is one of the biggest draws to the whole state of California. It is the longest stretch of undeveloped coastline in the US, boasting wild, winding, rocky passes and deep gorges spanned by impossibly-constructed steel bridges. It is considered by many to be one of the most scenic driving routes in the world, attracting as many people each year as Yosemite. And it has drawn scores of writers - from Jack Kerouac to Hunter S Thompson - and artists and photographers, notably Ansel Adams, and it continues to do so.

In 1972, California voters approved the creation of a coastal trail system that would provide unbroken access across around 70 miles of this coast for walkers, cyclists and horse riders. It was a hugely encouraging statement of intent. But even now and it has not been achieved - it has been repeatedly stalled over land acquisitions and bureaucracy. For now, cyclists ride the road like everyone else. It's a narrow two-lane highway with few places to pull over but in early November it was quiet, and the way the route hugged the mountains, which emerge abruptly out of the ocean, was thrilling. The road would sometimes skirt past the waves and at turns rise high over a pass, with the morning coastal fog hanging beneath us, making it feel like we were flying over the clouds.

The natural wonders extended to the fauna. At Julia Pfeiffer Big Sur State Park I left Killer in his tent to take a solo evening hike a couple of miles into the hills to find a waterfall, following a tip from TK. Signs at the camp had warned me of taking such a trip alone, given the presence of mountain lions in the area, but said I should be OK if I 'made a little noise to let them know I was there'. I had read in Bill Bryson's *A Walk in the Woods* that mountain lions had 'taken to stalking hikers' in California and I read somewhere else that as many as eight people a year are killed here by lions. I was far from devoid of fear of such a fate, in fact I was pretty much crapping my pants (known to us initially as 'Twanohing' after the incident on night 1, and later replaced by 'Pelicaning', and no doubt to be renamed a few more times on the trip), and yet I was doing it. I scoured the surroundings for signs of an attack as I walked up. Having Brian with me was not enough, I decided, so I carried a big stick, which I occasionally knocked against tree trunks or fence posts, and whistled an unformed tune, staccato-like to confuse the lions rather than melodic to lure them. This was all fine while there was no one else around but when I got to the waterfall and found five other hikers all looking at me in confusion, I had to carry on the strange one-man band, as if this was all perfectly normal and not the mad noises of a nervous man.

Off the coast, whales are often spotted in the bays as they migrate to new feeding grounds, but we were too early for the Grays and too late for the Humpbacks. But we were just in time to see another migration in action; Monarch Butterflies, which had started to gather in the trees of Big Sur in their scores to enjoy the winter sun. These winged wizards make a 3,000 mile migration that takes four generations to complete. I couldn't imagine being born and knowing immediately your responsibility to continue a journey started by your great grandfather. I was at times still confused where I was on my own journey.

Another big wildlife tick was the elephant seals. We had contemplated a visit the next day to the castle of William Randolph Hearst - the one-time richest man in America - who was one of the first proponents of the sensationalist approach to news we had witnessed in Carmel and whose life had inspired *Citizen Kane*. But we dropped the idea the instant we saw a beach covered unexpectedly in mesmerizing, wriggling and barking blubber at the foot of the castle's mountain pedestal.

It was peak season and as many as 17,000 elephant seals had found their way onto the local beaches. The largest bulls can reach 16 feet in length and weigh up to 5,000 pounds. They flap over each other, growl and fight but in early November they also mainly do a lot of relaxing, flipping sand lazily on top of themselves. Volunteer guides had gathered to help educate the public, to ensure people maintained a desire to respect and protect them. It was almost supernatural to see what felt like it belonged on an Attenborough documentary fill my eyes in real life. So uplifting that such a scale of nature should be happily continuing the habits of decennia, almost in secret, on a sandy beach between the modern mega cities of San Francisco and Los Angeles.

The campgrounds offered a chance to pause and take it all in. At Julia Pfeiffer, it had rained - the only drops for days - so we played Shithead by passing cards between the flaps of our tents. And at Kirk Creek State Beach we looked out to sea from a long-grassed field and drank a beer with our choodle, a feeling of serene happiness flooding our faces from the nature around us. The beer was our only small nod to the huge celebrations taking place across the country to mark Halloween. It was also a toast to our first puncture, remarkably coming after more than 1,100 miles on the road.

When wanting to go at our own individual pace along long stretches of less-heavily trafficked road, we'd often listen to music. At these times, it was not unusual for us to be separated on the road by a mile or more. If the gap got too big we'd pause to let the other catch up, but that day I hadn't noticed Killer slip behind me. I pulled over and waited. Twenty minutes past. From my rocky promontory, I could see the road snake back along the jagged coastline for some miles, but the haze was limiting the clarity and Killer was not to be seen. Ah, but only if there was some better way to scan these faraway bends for signs of life, I thought. If only some piece of equipment about my person might lend me some sort of zoomed, telescopic perspective. I was just unfolding and focusing the binoculars in smug proved-rightitude when a car pulled over and a man slapped his door to get my attention. "Hey! Your buddy back there has a flat. I think he wants you to double back. Bummer." I eased the binoculars back into their case and slowly returned them to my handlebar bag. Until next time.

Killer was waiting in a lay-by with a huge grin on his face. The bike was upside down, resting on its handlebars and saddle, with the panniers still attached and water dripping out of the upended bottles.

"Our first puncture, Bone, how exciting! OK, I've readied the bike. What do I do now?"

The bike creaked and then fell onto its side.

A note from my diary now to demonstrate even my own naivety over such mechanicals.

'Lucky that I headed back to help him as, thanks to my expert knowledge of bikes and the fact I was in possession of our only tools, we had the offending wheel repaired and returned in under 45 minutes.'

Anyone celebrating changing a tyre in three quarters of an hour is far, far, far from displaying qualities even approaching amateur level - let alone expert - but, perhaps comfortingly, we had no barometer of what was good bikemanship by then.

We tipped the bike up again and removed all the bags and bottles. We let out the remaining air, eventually loosened the brakes and the wheel nuts, pulled off the wheel, levered the tyre off, pulled the inner rubber tube out (to be inspected and patched at that night's camp), replaced it with a new one, reattached the tyre, and eventually got the wheel back on. It was an incredibly satisfying sequence of simple mechanical tasks but for which each one took around ten times longer than it should. That mattered not to us. With the wheel back on, we stepped back and gazed at the bike like we'd just cracked alchemy.

As we stood there, three Dutch cyclists pulled over to check on us, but we reassured them we had it covered. The tallest of the Dutch, and the only one who spoke, had a curious mouth, that bent back on one side as if he'd been snagged on a fish hook. (I'd not be mentioning this if it wasn't relevant to someone we would meet many miles further along the road). Was this the cause or consequence of his distinctive manner of speech?

"Yesh, looks like you have all thish under control," he said.

"Oh yes, ha ha, not a problem for us," said Killer, stepping in front of the again-dripping bottles.

"What nice weather huh?" the guy went on. "We are averaging about 70 milesh a day now."

"Oh yeah? Well we're doing over 200," said Killer slowly, as the bike toppled over once more.

The Dutch nodded to each other awkwardly and rode on. In fairness to Killer's lack of enthusiasm for 'other people', we had both become quite lazy about making friends with cyclists, particularly ones we sensed were 'un-Greve'. We had gotten so into our routine of choodle, Shithead and bed, that it was now not unusual to stretch and yawn as soon as the sun was down, with an eye on returning to an indulgent night of being wrapped in a sleeping bag, reading a damn good book with our head torches on.

"Oh look at that. 6.30 already, I think I might...er..."

"Well yes, we'd better get some, er, rest..."

Killer had finished *Jaws* and the *Godfather* and was now moving onto *The Count of Monte Cristo*. In the latter, the protagonist parades around Paris theatrically, women swoon and he attends the most lavish parties whilst he also enacts revenge on the three men who had had him wrongly imprisoned in the impenetrable fortress prison, the Chateau d'If.

Killer would occasionally chuckle from his tent and utter statements like, "Oh, that is TEXTBOOK Cristo, bloody brilliant!" And then he would call to me, "Bone, we really need to be more like 19th Century French Aristocrats, they are fantastic."

I had read *The Girl with a Pearl Earring* - a picture of Scarlett Johansson, who plays the title role in the film, stared at me, full-lipped, from the book's cover every night before bed. With a basic existence of tent life, and with only Killer and Brian's company, such images were intoxicating. I was now working my way through Killer's back catalogue, but I drew the line at reading *Inside Alcatraz*, which he'd purchased from the prison gift shop (a uniquely American retail opportunity). And there was one more book that rested at the bottom of my panniers that I would carry for the full trip. Slavomir's *The Long Walk* was there to power me, simply by its presence, and I would dip into it when I needed a boost.

The characters we encountered reading at night invariably found their way into our daily imaginatings and impressions. With every new book read, the community of characters we had gathered into our touring troupe grew still bigger, all mingling together with the ones we met on the road, to form one unlikely ensemble, which we called the Limenagerie. Brian chatting to Vermeer (who naturally sounded a lot like the Dutch cyclist we'd just met), with Gordon breaking up a fight between Jaws-hunting Chief Brody and whale-hunting Captain Ahab over Monte Cristo's lover Mercedes. The literary additions added some depth to our discussions but in fact one of the maddest and most spectacular of all the characters we met was in the 'real world' (whatever that term meant for this man). And that was Dedric, awaiting us the next night at San Simeon.

We heard him before we could see him. Stirring on the wind above the faint hum of cars came the unmistakable enthusiasm of

Bruce Springsteen, played out on a tinny CD player. *BORN in the USA, I was…* It was getting closer. And then, there he was.

"Oh for fuck's sake," said Killer.

The man was pushing a shopping cart, mushroom-loaded with his worldly possessions. He looked like the man in the dystopian no-one-gets-outta-here-alive film, *The Road*. Only he was shirtless and long, silver, wet hair fell behind him.

"That's you in two months," I said softly to Killer.

He waved as he passed. "Nothing like a good wash to make you feel fuckin' human again."

The trolley bumped on the gravel path. As it did a pleading meow emanated from somewhere within.

"Oh that's my cat, Castro. We're on this journey together. Dedric and Castro."

Yes. Dedric and Castro.

We returned the wave and said hello. He parked up by his tent and started rummaging, swearing as he pulled at blankets and boxes. "Ah ha." He'd found something. He opened up the CD player and inserted a new disc. It was the Rolling Stones. He'd picked up on our accents. No one else, no real human in the rest of this land had, but here, this guy, Dedric, he'd clocked us in a short 'hello'.

"Something to make you feel at home." He turned up the volume as high as it could go and started combing his mullet proudly. If we were to find out later he was anything but content with life - *far fuckin' from it* - I like to remember that moment and think there are times in everyone's life when you do find something that truly makes you happy, even for a minute, even if only a comb through clean hair.

We had agreed to go and join him round his fire later after chaghetti (no noodles in the store should have been an omen). We wrote our diaries and Killer's final line was, 'God help us'.

Dedric was standing by a big fire. He pointed to a pot of warm coffee and we poured it into our own mugs. The ever-impressive hospitality and generosity of the Americans extended even to this man and his cat. Dedric could *guaran-frick-fuckin-tee* many things, but not his sanity. His words came tumbling out like a waterfall, the sense mixed up in the stream with the flotsam.

"Just that, you know, just that, do you know what I mean, it's fuckin' bullshit, you know, these people, like just by Highway 77, east one block on Ranch Street, you know, there was an autobody and repair shop, my job, but fuckin' hell, gone, you know, gone, and fuckin' hell no bastard is gonna give me another... and I, I just sold my truck, that was my home, and took off on Monday."

I looked around at his world, now spread out to air like a garage sale of shipwreck salvage.

"It must be pretty heavy with all your things?"

"Yeah, about 400lbs. But it's all I need, I even got a TV in there. I already gone and done 587 miles with this fuckin' cart in Texas before so I thought, you know, what the heck and fuck you, I'll do it again and am taking off, but more this time. Ain't no fuckin' jobs man. I done auto work for 30 years. What was I gonna, you know, *do*, wait for nothing? I need to go, get going."

He'd sold his car for cash and was headed to Carmel, before planning to set a course for Nevada and then carry on all the way to the East Coast. From there, the world. He stared into the fire.

"I'm gonna see if that Clint Eastwood can help me first, you know, I just wanna catch a fuckin' break man. Maybe get in his next movie."

"I think Clint Eastwood is no longer..."

"It's fine, Killer," I stopped him.

Dedric muttered a few more hopes then petered out, occasionally stuttering half thoughts. We tried to make sense of him where we could but beyond our sympathy there was little we could offer him. We slyly tipped out our bitter coffees and said good night.

I had heard that transients were a big issue in the campsites of southern California. The people were moved along and the sites were closed periodically (as we would find over the next few days) to detract them from being used as bases, but Dedric was our first encounter and indeed the only other camper in the whole park.

I jokingly told Killer that he should sleep with his head to the north. "He'll instinctively come from the south when he comes to kill us."

I zipped up the tent and lay back. But then a realisation.
"Oh shit!"
"What is it Bone?"
"My washbag. I left my washbag beside Dedric's campfire. Shitting hell."

Killer laughed loudly. "I appreciate the sacrifice. I won't forget you old friend."

"Do you think it's easy for a homeless man to get a FUCKIN' job?"

Dedric was now pissed off. His earlier talk had got himself animated. He had found his groove now and he held me hostage with fast and furious talk for a further 40 minutes. It seemed like he had added a little livener to his coffee.

"Do you think a 45-year old white man gets the same privileges as a young Mexican woman with ten kids? I worked in auto shops for 30 years but you know, there's no fuckin' jobs. They make cars too perfect and all the fuckin' carpenty is production lined. You know. I got skills." He shook his head.

I was just contemplating how to react when he went on, in an unexpected direction.

"And do you think they landed a fuckin' rocket on the moon?"

I was lost momentarily but I sensed he was trying to get to the heart of his complaint, *the fuckin' government.*

"Bullshit. Have you seen how fuckin' fast that thing goes?" He pointed to the waxing lunar disc, as if in evidence. "It's travelin' at like a hundred thousand miles an hour. Do you think you could land a rocket on that thing? Bullshit man. I guaran-frickin-fuckin-tee

138

they did not. The government just fuckin' lies to us man. I know it because I was at a motel in Texas in '84 and I saw this guy coming out dropping blueprints everywhere and I knew it was, you know, *the man*."

"The man?"

"Yeah…. Saddam Hussein." He said it plainly, almost dismissively as he took another sip.

"Oh."

"Yeah. We drank some coffee together and he told me everything. I mean he didn't tell me his name but I recognised him from the TV."

Dedric then waved his free hand as if he'd said too much, and he wanted to change tack again.

"Anyway, once I get to Washington, I'm gonna fly a jet the fuck outta this country and find the King of England and show him how to build a fuckin' great house with wood, you know, and a toilet that works. Then I'll see Mick Jagger and maybe he'll teach me how to be a Rolling Stone. Even if I get shot down by a fireball on the way at least it will be God's hand and not some nut in the fuckin' white house that kills me, like they're trying to do now by screwing me. Listen man, if it's Hinduism or Buddhism or whatever, if you kill yourself you'll come back as a chicken, if you kill other people you'll come back as a cow and they're all fuckin' cows man."

He swigged back his coffee angrily in punctuation then took a deep breath to calm himself. Amongst all the mad ramblings, there was a singular point - *I just want a job*. I said good night. I felt sorry for him. He may have been prejudiced, he may have had delusions but within him there was an enduring quest for purpose that comes from honest work. Without that, he would go on his mad, angry adventure. Every one of us has a story to tell, if we will just give them the opportunity to tell it. I like to think that Dedric made it to Carmel. I like to think of him combing his hair, listening to Mick Jagger, standing on Bill's porch, maybe even preparing to take Bill for a drive into wine country.

I went to bed with two realisations - firstly, I was determined never to end up on my own and insane (something I had at one time entertained as being a possibility). Secondly, I would always see the potential in others, no matter how long their mullet. It was worth listening to people like Dedric, as you never knew when you would meet someone that colourful again. Well, as it turns out, we only had to wait until the next day.

Jimmy jumped around and waved his arms madly, to articulate his enthusiasm for everything. He shouted and laughed to himself.

"Oh I love your accents man, that's way cool, way cool man."

We had cycled 55 miles to Pismo State Beach campground at Oceano, passing Dedric's former employers in San Luis Obispo and giving them a cheery wave. Jimmy was parked up next to us. He would occasionally just rev his truck like a new toy and then laugh and dance around barefoot like a happy fool (and he continued this through the night). He was shirtless and fat, aged 52 (he told us repeatedly), with a large, ruddy, sweaty face. He had a scattering of missing teeth and lesions on his skin.

"Why do we always have to be camped next to some mad loon?" asked Killer, barely disguising his volume.

"I'm just hiding out - it's my first time camping man and it is way cool," Jimmy continued. "My mum just died so I'm hiding out and my two brothers died earlier this year. I got skin cancer. The doc says I'm next and I wanted to go camping. It's my first time and I love it. LOVE IT. Ha ha."

Jimmy's story was tragic and yet somehow he kept dancing around and waving his arms like he was being tickled by an invisible bear, which maybe he was.

"I'm gonna take all the money out my bank later. Just enjoy life man. I got no health insurance so what can I do. I just bought this truck. Isn't it great. I just bought it. Bought it off this crazy guy."

I felt dizzy with the enormity of the potential coincidence. "Er, did you buy it from a guy with long silver..." but I stopped as Jimmy was already nodding.

"Yeah, crazy guy, ha ha."

I shook my head. Maybe someone up above was just lining up all these Americans, each one connected and passing on the story, each with a role to play in revealing the country to us. It was up to us to stitch it all together and somehow make sense of it.

Camped immediately next to us was a couple whose normality led to them being infinitely less interesting than Jimmy when it came to recording extensive conversations in my diary. Becky and Colin. They had immediately got on our wrong side by asking, "Are you following Tom and Vicky's route?" while waving the guidebook we were also using.

"Ohhhh, you mean *Kirkendall* and *Spring*," Killer said, "then yes."

Killer and I discussed this at length later.

"Who do they think they are, calling Kirkendall and Spring by their first names?" I asked Killer in mock anger. "Are they friends? Do they deserve Kirkendall's love? Er, nooooo."

"I hate them."

"I looooathe them."

We laughed loudly at how ridiculous our roleplay had become. In truth, Becky and Colin were exactly the sort of people we had hoped to meet in campsites; people with the same naivety and excitement for the adventure as us, and even though they were Americans themselves - from Colorado - they shared the same warm, outsiders' curiosity for the characters they were encountering. Step out of your back yard and head in any direction in America it is all change, they said. We'd noticed that too, and yet perhaps being further removed enabled us to also see there was something that did connect all of these people and places; a desperate need to find out what it meant to be American.

We did differ from Becky and Colin in one clear way, in that particularly American trait for sincerity that us Brits struggle with. When Colin introduced us, he said: "Hey honey, I want you to meet two great guys from the UK; a journalist and a school teacher. Isn't that neat." Uttered by one of us, this would have sounded like a sarcastically-toned cutting insult, where 'great' was implied to mean 'shit' and 'neat' was implied to mean 'really shit'.

I had been working at a school before we left the UK, partly teaching English to overseas students and partly looking after the boarding house, but - much as I hugely respected the profession - I didn't see myself as a 'teacher'. So it was strange to be introduced as one. I wanted to be introduced as a writer.

Colin then realised something and looked a little disappointed when he said, "You must be the two guys we heard about at Pelican Point."

They'd arrived the day after our runner to find an angry owner, now distrusting of - and swearing at - all people on bikes.

"Well, we were never *really* there," I suggested mysteriously, feeling a little guilty still myself.

They told us it was going to storm in the night and we should stay put for another day. We looked at the clouds for some time, trying to shoot them down with mind bullets but sure enough, it grew black and forced us into our tents. Another sodding delay. A break in the weather the next day allowed us to venture into town at least but doing so only resulted in Killer losing his wallet.

"It's game over, Bone," said Killer when he realised. "If some fucker spends all my money then I have to go home. The end."

It sounded dramatic but he was right. We'd considered the prospect of calamity and disaster ending the expedition, but not something as simple as a slippery pocket. It may have been a few hours missing before he'd noticed and called home to cancel his bank cards, so we held out little hope of his finances still being intact. But as Killer called, I checked our emails and halle-bloody-lujah there was a message from our Oceano saviour. A woman had found the wallet on the street, spotted our contact details on our 'business cards' (another moment of mock aggrandisement from yours truly), and was emailing to see where she could return it. She soon turned up with her boyfriend at the internet cafe and handed the wallet to Killer. He immediately looked inside to see if everything was there, before realising how this might appear to his guardian angels. They stood there for a while and we all just nodded and smiled in silence. It was awkward. Were they waiting for a reward? They bloody deserved one. But money was in short supply and so we gave them a cheery wave and cycled off. Ding ding.

The extra day's delay gave me a chance to consult with Kirkendall over the route ahead to Los Angeles. We had a few beautiful Californian towns to pass through and soon we would have crossed all the peaks of this western coast. I could almost picture Kirkendall's face slowly wiping a tear back as he wrote that in the book. No more hills. The route would also get more urban, he warned us: busy, lots of traffic. But first we had a final hurrah. 'Two large climbs, each over 950 ft, stop the ride south of Oceano becoming tedious,' he noted. The me of a month ago would have laughed at this (or more likely cried) and perhaps dreaded the pain of the ascent, but I was finally understanding 'Tom'. Hills *are* awesome. They break up a long day's ride as much as a coffee stop. It gives your body something new to focus on and the slower pace cause your mind to drift off in different directions, and there's then a rush of endorphins as you reach the summit. You look out on something that only someone who has laboured for can really appreciate. It might even give you the chance to trick your riding companion…

Jimmy waved us off - or rather danced us off - and a few miles later I charged up the first hill, with a joke in my mind that was worth exhausting myself for. Killer was confused to see me disappear up, legs spinning, and by the time he got to the top, he was even more confused to see my whole face different; my scraggly beard - regrown since Greve - had been refashioned as a neat Freddie Mercury handlebar moustache.

"Oh hi Killer, nice view huh."

Killer laughed, seeing me hastily hide the plastic razor in my handlebar bag.

"I knew Bone was up to something. No one cycles that fast uphill because they enjoy it."

"Oh, I actually think I might."

Out of Oceano, the route had turned inland on a 40 mile detour to pass the huge, coastal Vandenberg Air Force Base, a space and military missile testing area. This was where America's ICBMs were developed. This included those called, with no sense of irony, 'Peacekeeper' missiles, which were part of the country's strategic nuclear arsenal at the time. These were missiles capable of travelling 7,000 miles and delivering a 300-kiloton thermonuclear warhead - that's 15 times larger than the bomb dropped on Nagasaki.

But on our side of the fence, all we saw were huge swathes of peaceful agricultural land. Endless fields of vegetables irrigated by giant sprinklers, hispanic-looking workers toiling and pickup trucks parked up at the side of the road as people set to work. Beyond the hills, we descended at speed down to Lompoc where I showed off my new facial fashion in KFC and - having just enjoyed his third puncture in three days - Killer suggested we stock up on bike inner tubes at Walmart. I became strangely and unreasonably angry at this suggestion. I wanted to be back out on the road and baulked at the comment.

"Oh yes, let's spend our free time in a sodding supermarket."

It is testament to Killer's character that he rode this off and perhaps telling of our friendship that I felt I could tell him when he was pissing me off. But this was no ordinary supermarket. In Walmart we found the inner tubes were two for $3, and a range of other everyday Limey essentials at ridiculous prices. We took some time to contemplate and select the right combination of chilli and noodles for that evening's dinner. And we found tubs of powdered gatorade, to scoop into our daily water bottles.

However, I should have stocked up on immediate snacks also. The next hill had looked easier on paper, a less abrupt climb, more gradual ascent for 14 miles, but really these tricksters were the worst. It looked deceptively like the flat as you rode along but the subtle incline grinded away at you, wearing you down without the satisfaction of a clear summit. But down the other side it was different, the road fell away straight and sharp, like the long slide at a fairground. We braced ourselves and let gravity take its course. As I noted the numbers flick past 40 mph on my speedo and as the bike started to wobble with the G-force, memories of the devil's pumpkin came back with frightening clarity. I think I might have let out a little yelp of terror. Maybe even a little Pelican.

At our intended stop of Gaviota State Beach it was empty. We had rejoined the US 101, and with the traffic we also had that glorious ocean view. But a sign said 'Closed for a few days' and we had no way of knowing when it had been hung up. We contemplated camping for free, behind the barriers, but Kirkendall had said there was a nice Hiker Biker site ten miles further and we got excited about the prospect of our first 75 mile day. The sun was low but our legs pumped with adrenaline to take us around the coast to Refugio State Beach. But no camping there either.

"Sorry, guys, the site is closed - try El Cap a few miles further," said the ranger. And so we pressed on to El Capitan as a golden sun slipped into a silver sea. We pulled in, pitched up and high-fived our first 80 mile day. Even better, there was no one else around. It was the wilderness, and it was all ours.

We covered another 95 miles over the next two days. Funny to think this was by now known as 'taking it easy', as we took time to explore the sites along the way. At Santa Barbara we wasted no time in heading straight to the Mission so we could recreate images of Kirkendall casually walking up its elegant steps, his strong legs shining in the summer light. The weather was being kind to us too that day; a gentle warmth and only a whisper of cloud.

"No, give it more calf Bone," said Killer, trying to pose me correctly.

"It's not possible Killer. He must be tensing in his picture."

"Kirkendall doesn't tense! My god, I love Kirkendall. Why can't *you* be more like Kirkendall?"

The Mission was spectacular - I could see why TK adorned his book with side trips to see them. They were also perhaps the oldest things you can still see, so a huge magnet for these Americans, as we'd come to understand them. This one was built in 1786, by Franciscans, and founded on the feast day of Saint Barbara, a girl beheaded by her father for following the Christian faith. It was perhaps a strange story from which to convince the local Indian tribes of the exciting possibilities of your cause, to remind them that people turning to this church have been known to lose their heads.

Invariably, it didn't take long before Dr John Santa Barbara turned up, offering his trademark wisdom for where to stop in town to enjoy its distinctive Spanish flavours, and how best to progress beyond it, including a 'great little restaurant' a few dozen miles inland.

"Oh, thanks but we're actually heading south."

"Yeah, well think about it, it's nice."

"Ok, er, thanks for the tip."

"Hey don't sweat it, I just like to help guys out, especially when they are from as far away as... New Zealand?"

We cruised along State Street, and at the pier we luncheoned on burgers, pointed at seagulls and enjoyed the beautiful beach life. That was until the burger seemingly caused an ill-tempered reaction in my ileum and I returned from the toilet whispering to Killer, "We must leave. I have no words for what happened in there."

The roads switched between gentle coast paths to city streets and freeways. This was well and truly 'Southern California' now. Perhaps it was the extra city traffic debris along the shoulder of the road that was punishing our wheels but, whatever the cause, we had our fifth puncture in five days. It says a lot about how the rhythms of cycling can become so mechanically subconscious that when the flow is disturbed by even so much as a prick of rubber, it was noted in my diary. A puncture, a pause, water bottles off, bike upside down, tyre off, hole located and patched, reassemble and roll on. And now all achieved in five minutes. It was a very pleasing set of manoeuvres and as it became more intuitive, it made us feel more authentic. But the puncture plethora brought with it a new phenomenon, ghost punctures. We started to 'feel' punctures that never existed. When the riding was as difficult as pedaling through treacle, you'd be convinced only a puncture could be slowing you down so much. You'd look down to assess, you'd pull over and squeeze the tyre but nothing. The cause was man not machine.

As we prepared to roll on from the latest repair, we paused to quickly compare Kirkendall's route to the ACA and a makeshift gathering formed around us. Two old duffer cyclists converged from the north and one more joined from the south, appearing instantly like some sort of geriatric superhero force. They engaged in a detailed debate about the options but spoke with all the clarity of the Mad Hatter's tea party.

"Well they could go that way but I don't know where it leads."

"Or that way, but there's no road there."

"Well I think they should go this way, but it depends where they are heading."

I tried to interject a few times to say that we had a good route map and had already decided where we were going but they were too focused (and too hard of hearing). We cycled on, leaving them still discussing and debating. As I suspected, they really didn't need us there to enjoy their nonsense.

We made camp at Carpinteria State Beach and then pressed on to Leo Carillo State Beach the next day. Three state beaches in three days and with it, we suspected, the last wild open camping of the western coast. They were low, long sandy bays with a scattering of rocks that were crested at low tide and the soft dunes were backdropped by rugged green hills. It was in places like this that you could lose your eyes into the panorama and allow all the unmanaged thoughts that had been bubbling in the background to be finally wrestled with. And one in particular was long overdue a resolution.

Before arriving at Leo Carillo I had headed into a store to buy a phone card. The Chinese American store owner had got his PhD in Miami so he cheered enthusiastically when I told him of the plan ahead. He displayed his diploma on the wall along with a photo of his citizenship ceremony. He thrust some bags of beef jerky into my hands, saying it would keep me strong but he was mostly interested in why I needed a phone card.

"Well I need to make a call. To Australia."

"Oh sure, who's in Australia?"

"Er, well, this girl."

"Oh ok. Why are you here then?"

And in that brief exchange he had summed up and concluded what I had been labouring over for weeks. Suddenly, it all seemed a little more clear. When I came out to the US, the girl I was dating in Sherborne had moved to Sydney to find the brother she'd only just discovered existed. She wanted me to join her when I was done, and I had been unable to commit to the idea. The shopkeeper was right - surely if I wanted to be in Australia, I would make plans to go there. I couldn't turn to Killer for sincere advice on this so I walked to the beach and had an emergency meeting with Brian.

"I think it's over," I said.

"It's been over for a while. Don't you think?"

"No, well yeah, I guess... I don't know. I wasn't ready to say it out loud before."

"And you are now?"

"I think I can do it."

"You are taking different paths. But, if I'm honest, I don't think you ever really wanted to follow hers."

"What do you mean?"

"You had fun but I don't think you ever loved her. You just didn't feel strong enough to be on your own, to follow your own dreams. In fact, maybe staying with her was even easier than deciding what your own dreams were."

"God, you're right. And that was bizarrely efficiently put."

"Well, this story really isn't about her so I thought we'd keep it short."

I let out a sigh of understanding.

"I feel bad," I said.

"No, don't feel bad. You believed you did love her but really you just needed her. And I think the same goes for her. It's now time for both of you to cast off. You got this."

I felt mute with the truth of it all. Brian rested a giant soft paw on my shoulder and rocked me into one of his thick, furry hugs, before sloshing his giant bear tongue over my face and I told him he'd taken the imaginary conversation too far. I stood up to leave but he called after me.

"Hey. Don't you worry. It's gonna be alright. 'Cause I'm always ready, I won't let you out of my sight."

I recognised it as the lyrics to the Baywatch theme tune and I shook my head at his levity, despite it sounding quite appropriate, and he chuckled, before running into the sea with a happy splash.

I found a payphone and called the girl. The last time we spoke I'd stalled the decision on 'what's happening with us' by saying I found the whole planning too much while on this trip. (And what woman in her right mind doesn't feel special when guys blame logistics for not committing). But now I was honest. We both were. We would still chat over the rest of the trip, we agreed. We still needed that. But 'us', Australia... that was never happening. I felt relieved when I'd told her but at the same time, I felt like I had kicked off my stabilisers.

All I wanted to do now was get incredibly drunk in LA. Thankfully, we had the perfect host for such a mission: Ernest. He was a 40-year-old writer with a huge trust fund and a penchant for debauchery, and he just happened to live in Beverly Hills. When I had calmed a little, I called him to flag we were due the next day and he gave me the directions to his home, just off Sunset Boulevard.

"You'll recognize it because of the big blue Mercedes out front. It's near Ozzy Osbourne's house, if you know where that is."

I did not.

"Great, well we don't want to trouble you too much. We'll just stay a night." I said.

"No man, you're staying the weekend, we have some parties to go to. Anyway, I gotta go - I can't concentrate: I'm hungover and I'm listening to the Beatles. And I haven't even done my meditation yet."

7. From Hollyweird to San Diego

Los Angeles, CA to San Diego, CA

Life moves pretty fast. If you don't stop and look around once in a while, you could miss it.
Ferris Bueller

We had been warned by Dr John Orick and every one of his namesakes since - including the latest incarnation in Santa Barbara - that cycling in LA was suicide. And the closer we got to the city, the more obvious it was that ignoring their advice might be the last stupid thing we do. 101 had become Route 1 again, which suddenly became something more appealing in name than in reality - the Pacific Coast Highway, or PCH. The road expanded with every mile, until there were eventually four lanes on each side. Everywhere around us were cars; overtaking us with inches to spare, blindly pulling out of junctions or just parked up but then opening their doors without warning as we passed, nearly ramming us. Along the way, we also spotted a few Malibu mansions that were quickly going from 'ocean view' to 'oceanside', proving time and tide get us all eventually. And we did start to see the city's famous beaches stretch out, twinkling in front us. But these distractions were just temporary glances between a firm focus on the road ahead and near-Pelican experiences.

By the time we had reached the junction with Sunset Boulevard, we had cycled 25 mentally exhausting miles. But this was nothing compared to the next leg. 'Sunset' snaked for over 10 miles, steeply up, past Bel Air, and into Beverly Hills. The cars all seemed to be sports cars with blacked-out windows, charging at speed in some sort of death race. Many of the drivers chatted away on mobile phones, and none appeared to see us. At times, especially as we rounded a blind bend, the car behind would be on us without knowing we existed, and we were forced on to the pavement to evade impact. In many places, there wasn't even pavement to escape to. Not even Kirkendall would take this road. He had advised that if we attempted to cycle in the city it would 'require the use of every riding skill you have' and that we would need to be 'constantly alert and concentrating'. This was, quite considerably, an understatement.

At one point, I needed to just catch my breath after a particularly buttock-loosening junction and I waited for Killer. He didn't show up. I waited for several more minutes but nothing. I kept looking back up the road. It bent around through a narrow gap and then I knew it dropped steeply on the other side. I walked back to the junction and started to ask drivers at the red light if they had seen a cyclist back up the road, but nothing, they just shook their heads. However, this meant little, as not noticing cyclists was something they did quite well. I could go no further back to check myself as I could not cross the road from where I stood. It would be like walking across the M25 with a blindfold on. In my mind, there was only one thing that could have happened - Killer was either dead or fatally wounded. I needed to get help.

I reasoned I couldn't have been too far from Ernest's so I pressed on and found his road and the blue car. It looked like Bill's beautiful machine in Carmel and I wondered if this was some sort of millionaire's Mercedes, maybe you get it when you join the club… No time for that. I had arrived sweating, filthy, shaken and bleeding from the leg where, in my haste, my shin had collided heavily with my pedal. I was therefore perhaps a bit of an unusual and unsightly guest to be ringing a Beverly Hills doorbell. It is perhaps then understandable that Ernest's mother Blanche - bedecked in crisp, human clothes, hair coiffed, neck pearled - lifted her eyebrows to the roof when she saw me.

"Hello, I'm Ernest's friend. Is he here?"

"Oh my, would you like a shower?" These were genuinely her first words to me.

"Thank you, but later. I've lost my cycling companion somewhere on Sunset Boulevard and we need to go and find him as I think he may have had an accident."

She then took in my whole ungodly ensemble, settling on my Tour de France yellow cycling shirt.

"Oh are you raising money for the French?" I loved her for this question.

"What? No. This is just a... I mean, no. Cancer. We are raising money to fight cancer. Is Ernest here?"

"Sure, I'll go and get him. Are you sure you don't want a shower?" I declined again and she returned a few minutes later.

"Ernest will be right with you." She pressed a fresh white towel into my hands, and scurried away.

Ernest and I jumped into the car and headed off down Sunset. Me, nervous, edgy, full of adrenaline. Ernest, almost sleepy with Californian coolness.

As I was fully expecting to find Killer's limbs laid out across the road, it was with some relief to find him wheeling his bike along a pavement, close to where I had looked for him.

"Oh hey man," called out Ernest as we approached Killer. "Looks like you need a drink."

So Killer hadn't died. He did come close though - a car had given him such a close shave that he was forced off the road into a bush where a piece of exceptionally placed metal had narrowly avoided his leg and slashed into his front tyre. But all the repair kit was safely stowed on my bike so he was forced to walk along the road - humming a protective mantra to the Limey gods - until he found a pavement. And as the directions to Ernest's were also with me, Killer then had no clue in which way to walk further. But he quickly formed an extraordinarily cunning plan to find someone selling maps to celebrity homes, which he would use to follow a path to the

Osbourne's, where he would ask the bat-eating rock devil which of his neighbours was the biggest drinker.

When we found Killer, he was slightly sweary at the state of LA's roads and then even more sweary when he saw there was no room for his bike in the merc. I tossed him the repair kit and pump and directions and we drove off, laughing at the fury creasing on Killer's face. In my memory of his expression in that moment, I see a foreshadowing. Killer was back in town two years later to interview Guns n' Roses for a rock guitar magazine. He was in almost the exact same spot when he was run over by a drunk driver, dragged 90 feet under the car and spent a month in hospital having a metal plate put in his leg. It was just a matter of time before Sunset - and America's automobile obsessions - got him.

Ernest's house was exceptional. Blanche is an art dealer and so the house also doubles as gallery space - large, sumptuous canvases hung on the walls, and fine sculptures decorated every room. This was also just the smaller of their two houses in Beverly Hills. In the other - nearby - such menial tasks as doorbell answering are performed by 'the help', saving you from unforeseen confrontations with grubby Englanders. They were one of the richest families in America and Ernest himself was one of the most interesting people I knew. He had moved to small town England to escape LA, to find time and space to write. What he largely found though were places to drink and discuss; he was often distracted from his writing by the lure of the pub. And when there was no one there to chat to, he'd just be reading in the corner, nursing a pint. Many people particularly enjoyed the fact that Ernest was one of those rare creatures - someone wholly at ease with themselves. He would walk through town in a cream linen suit, topped off with a Panama hat, a paperback poking out of his jacket pocket. Despite his wealth, in England he was modest and lived simply. The locals didn't find his intelligence snooty, they found him a delicious curiosity at most.

Ernest was 42 but looked like he was in his early 30s. For over 20 years he had done yoga for two hours a day, leaving his physique lean and muscular. As he welcomed us to LA, he wore white shorts, a white sleeveless T-shirt and a white gilet, all topped off with a tweed flat cap; a small nod to his Limey visitors. It would have been a mad combination of clothes on anyone else but on Ernest it had an enviable sartorial ease and you suspected this would be how all Los Angelians would be clothed from now on.

We decided to make good use of Blanche's washing facilities, which seemed to please her immensely. In the bathroom we looked lengthily at our curious new physiques. It was like a monkey being given a mirror for the first time. For a while we both just stood there and laughed. What was this skinny body, this flat waist, these muscles appearing at all angles on our legs. Was this one of those mirrors you get at the circus? Five weeks of cycling was already redefining our forms, and we had so far yet to go.

Ernest took us to a bar that is apparently a well trodden stop by both tourist and local. Barney's Beanery. We played pool, drank beers and smoked Marlboros on the deck, chatting loudly to other Americans. It was immediately reassuring to learn Ernest also found the loudness and directness of conversations with strangers in his home country unnerving. After a few years in Sherborne, he had only moved back three weeks ago, and was still trying to adjust.

"People come up to me and talk to me and I'm like WHAT DOES THIS GUY WANT? Your country messed me up man."

But it wasn't just the Brit in him. Ernest had always maintained a refreshing, objective eye on the goings on around him, laughing at the tanning stores we saw open at midnight, the people dolled up in cafes in case they got 'spotted' and the fact that everyone else seemed to somehow be in 'the industry'.

The guy next to me turned to his friend when a movie came on the TV above the bar.

"Hey, didn't you work on this one?"

"Oh yeah. With… shit, what's her name…?"

"Jackie, right?"

"Nope."

"Jess?"

"No."

"Carmen."

"Yeah Carmen, I think."

"Whatever happened to Carmen?"

"Oh don't ask man. She's shooting commercials for cat food or some shit."

"Ah that's too bad. Dog food would be different but cat food…"

"I know."

Ernest's sister Opal shared his perspective, and described the oddity around them as 'Hollyweird'. She also shared his giveafuck attitude towards attire, choosing to head out in a cotton onesie that resembled a child's pyjamas. She obviously made a clear distinction between the weirdness of the city and the perfect normalness of creative individual expression.

Opal was 40, but also could have passed for a decade younger. Back at the house, I had noticed that their kitchen resembled a low scale apothecary business, being festooned with health pills and potions that appeared to have stopped their ageing process. They may have baulked at some of the strangeness around them but had fully bought into the pharmaceutical support for California's healthy lifestyle.

At Barney's I asked her what all the bottles were and she went through them in turn, suggesting which ones we needed for our trip, talking at length about something to do with 'electrolytes'.

"Seriously? You don't take electrolytes? OK, so you are riding every day, losing a lot of salt in your sweat and in that sweat are so many essential electrolytes. You have to replace them. Sports drinks with electrolytes are good but pills are great. You need to buy some multivitamins that have electrolytes. What, you don't even take vitamins? And you eat what? Choo-what?? Seriously guys."

As much as I wanted to laugh I was left ashamed of my personal dietary habits. I asked Killer to order a pint of electrolytes at the bar.

We were joined by Kai, Ernest's old college friend. He wore round John Lennon glasses, which resided almost permanently at the end of his nose - they seemed to serve no function for vision but did seem well-used for emphasis: when concluding a point he would push the glasses up his nose with a long, wet inhalation, as if the gesture was a physical exclamation mark. "Hey, you guys should really try this Mexican beer called…." *breathe, push glasses, smile…* "Tecate!" It was to become a motion and sound that easily slipped into our daily impressions.

Ernest was getting restless and insisted on taking us to a strip bar on Sunset, er, Strip. Girls walked about everywhere in their underwear or danced on poles, across three different stages. They were all exceptionally beautiful but, for me, the most attractive was the fully clothed girl who brought us our drinks. She smiled encouragingly, sensing I felt uncomfortable to be there. Looking around, past the girls I increasingly just saw crowds of braying men, sleazing and laughing.

But not all patrons were the same. As with any other drinking establishment, Ernest enjoyed the experience on his own terms. He enjoyed long, interesting conversations with the girls (as well as long dances, it turns out). One girl bounced over, happy to see him, as if an old friend.

"Where have you been? I heard you went all British on us. How's the Queen?"

Ernest chuckled (and it wasn't until later that I thought 'He probably does know the bloody Queen…'). He asked the girl how her studies were going and then turned to me and Killer and said he'd got dances off her every week when he last lived here.

"I think I pretty much put her through college," he said offhand.

It was apparent that her study fund needed a top-up so we left Ernest to it and went off to find another bar but the bouncer told us all the bars were closed as it was after 2am.

"Closed??" asked Opal in disbelief.

"Yeah, closed. As in not open. This ain't New York lady. Hollywood's overrated."

Bars no, but manicurists, tanning salons and dry cleaners yes. Such was Hollyweird. Outside, a car pulled up. A limo. The rear window rolled down and a man leaned out calling to Opal, obviously believing only a certain type of woman wore pyjamas and a fur coat at this time of night.

"Hey, didn't I see you dance tonight? You were fabulous."

Opal pulled her collar up around her neck and threw her head back. "Thank you, darling."

We laughed like a gang of old friends and headed back. We drank for a while until Ernest returned and he confessed he'd spent $280 on dances on that one girl. Opal and Killer drifted off and it was then just Ernest, Kai and I by the pool drinking cans of Tecate. It was nearly 5am, 24 hours after I had woken up at Leo Carillo, and the subject moved to girls, real ones, the ones you have relationships with and that get you all confused inside. Ernest had a girlfriend in Sherborne he thought he might marry one day, maybe, and Kai had a girlfriend in Thailand he hadn't seen in years and wasn't sure when he would again. I realised that these guys - 17 years my senior - were still going through the same questions I was at 25. I wasn't abnormal for being confused and finding this relationship thing hard. But I also realised I didn't want to still be unsure when I was 42. Uncertainty was unhappiness, I'd learned.

Ernest had a meeting of 'the family' at 9am. It was a once a year meeting of the 12 members of the family to discuss and allocate that year's charitable donations. Ernest had decided to dedicate some of his share to a charity that built homes in Ethiopia but wasn't sure if he could face going to the meeting given his state. People were flying in from across the USA and Ernest couldn't handle the trip to the next street.

"You do realise that an entire African village is going to starve next year because the big white god got drunk on Tequila and Tecate?" I told him.

A few hours later, I heard Sgt Pepper playing at top volume and Ernest headed out. Killer and I turned on the TV and were amazed to see the team from Yeovil - the small town next to Sherborne, and where I had gone to sixth form college - playing football on this obscure American cable channel, the first channel we had clicked on.

Ernest had laid out a variety of newspapers - the LA Times, New York Times, USA Today. I was familiar with the latter and its lack of deep contemporary reflection but was pleased with the extensive foreign news and balanced reporting of American politics in the New York Times. This was all new to me. It reported on Michael Howard becoming the new leader of the Conservatives (I would then interview Howard in my new career as a journalist just a few months later). And I read that the California wildfires were finally under control and dying out but that the scale of the devastation was only now being understood. There was a cartoon of the former Governor Gray Davis handing Arnie the keys and saying 'It's all yours'. In a week or so we'd be crossing through the lands the fires were still being extinguished in.

When Ernest returned, he drove us down to the beach. The sand was occasionally dotted with lifeguard stations, exactly as you see on Baywatch, offering assurance to the cliché-comforted Brits. I half expected to see Pamela Anderson or Yasmine Bleeth jog past in slow motion, their swimsuits giving them painful wedgies, but in truth everyone looked like they could be on the show. Were the average, everyday Americans that we had met at every gas station coffee break on the road somehow not allowed here? What there were in abundance were cyclists, rollerbladers, dog walkers, and extreme frisbee enthusiasts, all enjoying the California beach life. I could see why this slice of LA life was appealing, but it also served to show more acutely that cycling was clearly a beachside leisure activity for the well-off and not an everyday healthily getting around kind of activity in any other part of the city.

We talked about writing. It was a rich seam with Ernest as he was always working on something, even if nothing ever seemed to be produced. His latest project was a dramatization of the life of John Wilkes Booth, the guy who assassinated Abraham Lincoln in 1865. Booth was one of the most famous actors of his day, the equivalent of a Hollywood megastar. His father was a noted Shakespearean actor who moved from England to Maryland in the 1820s and went on to found a family theatre business that would make them rich. Booth gave this up when he shot Lincoln in the head and then fled on horseback to try and find friends of the Confederacy. But instead he was found in a barn, smoked out and killed. As Ernest said it's 'one hell of a story'.

Since Lincoln, more than 30 attempts have been made to kill a US President (either in office or after or as President-elect). Two Presidents have been injured in the attempt - Theodore Roosevelt and Ronald Reagan - and three others have been killed. James Garfield was killed in 1881, William McKinley in 1901 and - most recently - John F Kennedy in 1963. Brian had pointed out in an earlier conversation how different this country might be if the right to *bear arms* was interpreted differently. A lot less shooting, and a lot more hugging.

It was a November afternoon and we strolled in T-shirts as far as Santa Monica. We looped back after checking the amusements through narrow shopping streets. We met a woman who had laid out a stall to tell the world about a Democrat called Lyndon LaRouche. She spoke eloquently and passionately.

"This is a man who deserves to be the Presidential candidate," she told me. "This is a man who wants a different

America. We must return to the old values. We must educate our young people. We must turn away from the brink of the nuclear war that Bush is taking us into. We don't have to follow this false message of fear."

As it turns out LaRouche would not get close to becoming the Democratic candidate. That would go to John Kerry but Bush would not be defeated. He was riding high as the man leading the fight against the invisible foreign terror. But it was the woman's comments on education that struck me most. Everywhere I looked in America I saw dumbing down and she suggested this was by design not accident. Eventually, I reasoned, people just won't realise they are dumb. How can the sleeping wake those that are asleep?

It was only later I learned that there was a whole movement behind this guy, the LaRouche movement. People like the woman we met were around the country setting up stalls, spreading his gospel. Whatever his message I was somewhat reassured there were powerful voices for change, at odds with the dangerous direction of Bush. LaRouche specifically had built himself around Marxist philosophies but drifted into quite alternative perspectives. I wonder how Ernest would have reacted if he'd known then that LaRouche once said he thought the Beatles were invented by British intelligence as a weapon to subvert the United States. Well, actually Ernest might have agreed with that.

Ernest had a family dinner that evening so he dropped Killer and I off at the cinema. We were excited for what we had thought would be a quiet night, and no booze. It was a Saturday night so the complex was teeming with couples on dates and groups of friends, although seemingly no other male duo in complementary 'his and his' dark jeans and fleeces. It was apparent that we were being taken for a dating couple also and at that time even in California it seemed to cause a few silent expressions of confusion. But Brian had taught us to ignore that.

The cinema in the UK is hallowed turf. Snacks really should be of the silent variety and modestly proportioned but here we were presented with a choice of vats of drinks and banquet items, ranging from nachos to hotdogs. I opted for a small (read jumbo) tub of popcorn and then followed the locals' lead in pumping hot butter onto it from what looked like a ketchup dispenser.

The film was *Kill Bill*, the latest Tarantino movie. We had hoped to discover Carmel Bill in the lead role as ninja assassin but sadly it had been offered to Uma Thurman instead. Inside, arriving late, we found the only seats left were in the front row. As we edged our way in - our matching outfits now being topped with his and his refreshments - the audience regarded us as if some suitably curious opener for the Tarantino madness to follow.

We soon discovered the American openness and fondness for talking loudly in public extended even to here. The guy next to me was a particularly enthusiastic observer of the film, calling out to the characters on the screen. "Oh no... watch out... I think she's gonna... Oh wow... Ha... what a way to die!" And at the end, applause ran through the audience as if we had been at an actual theatre with live performers. It is possible the noise of this ovation did in fact reach the actors in the nearby Hollywood hills, though.

Ernest picked us up and now had his cousin Tommy in the car. Tommy was a penis.

"Hey so like does everything look *bigger* here than in the UK? Ha ha. Like the houses, are they *bigger*? What about the cars, they gotta be... *bigger*? Yeah? I KNEW it."

Kai was also there, pressed up against me on the back seat.

"Have you tried Tecate?" he asked, as he pressed a can into my hand, before sliding his glasses up his nose.

When I asked Ernest if we were going back to the mansion for a glorious sleep, he just laughed. Our destination, it seemed, was Venice Beach, one of LA's most eclectic and eccentric neighbourhoods. Millions of people descend on Venice's promenade every year to enjoy the street hustle, performers and fortune tellers, or to gawp at the bronzed flesh rippling at the outdoor exercise zoo, Muscle Beach. We were headed to a house party where the owner had the appropriately Venitian job of high end stereo speaker designer. The party was to launch his latest designs, two of which stood about 8 ft tall in the main room, punching out asymmetric cool folk vibes. The room was otherwise empty and the speakers glowed under the focus of two spotlights. The owner would occasionally give people a tour of the speakers, pointing out the subtle innovations that made their sound worth the thousands of dollars price tag. Guests appreciatively nodded at the towers as if totems.

These guests oozed an uber trendiness; turtleneck jumpers and leather jackets, conversations about jazz poets and secret gallery openings. I had stumbled into an arthouse movie. I felt apologetic for crashing the scene but the owner seemed to enjoy the sprinkled spice of these two Englanders passing through on their transcontinental push-bikes. And indeed everyone we met was open and keenly interested in our adventure. Ernest had already warned us, "With your accents and your story you are going to be mauled."

I got chatting to a young guy who, when he heard I was British, got emotional about an 'amazing' book by Ken Follett that enlightened him to an 'amazing order of monasteries in the 11th Century'.

"I just love all that old English stuff, you know," he said. "It's amazing."

"Yeah. I know."

I told him about Sherborne; our castles, the Abbey, our local Saint, Sir Walter's head… "…and one day he was smoking his pipe by the lake and…ha ha ha." By this stage, his face looked like he was about to ejaculate, and when I mentioned our school was founded in 1550 by King Edward VI, and we had a school song in Latin, I feared he would combust.

Where were these intelligent and oddly interesting people when I turned on the TV in the USA? I started to contemplate the curious and dangerous habit of platforming ignorance. To return the educational exchange, my new Follet friend not only enjoyed outlining the options for our route ahead across country but wanted to ensure we understood the potential dangers they came with.

"I tell you what. You'll probably hit New Orleans. I was there last year. A guy jumped into our car and demanded our money. My buddy - who was driving - had a gun and just shot him three times. Shot him in the chest. The guy died a week later."

He left the story there in the air, enjoying the effect of the drama. I looked to see if Killer had also taken this in but he seemed to be trying to explain the comparative proportions of British and American cinema snacks to cousin Tommy. I moved away to get a beer and a girl bumped into me. She was called Jaymie, was 21, and had moved to town from Oklahoma a few months before to discover the Californian dream. She already seemed so typically LA but I could tell it was an act, masking a country naivety that she was hoping no one would notice. It was there to be seen in the way she tottered in her glossy red stilletoes and left traces of her thick red lipstick on her wine glass. As she stumbled, she occasionally spilled her wine, although somehow never on her ice white jacket. With every new spill we'd move away from the crowd a little so as to not be blamed. And eventually we were on our own and I realised we were just staring at each other as we spoke. I also realised I was smiling broadly. It was partly the happy relief that came from knowing with more certainty that I had closure from the girl. But moreover it was that vain pride that comes from having someone beautiful look at you like they find *you* attractive; an invitation to examine them more intensely.

Ernest was leaving but Jaymie said she'd drive me herself if I stayed a little longer. Her car was a four wheeled drive all-terrain vehicle, the kind marketed at LA people who want to imbue they have adventure in them. She played Phil Collins on the car stereo, the lights of the city hummed a soft orange as we drifted home on the seemingly mile-wide freeway. She confessed she didn't want to say goodbye just yet and we drove for a couple of miles past Ernest's until we found Benedict Canyon and then went up Summit Drive, passing huge, multi-millionaire mansions. We pulled over. The valley was a glowing carpet of fog but it soon blew off and there was that view, the Hollywood view with LA spread out before us like a movie set. The day before I was a filthy, sweaty tent dweller and here I was, the King of Los Angeles. I loved my tent life but this was some experience. I tried to ignore the nagging feeling though that across this whole wide horizon, the simple pleasure of riding a bike was always an exercise in keeping your pants dry.

The evening needed an end and we started to contemplate it, navigating our positions across the front seats like teenagers. As we did, a car drove up the road and pulled alongside us. Its headlights had revealed the scene to the driver. I assumed it was cops or an angry resident, but a happy, surfers voice came from the darkness, "Way to go dude!" and he drove off. We laughed and fell back. Jaymie dropped me off for real and told me that even though she didn't really know me, she'd miss me like hell.

"It is so good to meet someone so passionate about what they believe in," she said.

I hadn't been aware of how much I had been talking about my motivations and hopes for this trip, or that I had done so with so much enthusiasm, but I reflected happily on how this appetite within me was burning so brightly. I was excited to again get back on the bike. But first, we had another friend to visit.

Ernest sketched the best way to get to the next stop, a southern LA neighbourhood called Manhattan Beach, on a scrap of paper the next morning. The 20 mile route was marked by several intersecting lines to indicate major highways, and was signed 'Good luck'. Was it just me or did the sketch map bear a striking resemblance to a picture of a gallows? As I looked at this and considered our upcoming death, I asked Ernest casually, "Um, what would you think of, er, maybe, driving us?"

"Oh sure, of course, let's go," he said.

We collapsed with relief into his car at having once again sidestepped the reaper and set off. We stopped along the way at the Urth Cafe for lunch. It's in Melrose, a neighbourhood known for its high proportion of enhancedly beautiful people, even by LA standards. And this cafe was the centre of gravity for the health conscious wannabe Hollyweirdo, paying well to see and be seen. I ordered a coke and the waiter laughed as if I'd taken a wrong turn at Compton, and pointed to the extensive range of health drinks available.

"I used to just come and sit here and stare at the beautiful women," said Ernest reflectively.

By then we had to add a name for beautiful women to our Limepedia. And this name was Jessica, in honour of recumbent Greg's 'most beautiful girl in the world', who he'd been writing to when we met him. There were inordinate numbers of callipygian Jessicas in Melrose and so they exceeded the tipping point that meant adding their name to the Limepedia was a necessity of navigation, rather than purely a symptom of our bubbling, immature desire. Every one of these Jessicas carried themselves as if they were famous; some dressed to the nines on a Sunday lunchtime, some dressed down but in a way that told you they had made a lot of effort to appear so relaxed about their appearance. And many wore large sunglasses as if they were trying to just get some goddamn celebrity privacy. We put on our shades to try and blend in but I don't think anyone was convinced by our cracked Oakleys and general hobo-chic look, with authentic tramp hair. And we obviously hadn't been to the 24-hour tanning salon. So we left Hollywood having not been asked to appear in a single movie, or even a pet food commercial. Killer and I reasoned we'd just have to write our own film and cast ourselves in it as the leads, with Brian involved too of course. We'd return to that thought later.

At Manhattan Beach we said goodbye to Ernest with hugs. In the city of sin, he'd truly shown us the way around. But moreover he'd opened his home, fully. And here was another - when we walked in, I recognised it from the last time I was here. I'd passed through LA three years before, spending one night while waiting for a connecting flight. In a bar, a girl had bumped into me - it seems to be an LA tradition - and when I had apologised in typical British fashion, even though *she* had walked into *me*, she exclaimed excitedly, "Oh do I detect an accent?" Beverly - whose surname was tragically not Hills - was a self-confessed Anglophile and pulled me into the limo she'd hired with a group of friends that night and I'd crashed at her pad so they could make me say 'tomato' and 'water' and 'pasta' and 'OK that's enough now'.

This time she was no less enthusiastic. Her already-huge eyes were exploding with excitement and eagerness to be a good host. She produced a freshly baked cake and made tea. She was the definition of American wholesomeness and had a perennial cheerleader's smile on her face. And the community of Manhattan Beach seemed to fit her mood - down by the pier we watched surfers happily catch breaks by our feet. The beaches were long and beautiful and free from care. The area had a villagey feel with laid back cafes, and people playing volleyball or pushing prams. Her life as an auditor at Deloitte didn't excite her so much, she said, but for now she liked what it afforded her.

We showed her some of the photos of the trip so far and she was laughing loudly - the Escape from Alcatraz, the matching moustaches, the getting stuck in Redwoods...

"Wow - you guys really like to have *fun*, don't you?"

She asked what was happening in one picture and I explained how we had enjoyed a mini fridge raid at Harrison's in San Francisco. She insisted on recreating it with her own fridge and her eyes twinkled a little more as she joined in ransacking her own supplies.

"Oh my gosh, I'm having too much fun!"

Coming from a long tradition of British sarcasts, I found Beverly's sincerity uncomfortable at first, but soon found it incredibly charming. It was a trait we would see in many Americans, including in Beverly's friend Chrissy who joined us for dinner. She wore crisp jeans, and a neat, plain pink jumper. She soon declared, "Oh my cheeks are hurting from laughing so much." And the waitress joined in when I tried to order a BLTA (Bacon, Lettuce, Tomato, and Avocado sandwich), pronouncing it phonetically for comic effect, as if it was a word I had never seen in this exotic country, "Can I get the, what is that, a 'blataaa'?" To which she replied, "Hey, that's funny."

Back at the flat, Beverly put the karaoke machine on the big TV and we took turns to sing along. Killer and I performed Backstreet Boys which drew some enthusiastic applause (for Killer's singing). It was good, clean, wholesome fun. I couldn't imagine doing something so simple back home without a raft of sarcastic comments about how geeky it all was and what losers we all were, whilst we all secretly revelled in it. I'd have to change that. Even *my* cheeks were starting to bruise.

In the morning, we waved Beverly off to work and then watched Baywatch - which of course just happened to be on TV - as we packed up and prepared for the next leg. In the episode, Mitch Buchannon, aka hairy sexcake David Hasselhoff, was talking to his son about being true to yourself, having just rescued him from a storm. The rising waters that nearly trapped the boy were a metaphor for what happens when you get in with the wrong crowd - evidenced by one nasty older boy smoking a cigarette and having an apparently total disregard for the creases in his T-shirt. The son thanks Mitch for this valuable life lesson.

"Dad, why is it that I feel like you're my best friend?"

"I don't know son, maybe it's because you're my best friend too."

In this one scene, our LA experience was concluded. Crime and temptation all around, and messages of the redemption of karaoke and fresh cakes alongside it. Funny to think that a few months after we passed through town, the wholesome all-American gal Beverly quit her job as an auditor, moved to the northern

California woods, married a leather-clad motorbiker, and started working for a 'Tattoos & Bikes' magazine. Well, if we were encouraging people to follow their dreams, I was all for it.

It was only three days from Los Angeles, or more specifically, from leaving Beverly's, to get to San Diego, but I had decisively scribed 'shit' in big letters in my diary on the leg's completion. This was not some dismissive score I had given the entire southwestern seaboard's scenery but more an encapsulation of the nervous near-death feeling we continued to experience periodically but painfully those short, trying days. It was the feeling of occasionally being nudged by the wing mirrors of giant RVs and edged off the road by their sheer girth that left us feeling as if we might at any time be sucked under their colossal wheels. Indeed, the last dash to San Diego may be mostly remembered for our occasional, high-pitched gasps of 'shiiiiiiiiiiiiiiiit'. If anyone ever asks me if I recommend cycling the Pacific Coast, I say yes, most emphatically. Just, whatever you do, please, for the love of Dr John, stop at LA.

The first day out was particularly hard. The open roads north of LA had given way south of the city to dense, built-up communities that melded into one another in seamless similarity. Threading through the urbanity was the heavy and frenetic freeway, lined with motels, fast food chains and surf shops. Every town looked the same and all had the same suffix, as they competed for visitors to their slice of the California coastal experience. We passed Hermosa Beach and Redondo Beach before getting lost at Long Beach. Seal Beach, Sunset Beach and Huntington Beach followed in the afternoon before we arrived at Newport Beach after 55 miles. Our stop, the first camping opportunity south of LA and with no other options for more than 20 miles, was an RV park that had the grand title of Newport Dunes Waterfront Resort. In Newport, everything liked to be grand. This was Orange County, known to many as the OC, and its status as a rich kids playground was just being brought to life in a new eponymously-named drama series while we cycled through. In the show, an idealistic family called the Cohens (essentially people we all want to believe are just like us) clash with the shallow, materialistic, and closed-minded community in which they reside.

And this was also our take on the community in real life. Having paid $18 for a small plot, we were then informed that we were not allowed to put tent pegs in the Astroturf type ground. After a number of escalatingly expletive curses in which it became clear the site staff thought campers were an alien breed to be tolerated but not accommodated, there followed a sweaty hour while we attempted to keep our tents upright by tying various corners of our tents to signposts, fences and any other surrounding objects we could reach. The only comfort came when we later visited the resort's ginormous pool and hot tub. They were floodlit from within, and so passed a golden glow to the steam that was rising from the surface into the night. It looked beautiful. In fact, it must have looked like some romantic idyll to anyone who passed by or, specifically, to a large man called Chris, who was lured in to joining us by the vision.

Splosh.

"How y'all doing?"

Chris was taking in the scene. Two athletic looking guys in tight lycra shorts (we had no swimming shorts) sitting together, alone, in the hot tub.

"Y'all having a nice time? I saw you here having fun and couldn't resist but come join." He sensed our trepidation. "Oh, I'm here with *my* partner Justin, by the way."

It was as if he was trying to say 'Don't worry, I'm here with someone so I'm harmless even though my eyes suggest I want to cover you in butter and eat you all up', but the emphasis on the *my*, 'I'm here with *my* partner', suggested more - he assumed Killer and I were also partners, and that we were all just a bunch of happy gay guys hanging out in a spa. By this stage we had stopped trying to correct anyone's impression of us. Almost everyone thought we were either brothers or lovers and that was fine with us.

Chris and 'Jus', as he was soon referred to, were staying in a large RV in the park. They were having pizza later and watching tennis on TV.

"You should come over. You'll see our trailer cos it's got a large satellite on the roof. Jus' would love to meet you." He had a twinkle in his eye that reminded us of another Chris - the desperate burger making Internet hunter from Day 1's camping, which instantly filled me with dread. I replied with a, "Sure, we'll see, maybe, but we are really tired."

Killer followed my cue with a stretch.

"Yeah, looooong day," he yawned.

Our suspicions that a conversational hostage situation would have arisen had we accepted the invitation were realised when Chris proceeded to tell us everything we could possibly know about Justin. It started as a romantic homage but descended into a counseling session for his frustrations as he told us 'another thing that upsets me about him', concluding with a story about how Chris had been bitten on the finger by a squirrel, had called Justin in tears to tell him and been met with gales of laughter as Justin then told everyone in the bar he was in, "Hey everyone, Chris got bit by a squirrel – ha ha ha ha, what an idiot huh."

It was time for bed.

The next campsite was 60 miles on, past Laguna Beach, San Clemente and Oceanside, along the Coast Highway (Pacific seemed to have been dropped from the PCH title post Newport). After another fraught day we were delighted to arrive at San Elijo State Beach. This was the last public campground before Mexico and it was full; perhaps it was busy as people gathered here before the final push over the border but perhaps it was also because it was a public holiday. 11th November is celebrated as Remembrance Day in the UK but here it is Veterans Day. On our ride that day we had chanced on a full military parade at a Marine Corps Base called Camp Pendleton. Pristine soldiers in blue-grey trousers, burgundy waistbands and low-sitting caps formed large blocks on a football field while whole families in ranks of folding chairs applauded enthusiastically.

We were amused to find zee Germans - that we had first met with Greve - were also at San Elijo. Anke was instantly recognisable by the deeply white tan marks from her sunglasses, which most humans would have been deeply embarrassed by but, as it displayed a certain German efficiency over the use of eye protection, caused her no bother. I noticed her shoes – shiny, stealthy slippers with metal cleats underneath to connect to the pedals.

"It improves the productivity," she stated.

Maybe this is what we need, I thought. Maybe, just maybe there's something that would be better than tennis shoes… Then she jumped in with a statement that instantly got etched into the Limey annals.

"But they are not so com-for-ta-ble," she opined in staccato, splitting the word into four long parts.

She spoke in robotic, laboured English, stressing every syllable in her speech. Years later, whenever he notes I am wearing new shoes, Killer still asks me to describe my apparel in four sounds.

Mikhail's patronage was also on display, evident by him donning gloves to prepare his Trangia camping stove for the evening's meal - to combat the soot stains that had plagued our days until we had given up on it entirely. He saw me also admiring their roomy two-person tent and asked me if we were happy with our own choices and, before I knew it, I was showing him around the Vango's key features like an excited salesman. I glossed over the lack of self-standing ability and pointed out the storage pockets, hanging loops, the vents, and the generous vestibule area.

"Yes, Mikhail, I think you'll find the Vango Phantom 150 is really top of its class."

I noted the weight, how well and easily it packed up and how snug I found the layout of my sleeping bag within it… It was then I realised that I had truly become a bore. There was nothing for it but a game of Shithead as the sun set, turning the sky a delicious stew of reds and pinks and gold, illuminating the last surfers still wrestling with the ocean waves.

As we neared San Diego, we appreciated our proximity to Mexico through constant impressions of Arnie in Predator, cycling past each other with rounds of 'Come onnnnnn, get to zee border!' We passed a blustery La Jolla, where scores of shags and Black Pelicans leaned into the wind from their dramatic promontories beside our path. We skirted the walls of Sea World, passed a huge aircraft carrier, the USS Midway, and threaded our way around the water into the centre of San Diego. It was in this bay that a few months earlier George Bush had stood, dressed like Maverick from *Top Gun*, thumbs up, in front of a giant, flapping banner that read 'Mission Accomplished', and surrounded by adoring men in uniform. He'd declared Operation Iraqi Freedom a 'job well done'. Baghdad had been 'liberated' and Cheney - the architect of the War on Terror - had said that Iraqi forces were engaged in 'the mother of all retreats'. The war would rage on for another eight years and this image, in this bay, would come to symbolise the futility and unpopularity of the war. But Saddam - and his weapons - were still missing; their elusiveness plaguing the administration. Amongst the bleak madness of it all, I comforted myself by imagining Bush and Cheney in the Oval Office playing a round of Bone and Killer's Patriot Points.

We didn't have high ambitions for San Diego; more a hope to repair, reflect and refocus before heading on, deeper into the expedition. A marker of our simple needs, and the fact any Bacchanalian aspirations had been sated for some weeks to come in Los Angeles, was evidenced by my 'To do in San Diego' list.

- Buy toothbrush
- Buy T-shirt
- Go to zoo
- Get survival stuff

Our basecamp for this mission was the USA Hostel on 5th Avenue. Just arriving here and lying down made me realize how utterly exhausted I was. Relaxing was not easy though; the hostel's communal lounge set the tone by being called 'The Party Room' and the raunchy student-like parties spilled back into the dorms until the small hours. So we headed out to find peace. The downtown Gaslamp Quarter around us looked pleasant and was buzzing, but without the money, energy or inclination to socialize, it was mere window dressing. In a Chinese restaurant, my fortune cookie motto read, 'You will soon be involved in many gatherings and parties'.

"I sincerely hope not," I remarked.

And so, for three nights in a row, without our tents to retreat to, we found the only escape was in the cinema. Dressed in our matching clothes, what else to watch first but a romantic comedy; *Love Actually*, the new film from the great Brit, Richard Curtis. The film explored the many ways that love manifests, although there was no representation for men who love imaginary bears. At times, we would be in stitches of laughter whilst the genius of the subtle comedy washed over the rest of the audience, who sat still in confused silence. The next film was *School of Rock*. Struggling musician turned unprepared teacher Jack Black transforms every class into rock themed learning before a final concert, declaring to the pre-teens, "Now, let's get out there and melt some faces!"

Without discussing it, we both listened to Stonegarth that night on our Jukeboxes when we returned to the hostel. The sound of high octane sex and snoring from our fellow guests seemed to add a new layer to the melodies, especially the ironically titled Bush-bashing song we'd penned before we left the UK, 'We will not be Terrorised'.

In need of new clothes, but apparently unable to break free from our mutual assimilation, we went into a store and both bought matching black T-shirts without knowing the other's intentions. In fact, it should be said that our telepathy had become so extraordinary that it had just become accepted as normal. Quite frequently one of us would remark upon something the other was thinking, without having voiced the thought at all. I was just thinking that at some point we would not need to speak at all when Killer turned to me and said, "I suspect you're right, Bone."

At San Diego Zoo, we saw Brian himself. He said he had just popped in to see some friends. He blushed a little when I asked if he meant the panda, undoubtedly the sexiest of all the bears. It was great to catch up in person. But how can we cycle for miles upon miles and get tired out walking around a zoo?

The need for 'survival stuff' sounded dramatic (and its vagueness hinted at our complete naivety at what lay ahead) but this was only in response to the repeated and escalatingly passionate pleads to heed caution in the interior from most everyone we met. The next leg would require, at the very least, a new set of thermals, a vast vat of Vaseline, a new head torch (the current one having met its amateur maker, forcing me to stuff a bike light under my hat to read), and more camping gas - hard to come by in the desert by all accounts. It would also require bucket-loads of fortune.

To locate the supplies money *can* buy we sought out the City Information Center. Outside, groups of men, mostly black, stood around, all talking to themselves. There were scores of them, all assembled in a line and having animated discussions but with no one talking to their neighbour, as if they had let go of reality and slipped into a constellation of independent madness. San Diego has the fourth highest homeless population in the US and many seemed to be here.

Inside, we asked desperately where we could find a camping store. The only one, it seemed, was a little out of town.

"Oh it's really only accessible by car, you have to get on the freeway and…"

We had handled freeways before but this one was even beyond us. At the news we just buried our heads and almost started to weep. But, by a stroke of stupendously welcoming serendipity, a man standing behind us in the queue stepped forward.

"Oh, I can drive you there and drop you back - not a problem." I wanted to thank whatever power had put Dr John Diego there, but something told me I ought to just simply believe more profoundly in the basic goodness of strangers.

We stocked up and returned to the hostel. Killer and I then spread out all our shared possessions in the party room and redistributed them one by one, to ensure we were evenly sharing the weight. Killer took the lock and I took the locking cable, Killer took the stove and I took the gas, Killer took a biro, I took all the maps... well, it was close enough. This was also an opportunity to get a look at the full extent of my burden, to see what I had been carrying. A catalogue commenced.

Large rear right pannier:
- Flip flops
- Waterproofs and rain coat
- Dirty laundry
- Clean clothes
- Towel
- Fleece

Large rear left pannier:
- Sleeping mat
- Small pillow (seriously...)
- Sleeping bag
- Wash bag and washing stuff
- Books - Slavomir, Jaws and Monte Cristo

Small front right pannier:
- Many many muesli bars
- Coffee
- Belt
- Batteries
- Bike tools

- Maps
- Battery charger
- Postcards
- Binoculars

Small front left pannier:
- First aid kit
- Spare inner tubes x2
- Gas canisters x2
- Chain lube
- Powdered gatorade
- Mug
- Cutlery
- Peanut Butter

Rear rack:
- Tent
- Locking cable

Handlebar bag:
- Digital camera (a weighty 2 megapixels…)
- Diary
- Archos Jukebox MP3 player (aka the 'brick')
- Wallet
- Money belt
- Sunglasses
- Maps and guides
- Mini bike tool
- Body lubes (lip balm, sun cream, groinal Vaseline smear)
- Torch
- Bike lights

I reasoned it must have weighed around 20 or 30 kg. I suspect that even Scott of the Antarctic probably had fewer possessions on his expedition. Although, we know how that ended.

We were ready. We had covered 1,700 miles in around seven weeks, crossing three states and completing the whole west coast of the USA. We hadn't been attacked by bears - in fact, quite the opposite. We'd met some characters, seen some outstanding scenery, and our health and bodies had just about held up. So far. We'd also started to receive messages that our progress was already inspiring people to imagine more, to travel with an open mind, or to act more charitably.

The first leg was complete and that was something neither of us had thought possible when we took that first pedal stroke out of Bremerton. The days of being delighted by managing 40 miles seemed many miles behind us, and the intricacies and boundless pleasures of cycle touring (on quiet roads at least) now felt well understood. But was this just a warm-up? We still had another six states to cross, and around 3,000 miles yet to cover. The nights were going to get colder, the campsites more remote, the mountains higher, the wild beasts more grizzly, the food and water less accessible, the bottom severely more bruised...

We knew this. We were aware that we were heading into the unknown, again. I wrote in my diary, "I feel both excited and daunted as I look at the vast expanse of America still in front of us and imagine how different it may all be." But in truth, I'm not sure we imagined at that moment that it would be quite as mind bendingly, limb testingly tough as it turned out to be. We mounted our bikes again and turned our wheels to the left.

"Who's idea was this anyway?" I asked Killer.

8. Into the desert

San Diego, CA to Phoenix, AZ

Real adventure is defined best as a journey from which you may not come back alive, and certainly not as the same person.
Yvon Chouinard

In the annual Race Across America (RAAM), cyclists (well I say cyclists, they might actually be cyborgs) attempt to get from the west coast to the east coast in the fastest time possible, including rest stops. In fact, they often don't even pause for 'rest stops', peeing freely as they pedal along and inhaling high-caloried snacks like breaths. The most elite average 22 hours cycling a day. It was a far cry from our approach, the one that allowed you to lift your head into a full windbreak position, and open your mind to what was around you, but we would soon learn by virtue of the terrain and temperatures quite how profoundly impressive their efforts are. Perhaps that was why their branded cycling shirts seemed to have genuine commercial sponsors on them.

A couple of months before we headed east ourselves, the 2003 event had taken place, also departing from San Diego but aiming for New Jersey.

"Strange that they didn't follow the ACA maps," I remarked to Killer when we learnt of it.

The winner that year was an American, Allen Larsen, who completed the near-3,000 mile course a few minutes under nine days. If all went according to our rough estimates, then in nine days we would be taking our first real break of this leg, soaking in a hot tub around Phoenix, around 450 miles away. It was an increasingly enticing vision as we headed deeper into the desert. But we really didn't have an idea how long it would take. In echoes of rolling out of Bremerton, our estimates of where we would be at the end of each day were back to being an unknown as we adjusted to a new reality, where time and distance seemed beyond our grasp, lost in the unfolding enormity of the American interior.

So yes, we had left the ever-comforting words of Kirkendall behind - just as our own calves were finally starting to resemble his - and were now back in the safe hands of the ACA on its 'Southern Tier' suggested route. It promised to thread us along the quiet ways where it could but in many parts, it warned, there was simply no other road than the Interstate; the American automotive arteries where road trains fly on autopilot barely noticing the two-wheeled obstructions slowly making their way along the hard shoulder. The dangers of these roads were marked by that year's RAAM seeing the event's first death since it was launched in 1982. A rider, Brett Malin, was killed by an 18-wheel truck in New Mexico. We would need to stay alert.

We had been so focused from the start on simply reaching San Francisco then daring to dream we might make San Diego that we'd never really contemplated the west to east adventure, and that we had to cross the entire country, again, but this time going a lot further. And whilst we would still be accompanied by a friendly philosophical bear, we'd also be joined by snakes, coyotes, hunters, rednecks, racists, misogynists, madmen, alligators, evangelists, bodily breakdowns and, to top it all, extraordinary levels of bottom gas.

But the greatest obstacle was the land itself, and it started immediately. It was TLP 50. Leaving the Pacific behind us felt like letting go of a guiding hand. It had been our companion and compass for the past six weeks and it would be another two months before we'd see sea again. We climbed steadily away from the city, into the mountains. The sky grew darker as if in solidarity with the land itself, whose hillsides were bare and blackened. The fires we had followed on the news were extinguished, just, but the resulting devastation was enormous. That month a dozen separate fires had been recorded in California that each covered more than 1,000 acres. The largest was known as the Cedar Fire, which was started when a hunter got lost and lit a fire to signal for help. The fire - fanned by coastal winds - spread at the speed of a runner. It covered 273,000 acres, destroying nearly 3,000 buildings and killing 15 people. Many of the victims died trying to escape in their cars. It was almost too huge to comprehend but it found form when we passed a patch of ground where just a week before a house had stood and all that now remained was a metal mailbox by the side of the road. I thought of this and the thousands of other families whose lives were changed forever by something that had at one time been just another bad story on the news but which now was tangible in front of me. Few knew then that such scenes would be a more regular risk every year as the climate shifted.

Arnie had declared a state of emergency. Side roads were blocked and we were waved on by rangers and police officers whose usual stone faces were marked by emotion. Just 25 miles on winding roads from downtown San Diego, we had planned to camp at a fishing and leisure area called Lake Jennings, but the gates were closed. There were a number of 'Do not enter' signs and a fastly-locked heavy chain, all guarded by men in a big Chevy truck. The land beyond smelled innocently of damp camp fires.

We had to take a motel that night and found one after 40 miles in Alpine where we cooked the comforting choodle by propping up the gas burner on the loo seat and shared a bed to save some money. I wandered along the highway to find a payphone and called my brother in Korea, where he was working as a teacher, to wish him happy birthday.

"You're a bloody Trojan bro, you're bloody doing it!" he cheered.

It was a good little push. But wouldn't 'you're a bloody Macedonian' have been more accurate? The Trojans get massively beaten.

"Never correct a compliment," Brian said, taking over my 'Quote of the day' and following it up by remarking to Killer once the choodle had settled, "There are few things more comforting than your own fart, very few things more disgusting than someone else's."

As we laboured higher up the hills in the morning, our breath condensed in front of us. If anything, the landscape was even more apocalyptic and the clouds above us were now black. After ten miles, the sky finally broke, dumping its full weight aggressively on us. We continued until spotting a diner; its windows opaque, steamed up against the cold outside. We warmed ourselves with three refills of coffee and deep bowls of chilli. Killer surveyed the half empty room.

"Imagine what this place could be if they simply mixed some noodles into this concoction."

We then held a good pace for the rest of the day and whilst we had already started the day at 2,000 ft, we were pleased with our progress over three 4,000 peaks as we headed across the parched Cleveland National Forest and made it to Live Oak Springs. The days of living in fear of Leggett Hill were long behind us.

"Oh if Greve could see us now." I told Killer. "I think he'd really appreciate our warm legs."

The campsite was $17.50. For this price you'd expect some sort of spa treatment and a hot stone massage but the site consisted of a scrap of wasteland where groups of men stood chain-smoking and staring the cold away. One man was rummaging around, collecting cans and bottles from the bins to sell.

"Are you done with those?" he asked, pointing at the bicycle water bottles.

"You don't get many cyclists here, do you?" I replied.

As he left, Killer turned to me. "For a few dollars more we could have stayed in another motel. I promise to control my flatulence next time."

"Unfortunately, at this price, we cannot even afford to keep staying in Mad Max themed campsites, let alone gassy motels. I think the desert ahead will be our free campground - we'll have to surrender ourselves to the will of the wilds and all its beasts."

I then started recounting all those potential beasts in my head. There were quite a few of them.

"That or we work on our Love Actually-type foppish grins and knock on doors until kindly strangers take us in," suggested Killer, half joking.

In the film, a geeky Brit travels to America, where his delectable accent is immediately detected in a bar by a bevy of beautiful women who take him in and lavish him with sex. But we were far too politely British to enforce British charm. And who knew what sort of people we'd encounter in the desert towns ahead. I suspected swimwear models would not be amongst them.

The next morning, a neighbour walked over. We had met him the night before when he simply announced he was aged 73 and when he found out we were from England, he said: "Oh yeah, well fuck me, my great grandfather was from there." And then he had left abruptly. So we hadn't expected much from him when he returned. However, like Dedric, Jimmy and all the others before him, this man was to etch his name into our diaries with his utterances.

"Good morning. You heading east eh?" he asked, still marching towards us purposefully.

"Yes, that's right, we are going to..."

But he wasn't interested in the answer.

"Yeah yeah. Hey, you know that I said my grandfather was from England? Yeah, well his name was Braddigon and they named a road after him. You ever come across a Braddigon Lane?"

"Um, I am not sure I have... er...In what city?"

"Oh I don't know that," he said, as if it was a ridiculous remark. "Anyway, it's called Braddigon Lane. I think I might try and find it one day. Yeah, Braddigon Lane. You sure you never seen it? No? You see, I'm named after him - my name's Braddigon too. My brother's also named after him in a roundabout way..." And here it comes... "Yep, my brother's name is Lane."

Braddigon turned and left abruptly once more, walking swiftly through the invisible doors to the Limenagerie.

If Live Oak Springs felt like a sort of frontier town that was because it stood rested at the precipice of a near 4,000 ft drop, from cold mountains to baking desert. The elevation marked in the ACA looked too enticingly severe to be real but a few miles along the road and there it was. At the In Ko Pass, the road left all green behind, wound down through scrubby, broken, beige rock to the golden brown expanse of the Yuha desert that then melted into a bright white horizon. At the top, it looked like we were sitting at the apex of a rollercoaster. It was a hard drop. And at the bottom a different America awaited.

We had found the Interstate, I-10, so we donned our headphones to help maintain calm as strong crosswinds threatened to knock us into the path of colossal industrial trucks that tore down the road with the considerable accumulation of gravity.

The descent lasted around 25 miles and having started the day in fleeces, wooly hats and long trousers, we could feel the change in temperature immediately when we reached the scrubland. Killer wisely proposed both 'shortage' and 'shirtage' and all warm clothes were removed and tucked into the panniers for another time. The day had looked simple on ACA paper - descent and then flat - but the winds and the beating sun made it a demanding ride. Added to this, the road was cracked like a fallen mirror with tufts of weed growing in the gaps, making riding hard and suggesting that some severe temperature extremes - as much as a 30 degree shift daily - were now upon us. We were now on the same latitude as northern Africa.

At Ocotillo, the first town on the flat, the route took us off the Interstate and onto quieter, local roads. We passed a few small unknown towns before entering impossibly rich arable land. This was the Imperial Valley, it's towns and fields all laid out almost exactly 100 years before and all maintained by diverting unreplenishable amounts of water from the Colorado River. I didn't know much about the sustainability of water cycles back then, but even to my naive eyes, it all looked impossible; such verdant abundance in one of the driest places on earth. We were surrounded by soft fruits but our heads were slowly baking within our helmets like chestnuts.

"Holy shitting Neptune!" declared Killer.

"Yes it's frickin' hot isn't it," I said, panting.

"No, more than that. Look!"

Killer was pointing at a huge industrial tower, part of a sugar refining factory complex. The words 'Sea level' and a thick line, were marked around 150 ft up the tower.

"What the…?" I started.

"Is this why I feel like I have the bends?"

"Oh, I don't think it works like that Killer."

"Yeah, well explain why my head is on the verge of explosion."

"Because you are wearing a child's BMX helmet?"

I romantically imagined the vast seas being held back by the ridge of mountains we had just traversed. Indeed, this whole valley had at times been under water, it was once where the Colorado entered the Gulf of Mexico but millions of years of dumping the load the river had swept up when forming the Grand Canyon meant the sea was now at least 60 miles due south. Imagine a river carrying away flecks of rock in teaspoon sized trips, and imagine the time needed to carve away mountains and push the coast three marathons away. You can lose yourself in the profundity of nature if you allow it.

After 50 miles were up, we stopped for hotdogs, Gatorade and the daily choodle shop. With so few roads and with the sun blazing in front of us, it was impossible to get lost but we wanted to see what lay ahead up the road, so perused the maps and discussed its erratic contours.

A woman started walking over to us. She sighed, rolling her eyes. "OK, where y'all headed?"

"No, it's fine." I said. "We know where we're going, we're just surveying our *rowt.*"

"Sure. Where y'all from?"

"England."

"Oh great. I met a lovely couple from Denmark a couple of years ago."

We looked at her blankly, silently.

"Uh huh, Denmark," she repeated, and then walked away. In these parts, the search for a connection was finding new stretch. It was also a good introduction to the standard of conversations we could expect for the next few weeks.

After 75 miles we were trying to get out of the town of Brawley and past the farmlands. I was exhausted but we were spirited by the prospect of our longest day and when I spotted the tundra in the distance I became excited. After 85 miles we left the town and crossed the valley's giant irrigation canal. The shift was immediate and we were in the desert again. A few miles further and we pulled over and made camp amongst the dusty low shrubs a few metres from the road, hidden away. We were tired but ecstatic with our progress. I quickly made the choodle in my porch, using my head torch to guide my cooking.

We had spent some of the day imagining opening the UT bar, a place that served choodle exclusively – all the flavours of the world would be catered for but would only ever be represented in choodle form.

"Can I order some fries?" a confused customer would ask.

"OK, where's that on the menu, sir?" our talented waiting staff would reply, taking their cue from the cafes of Seattle.

Our daily intake of choodle never got boring. We would spend all day looking forward to that simple evening meal of chilli and noodles and would be beyond excitement when we would find a new flavour of noodle or brand of chilli to try in a supermarket. That night, our Stagg chilli (the best) was accompanied by the warm comforts of lime chilli shrimp flavoured noodles and a hit of Tabasco. Damn good choodle.

"Stick it on the specials board, Bone," roared Killer.

We had even affected - naturally - a ritual to the preparation and eating of the sacred choodle that had all the markings of a Japanese Tea Ceremony. We would take turns to cook the dish, ensuring it was both stirred and reverse-stirred for maximum flavour dissemination, then divide it into two pans. The other Limey would then pretend to assess the division intently before always choosing the same pan to eat from. The non-cook would take the first bite, assess the flavours swimming about his mouth, pause to calculate his enjoyment and then let out a knowing smile and nod.

"Compliments to the chef," he'd say.

"Oh you're totally welcome," would come the reply.

There would then follow a deliriously happy gluttony of choodleage, the last scrapes of sauce savoured as if the last meal on earth. Oh choodle, beloved choodle. (And I write these words some years later, recalling our true happiness, as a man who is now not only a vegetarian but also a lover of kale).

I pulled out a folded piece of paper from the back of my diary.

"Killer, I've been waiting some time for this moment. I actually never thought I would get to read this to you in this auspicious setting but do you remember the quotes we made up for the unnecessary press release announcing this expedition?"

"Um, I said something about 'I was only joking'?"

"You said, 'A lot of our friends think we are going to die out there in the desert...but it *should... be... easy.*" I emphasized the last words.

"Well I guess now we get to find out."

On cue, a coyote howled in the distance.

"He'll never find us," said Killer.

"He is two miles away and has already smelled us," I replied. "And coyotes love choodle."

Sated, we drifted off to the howls. They at first felt comforting, like a sonorous reminder that we had made it to the wilderness and were on our way across the country. But we were woken up frequently that night when the noise got closer and on two occasions when loud rummaging noises seemed to come from around our tents. To assuage my fears I told myself it was Brian, looking for some scraps, but I stayed silent. I suddenly realised that if anything happened, no one would know for weeks that we were missing and then no one would know where to find us. We would just disappear. It's strange that I found the thought more intriguing than worrying.

In the morning, we discovered something had chewed one of Killer's water bottles and his flip flops. Killer did a mock howl but ended it with an upward intonation. I think he was trying to make it sound mysterious, as in, 'Maybe it was me, the coyote, maybe it wasn't...Howoooo?' But it ended up just sounding like a greeting from Julian Clary or Kenneth Williams. Killer carried on as if this was his intention all along.

"Looks like we were visited by Mr Camp Coyote last night, Bone. Howooooooooooo?"

I am not sure why the menagerie of our imagined beasts was largely sexualised - something to do with two men alone in need of female companionship perhaps - but Mr Camp Coyote became a regular visitor in those desert nights, with his curious howl. And he would soon be joined by Mr Randy Rattlesnake and Mr Sexy Scorpion as the roadkill by the side of the road shifted from the domestic pets of the west coast (I actually had kept a 'cats v dogs death toll' in my diary. The dogs won and, that is to say, they lost) to the arachnids, serpents, lizards and aardvarks of the desert states. I had always wanted to see an aardvark. I had no idea they were so flat in real life.

We spent most of TLP 53 battling strong winds that, at points, had us struggling to reach 5 or 6 mph on the flat before then throwing more mountains into our path. Added to this Killer felt unwell. Maybe he did have the bends. I rode behind him, watching his cranium, somehow imagining in my heat delirium that it would ignite if I looked away, and that I would miss it.

It was a hard slog. We had carried extra water in our 4 litre water bladders the day before, which we had needed to drink and cook with, but we were now out of all food and water and were desperately counting on the store marked at Glamis 20 miles up the road being open. In such places in his book, Slavomir and his friends would suck on pebbles to force saliva. Luckily, we hadn't gotten to that point yet.

The scrubby desert then gave way to seas of magnificent sands which swept away from the road as far as you could see in every direction. This was the Algodones Dunes Wilderness Area, the largest dune system in the country, and also formed by millions of years of shifting Colorado. We were peddling in the middle of a golden ocean and everything about it seemed beautiful and peaceful.

But this blissful illusion was soon dismissed closer to Glamis as increasing numbers of dune buggies and quad bikes raced at fierce speeds across the sands and then rose up the waves, launching themselves into twisted jumps and impossible tricks.

At the town itself, it turned out that Glamis was just a store but, thankfully, it was open. It was like a wild west saloon, all misshapen wood and darkly lit. And it was huge; there was a long bar and large diner, and even a gift shop. There were just a handful of people, but there was a distinct feeling of waiting for something bigger. On one wall, we spotted framed photos of the same dunes we'd just passed but swarmed with people and vehicles.

Dr John Glamis spotted us and bowled over.

"Yeah, that's here," he said, almost spitting the words. "This time next week there'll be more than 100,000 people here. Thanksgiving. The annual race fest. F-U-C-K-ing madness."

"That many people… here?" I said, looking around.

"Yeah. And a handful of them'll die. About six every year. Drunk racing or just dumbass driving."

And then he half turned his head whilst still looking at us, and spoke loudly as if to address the whole store.

"I'm getting the HELL out of here before the CRAZY ensues. It's supposed to be a GODDAMN nature area."

He turned back to us, puffed out his cheeks and took a deep breath before a wholly other thought hit him. "Hey hey, you're British, did you know this place is named after the Glamis castle in Macbeth?"

I was still trying to work out how an angry local got to know about Shakespeare's influence when Killer tilted his head, closed his eyes and placed a hand to his chest in oration, "*Stars, hide your fires; let not light see my black and deep desires.*"

John puffed his cheeks again in confusion.

"Maybe you're more of a Hamlet man?" suggested Killer.

"Right. Anyways, where are you headed?" asked John.

The desert felt a million miles from the tropical-beached checkered flag and the surroundings lent a question mark again to the word… "Miami?"

John looked to the east. "OK then guys. Just make sure no rednecks don't try and run you over." He walked off without looking back. As he did, Killer worked on removing a hotdog ketchup dollop from his chest. "Out damn spot, out I say!"

It was the first mention of rednecks. We had used the word ourselves on occasion as a joke, referring to an amalgamation of mythical villains that we would defeat as easily as if in a computer game. We had forgotten that people - real people - might actually pose a threat to us, and this man was suggesting they lay just ahead. The challenge was growing daily.

Beyond Glamis we found a railroad crossing closed with a clanging bell and flashing warning light. We waited as a freight train trundled past for what must have been ten minutes, the double-stacked carriages stretching far beyond the horizon of even this vast landscape. With so few roads, we were having to tack around 60 miles north to find an eastward highway. As we did, we were stopped again, this time at an official immigration checkpoint. Armed border guards in aviator-style sunglasses and pressed uniforms, who we'd seen cruising these local roads, waved us over to their office. The building resembled a small petrol station forecourt and I was tempted to instinctively ask for some Marlboros and a copy of Razzle. We were asked a few simple questions as to where we were headed and they grew suspicious of our intentions when I added an even weightier question mark to 'Miami??', but they waved us on regardless.

"Take care on the roads," said one of the officers. "There's a lot of people - around half a million a year - trying to cross the border illegally. And not all of them are nice guys."

He fixed a stare at us but all I saw was our slightly confused faces in his mirrored glasses. Just across the sands - and even within them - there were people dreaming of creating a better life for themselves. I imagined most of them were desperate and brave, not bad.

After 50 miles we again peeled off the road at dusk but this time into a more sheltered spot, behind some tired-looking brittle trees in what appeared to be a dried out river bed. The whole place around us looked like a dusty, rock-scattered Martian landscape, never before troubled by man. We were exhausted, totally exhausted from the headwinds and hills and touched by sun stroke. I stripped completely naked and collapsed into my tent to cool down, gulping my precious water reserves to fight a pressing headache and knowing that if the desert's beasts wanted to invade my lodgings I would not be able to even raise a penknife to them. I drifted off mumbling something indecipherable about the attack, "Get them, Brian. Get the snakes…"

The deep cold of the morning restored us enough to go another few miles to the first town, Palo Verde, to stock up on essential provisions, like chocolate bars. We stopped after another 18 miles in Blythe to use the internet. I emailed home and checked the weather reports. The forecast was arid and exhausting, to say the least. In the news, I read Walmart had been accused of offering extremely low wages and a lack of adequate employment benefits. A police operation to investigate this led to the arrest of more than 600 illegal immigrants working at Walmart stores - people who had perhaps crossed these very sands and who saw even these poor conditions as life-saving for them and their families. It was all around us but we couldn't see it.

I was about to exchange notes with Killer - who I presumed was also carrying out essential Limey research on the computer beside me - when he let out a laugh of delight.

"Bone, did you know that Steve Guttenberg used to be Mayor of a town we passed through near Malibu? Isn't that great!"

"Er, Steve Guttenberg who was in the Police Academy films? Is that in the news?"

"Yes him and no, not news, I've just been looking up facts on him on this incredible website."

"Handy."

"I really think Mr Guttenberg has been ignored for too long since that breakthrough dramatic role. I have just decided that I am going to form The Official Steve Guttenberg *Re*-Appreciation Society when we get back."

Killer was now beaming with the successful application of his time on the internet. Whatever emotions he was still keeping deeply buried, I sensed that worry about the adventure ahead was not included. But I didn't question him. In fact, I found myself fully supporting his re-appreciation dream.

We moved on, channeling Guttenberg with the occasional line from Police Academy - 'Mahooooonnneeeyyyyyyy'. We stopped briefly after a few miles to enjoy some luxurious shade in the lee of a tin shack and then pressed on to cross the Colorado River. Half way along the bridge, Killer clapped me into our new state.

"Welcome to aRIZona," he cheered.

It was farewell to The Golden State and hello to The Grand Canyon State, but sadly we would be travelling too far south to take in that wonder. Another nickname though for Arizona is The Copper State and we would see plenty of that a few days later. The 'clapping-in ceremony' for entering a new state was now accompanied by the 'application of the state sticker to the bikes ceremony'. Arizona's flag was one of the finest, the bottom half deep blue, the top red and with yellow sunbeams emanating from a central, copper-toned star. Of course, the design was deeply symbolic, representing the river we were standing above, the region's mining industry and the number of sunbeams corresponded with the original 13 United States. But, to me, it was just a flag that said, 'You're a long way from home now' and it excited me immensely.

The scenery enforced this feeling. We were heading for the town of Quartzsite and the road approaching it was another glimpse into the vastness of the landscape we were entering. The town sat shimmering white in a long valley and looked like it must be just a couple of miles away but it was in fact at least ten miles before we came even close. We would experience similar distance and scale shifts in the days ahead - there would be a few times when we would point our bikes along a road towards some far-off, hazed target and would labour for what felt like hours without drawing it any closer. And on some of these roads, we'd have no idea if we were descending or ascending. In this huge place, where the sides of mountains looked like flat horizons you could only tell if you were going up or down by the experienced 'feel' of the ride. And it felt tough.

We were on the Interstate again and were forced to balance the threat of avoiding scraps of broken metal and glass along the shoulder with the threat of the gargantuan road train trucks that bore down on us. The only positive was the trucks carried us with them in their wake, as they had when we entered Toseland's

Aberdeen, offering temporary - albeit hair-raising - respite from the fierce headwinds.

Quartzsite found form as a strange assembly of huge truck stops, makeshift precious stones selling tents, snack stops, dusty shacks and parking lots. In the past it had been a fort and trading post but gets its name from being a quartz site (see what they did there) and therefore an important mining area. It hadn't always had the best reputation - one visitor in 1875 (which I had read whilst Killer was researching Guttenberg) is reported to have said it 'reeks of everything unclean, morally and physically.' I couldn't see much immediate charm in the place but it seemed harmless enough, with tourists driving in to see and swap precious stones. And from the looks of it, they were spoilt for choice - signs everywhere shouted 'Rocks Here'.

Quartz has fascinated scientists and artisans for centuries for its ability to fracture light, power watches or be carved into objects of any imagining. There are many varieties - from rock crystal to amethyst - but the only one that mattered to me was Rose Quartz, a pleasing conflict of soft pink and hard edges. It's the birthstone for May, my birth month, and my mum had given me a small crystal before I left, for good luck. It travelled with me everyday in my handlebar bag. I reached in and ran my thumb along the sharp grain, charging myself with her good wishes.

We would have pressed passed the town and into the free desert again (if we could limit our daily spend to a dollar or two we were very happy), but we had agreed to meet up with 'The Three' that night.

We had encountered them in the morning at Palo Verde where a cheery voice came at us outside the store.

"We first heard about you two days ago."

We turned to see a middle aged man with a generous, Gordon-worthy moustache smiling knowingly at us. Beside him was a boy and a girl in their early 20s, also looking at us. All of them stood proudly by their fully-loaded bikes. They genuinely seemed delighted that they had found us. Cyclists in these parts, at this - or any - time of year, were not a common sight. In fact, we would go entire weeks for the rest of the journey without seeing a single cyclist in town or country. Here at Palo Verde, we were very happy to make contact. I could tell by their baggy shorts and T-shirts they were taking as enjoyable an approach to the road as us, not RAAMing their way through.

The older man was Jack, a retired teacher, and the others were his son Brooks and the son's girlfriend, Lindsay. They were travelling from San Diego to Phoenix and had left the same day as us, planning to average around 50 miles a day. Jack explained to me, extensively, at that first meeting, how he had heard we were just ahead of them in every town they had been through but they hadn't seen us until Palo Verde. I held in a laugh as he repeated this tale word for word when Killer arrived on the scene, even though I was still standing there.

At Quartzsite we found they had already set up camp, had paid our fees and had two cold beers waiting for us. We pitched up and went to wash. I noticed my face was caked in dirt, and my shorts were striped brown and white from desert and sweat. Maybe there was something still 'reeking' in Quartzsite. The dust had even found its way into my sleeping bag. We were becoming a part of this landscape. And the nature around us was the main topic of discussion that evening.

"What did you think of the Colorado?" Jack wanted to know.

I thought for a while. The Colorado was the name of the most exhilarating ride at the water park of my youth. I had always imagined it as a broad and cutting torrent. But that day I had noted it drifted lazily and more narrowly than I had thought possible.

"Remarkably unremarkable," I replied.

"Exactly," he nodded, pleased with my answer. "You expected something else, right? Yeah well that is long gone."

He then went on to confirm my suspicions, first raised at Imperial.

"All that food you saw growing a couple of days ago... well, let's just say that sort of intensive irrigation does not come without significant ecological impact. And in fact what you saw is just a small fraction of it."

He talked of damming, overdevelopment, disputed water rights, the poor treatment of the Hispanic communities that lived around it, the irreparable effect on ecosystems, the lack of minerals reaching habitats - now dying - downstream. Lindsay and Brooks worked as ecologists and would shake their heads as Jack talked about the 'ecological exploitation'.

"But just wait until you see the Rio Grande, which I guess you'll cross in a week or so. That's something else again. And what is the government doing to find solutions?"

"Less than they're doing to find non-existent weapons of mass destruction?" I suggested, daring to push politics amongst these friends.

Jack nodded slowly. "Exactly," he said again.

Even if it felt we had been talked *at* for quite some time, it had been worth it for the education. It was a reminder that every piece of land we pedalled through has - and yes, I know this sounds like a major cliché - so much more to it than meets the eye, and so many different people's lives attached to it.

I looked at everything around us more intensely now, rather than just passing through it I felt a real part of it. The path past Quartzsite was marked by mountain passes and low-growing scrub; spiky bushes aside scatterings of broken rock. In some places it was also clustered with huge Saguaro cactuses that looked like cartoon green men holding their arms up to invisible Wild West gunslingers. Whenever we were advised to carry extra water here because the next town or store was more than a day's ride away, it caused some celebration in my soul for the wild places that still existed.

And there was something transformative about the size of it all, the impossible-to-comprehend enormity of both space and time that gave scale to your own existence. In brief blazes it illuminated you but I also felt that the full scale of it had the ability to annihilate you. As we spent more time here, it felt like the big ideas I had come to America to find were taking shape, but then what is it about these important ideas that makes them the hardest to get hold of? At times, it felt like they were falling through the holes of a butterfly net. But I was getting closer.

The beauty extended from landscapes to lightscapes. Every sunset and sunrise revealed a thick soup of pastel pinks, blues and yellows that filled the entire sky, and lingered. At these times, the mountains were jagged silhouettes, looking as if a piece had been torn from the bottom of a paper sky. In Moby Dick, Herman Melville spends an entire chapter trying to express the whiteness of the whale. Without that context, it is impossible for the reader to understand how the creature had so haunted the crew and fed Ahab's obsession. I would need to write entire volumes on the kaleidoscope of desert colours to convey their impressions on me. It was profoundly restorative. And once the evening show was over, there was another. I had never seen such stars.

It was impossible to capture any of the strong emotional associations I felt here in a photo, of course. We did take photos, perhaps once every other day, when we paused. But they were taken for ourselves, in the moment, not curated to show some dreamy version of this trip. In each one, we are active, engaged, doing something. Each picture a story. I look at them now. In a photo of that desert I prepare the camp. I lean over the panniers to fish out the sleeping bag and arrange it inside the open tent, which stirs in the light evening breeze. The stove is resting on the ground, ready to receive the choodle pan. The dirt on my face looks like a desert camouflage. I don't look tired. I look content. I look resolute.

Free from any form of telecommunication technology, we were utterly alone in these places and that feeling danced inside me. We may have been two of the last humans to enjoy such a private experience in America or, rather, with America.

But, of course, we weren't totally alone. Brian visited us most nights, even if only briefly.

"Did you see the Colorado Brian?" Killer asked. Brian replied with a low, muted moan.

For the next two days, we joined The Three on the road, at times riding with them, at others drifting away and seeing them in gas stations for coffee. But at night, we would always peel into the desert on our own to find free spots and to find our place within the wild nature, undaunted by the various animal tracks around.

One reason for leaving The Three to it was their riding style, all close in single file, taking turns at the front, efficiently conserving energy and maximising their work rate. We had to admit it was a much more effective way to get across these huge distances but it didn't really work for us. Neither of us wanted to be a slave to the other's pace - if we wanted to cycle side by side and chat and sing occasionally, or if we wanted to disappear miles ahead with our headphones plugged in and wait for the other Limey brother at some viewpoint, then that's what we'd do. And besides, the idea of staring at Killer's arse all day and feeling the effect of its frequent reverberations wasn't too appealing.

One of the places we caught up with The Three was at the town of Hope. As we left Quartzsite, the road looked flat but we felt we had been rising and sure enough the maps revealed we had come up 1,500 ft by the time we got to Hope. There wasn't much to it; it was a typical desert community - a gas station with a small mart and an RV parking area. But Hope did have something else – a Vietnam Vet to chat to. He sat at the bar like an abandoned film prop, wearing a long beard, an American flag bandana and ripped denim shirt. He asked us for some change, "I'm just a 'vet trying to get by..." he said.

"Do you live in hope?" I asked him, to which he nodded, thankfully ignoring my crass joke. Indeed, the main enjoyment to stopping at Hope was the wordplay. When we arrived, Killer had called out to me, "Hey, I've found hope". And when we went to leave I asked Killer to hold my bike while I sprinted off, shouting, "I have to go. I am running out of hope." Devoid of few other distractions, such simple things continued to throw us into fits of schoolboy-sized laughter. But our efforts were dwarfed by a large sign about a mile down the road that simply stated, in fading paint, 'You are now beyond Hope'.

We cycled off and on with The Three for the rest of the day and then let them drift ahead of us as the sun went down, and that was our simple goodbye. I was still thinking of Jack's lecture as I drifted to sleep when I was startled by a cry from Killer of, "Robert Duvall! It's Robert bloody Duvall. Oh, *now* I can sleep."

I would be worried about Killer making random outbursts if I wasn't more worried about the fact that I knew exactly what he meant - Jack had an uncanny likeness to someone and resolving the riddle of who that was must have been troubling Killer as much as it had me. Killer had aired the unspoken thought we shared and my total comprehension of his simple utterance confirmed we were farrrrr too familiar with how each other's minds were working.

"Yes! That's him! We'll have to cast the rest of the movie now," I said. "We'll have to find others to play all the other characters from…" I then switched to my dramatic voice, "*The Limey Project: The Movie.*"

"Oh god, you're right. Well farewell sleep, until next time."
And then a rustle.

"Um, not to interfere," said Brian who'd clearly been listening in, "but have you considered Rachel Bilson from The OC for the part of Lindsay and perhaps the comic actor Ben Stiller for the role of Brooks? The likenesses are quite strong."

Killer and I laughed.

"OK, OK we will consider it," said Killer out loud, and then whispering to me. "I think he might have cracked it, Bone but let's not give him a big bear head. Anyway, let's cast the rest in Phoenix."

The run in to Phoenix on TLP 57 was fast and fun. The wind was finally on our backs for much of the day and we ticked off another 'must see' as huge numbers of tumbleweeds blew past us. We cycled on town roads, cycle paths and next to canals. We passed kids playing 'soccer', families out for walks and general signs of civilisation. After days where desert was our new reality, this had all the normality of having come through the looking glass. We traversed endless miles of urban sprawl but any signs of the city of Phoenix itself - the largest city in the state - alluded us. We kept checking our maps, thinking we must have miscalculated and overshot but we were on the right path – the ACA had simply arced us through the suburbs rather than the centre. Phoenix covers 100 square miles and so there's plenty of suburbs to get lost in. At a gas station in Mesa - named a town but really just part of the city's eastward sprawl - we stopped to get our bearings and it wasn't long before we had attracted attention.

As Killer went in to use the toilet, the usual opening gambit was launched at me, "Where y'all headed?"

The voice was a slow, thick drawl. It came from a man, about four and a half feet tall, wearing tight jeans, sunglasses, a cowboy hat and a leather jacket with pin badges crowding his lapels.

"Miami," I said reluctantly, but emphatically.

"Oh - that'll take you a couple of days," he nodded.

I laughed but he looked at me with a stare to show he was not joking and then pointed at his own bike, which was resting against the wall behind him. It was a battered old mountain bike-looking thing with two wire baskets strapped on as rear panniers and a Stars and Stripes flying off a short flagpole at the back.

"I gone and done 18 or 20,000 miles on that there bicycle in two years."

He rolled a cigarette and started smoking it through deeply stained teeth, then he looked at me above the rims of his glasses to suggest it was my turn to say something.

"OK, er, yeah, we have had a good trip so far but everyone has been warning us about Texas."

"Oh you can cycle across Texas in a day - I done it. Yeah. And Mexico. I did that in a day too."

The man was Dedricly insane, suggesting he was able to travel at many times the speed of the professionals racing across America. I looked around to see if anyone else was witnessing this dialogue but there was no one. Killer eventually arrived, took one look at the man and then turned to me, saying loudly, "Let's go Bone, we don't have time for this sort of thing."

Whilst Dr Johns tend to only impart useful information, Dr John Mesa was given his name for helping us to understand that you can't act on the word of *every* friendly madman you meet. Anyway, we didn't aspire to such an impossible pace. We hadn't come to eat up the miles but America itself; its people, culture and, yes, junk food.

Within a few more blocks we found a Travelodge motel and made camp in the luxurious twin beds after hot showers. We ordered delivery pizza, drank beers and watched three Morgan Freeman films back-to-back (an act known as a 'Morgasm'). We then slept deeply for 13 hours.

9. Landscapes within landscapes

Phoenix, AZ to Three Way, AZ

Great things are done when men and mountains meet.
William Blake

Ahead of us lay some of the most spectacular scenery of the trip. But we were struggling to get out of Mesa. We had always planned on staying a full day but that drifted into a second very easily. We were exhausted and the free coffee and donuts every morning from the effervescent Indian manager did not help. The simple gesture of telling him he made the best coffee and purchased the best donuts on earth was enough to ensure top-ups and seconds, or even thirds. We had covered almost 450 miles in eight days. When setting out from Seattle - in gentler climes - we had covered 200 fewer miles in the same time. I reminded myself of this fact as I flicked between the various MTV channels, funneling Pringles into my mouth.

Yes, this was a chance to further immerse ourselves in American TV, catching up with some of the bizarre shows we had come to love from every other motel break, and discovering new oddities. It provided an extreme alternative to the isolation and innocence of desert life, but all of it was America.

On MTV, as well as the music videos (which largely seemed to be of Pharrell Williams and people trying to be him), we watched as a computer geek was transformed into a ladies man, and were shown how he had to be someone else if he wanted to achieve anything at all. And some of the former stars of Jackass were now in a show called Wild Boyz! - they were on the hunt for extreme animal encounters, allowing themselves to be bitten by scorpions, attacked by panthers and bitten by bears.

"Oh it's my friends Tony and Big Dave on the telly," roared Brian with delight.

One show that seemed to be on perennially was The Wade Robson Project, in which the eponymous host - spiky-haired, goateed, baggy-trousered Wade - oversaw dancers competing for a $200,000 prize. Wade was clearly the competitors' guru. As the choreographer for everyone from Britney Spears to NSYNC he had set the style for how bands across the world approached movement to music. And he seemed to have his own language for dance judging - every time he complimented the performers enthusiastically on their 'musicality' or said he really liked 'the way you got low and then got high and then got low again' they would purr, and every episode ended with all the competitors imploring Wade to do a final freestyle performance for them as the credits rolled. He'd brush it off, embarrassed, for all of two seconds before throwing his shapes and the crowd melted into puddles of ecstasy. In the ad breaks he'd be back, promoting Juice batteries like a human Duracell bunny - even I was convinced they were the coolest batteries I had ever seen.

Of course, Killer and I tried to emulate his judging patter. As dancing was beyond us, we applied our impression of Wade and his words to everything from how our Limey partner had poured the coffee to how they had commanded the TV remote to find the perfect channel. This generally involved saying, 'I liked your musicality'. A lot.

But there was something else. There was something about Wade's dancing that seemed so familiar; the quick, sharp moves, the physical twists and jabs. It was only later that I heard he had learnt his skills when he met Michael Jackson aged seven, and became his protégé. It was only in 2019 after a mental breakdown that Wade asserted in a documentary that Jackson had forced him soon after they first met into a seven-year sexual relationship. Suddenly, the way the world moved to music seemed to have been tainted. America's almost constitutionally architectural relationship with celebrity was tested, but only briefly: Robson received death threats from hard core fans and many people have turned a blind eye to the crimes to continue to enjoy the music.

As well as the regular shows, we started to grow an appreciation for those ad breaks too. One favourite genre was the info-mercial - we would marvel as the host guided a guest or entire audience through the mystifying awesomeness of some weight-loss cocktail, underwater cooker, multi-functional coat hanger or state-of-the-art toenail clipper. Stuff you obviously desperately needed but had never known. In one ad, an audience sat at dining tables, arranged in a crescent around a central high table where a man with a blender stood, elevated above them like an emperor. As the blender demonstrated its magical ability to, er, blend things like every blender tends to, the audience nudged each other in disbelief, cooed and then started clapping like drugged circus seals.

Another type we particularly enjoyed, as it lent itself wholesale to our daily impressions, was the 'marvellous medicine' advert. Whether it's a pill for dieting, headaches, depression or insomnia, the approach is always the same. A woman's soft voice will explain how their life has been revolutionised by the miracle of the pill. At the start of the advert the images are of her clutching her head in agony, perhaps a bemuscled husband rests a caring hand on her shoulder and shakes his head, if only there was something he could do! Why not try this pill, he suggests, with the deftness of a mime that could be deciphered from space. By the end, she is dancing, jumping on the bed, kissing her spunky husband and playfully hitting him with a badly-stitched feather pillow. As the shots of the happy woman continue in slow-mo, the voice-over switches to that of a quiet, fast-talking man listing the number of possible side-effects for the medicine, which often not only include the illness you want to relieve but much worse - the final risk listed is often 'death'. One headache pill actually said, 'side-effects may include headaches'. The cultures of legislature and advertising had got drunk, had sex and birthed a chimera, the likes of which I have only ever seen on American TV.

We were reminded that the world itself was not too dissimilar from the one we were observing through our box-shaped window. When we eventually did make it out of the room, we found a 'family restaurant' for lunch. The head waiter had a cordless mic and would occasionally announce a birthday to loud whoops or go over and chat to a group of patrons, casually engaging them in some hilarious banter and positive fluffing to keep the atmosphere topped up.

"It sure is great to see so many wonderful people in the restaurant today. We really hope you have the *very* best Sunday with us!"

At one point he announced the daily quiz question, with the chance to win free desserts - "What is the Italian for sparkling wine?" We listened as he updated us that 'vino' and 'champagne' were sadly not correct guesses. He kept repeating the question every few minutes. "Anyone, anyone? No? So, just to recap - we have had several guesses so far and they were…"

"Just go and put us out of our misery Bone," implored Killer. "If he goes on any longer, I fear side effects may include strangulation."

Reluctantly I got up, whispered into the waiter's ear and then returned, placing two chocolate brownies in front of us.

"It was decent of us to let them have a chance but eventually you have to just step in and help these people out," said Killer.

The reason for the lunch was celebration. We had managed to find, in a small three-sentence report in USA Today, on around page 63, that England had won the Rugby World Cup the day before. Jonny Wilkinson had launched a drop kick in the final seconds to snatch victory from Australia. The whole country had come together to spectate and enjoy a new-found national fervour. Here, in Mesa, people knew as much about this 'rugby ball' as they did about spumante wine. We called home and bathed in our families' retelling of the match before further celebrating in a vast guitar superstore where we pulled models from the shelves and played celebratory riffs of Stonegarth.

"That's a cool tune dude," said one of the shop workers.

"It's called Afraid. It's about a duck learning to fly," confirmed Killer. "But don't worry - he flies."

Back at the motel there was then just enough time to write the next article for the magazine. Killer was happy for me to write it entirely and as I typed up the words, I knew that writing would feature prominently in my post-Limey life.

The only remaining task was to cast the rest of *The Limey Project: The Movie*. Needless to say, Brian Blessed was cast in the role of Brian. The part of Paul Bunyan went to Sylvester Stallone, and the Governator insisted on playing himself. Dr John would also, of course, be played by musical Dr John, except when he was off stage and on the bike, dishing out his invaluable advice, then he was Steve Guttenberg, re-appreciated. It got a little meta when we started holding auditions for the other roles, some of which were closely contested. In the end, it was decided that diminutive duo Bill and Patsy would be played by Danny DeVito and Danny DeVito in a dress, Ernest by Jude Law, Greve by Richard E Grant and Tom Selleck, the Germans Mikhail and Anke by the Germans Boris Becker and Martina Navratilova, and Dedric by Patrick Swayze (we wanted Dedric to dance a little as he pushed his cart...). That just left Bone and Killer - these lead roles were assigned to Christian Bale and Johnny Depp, respectively (fairly kind on those actors, I thought). This was a satisfactory start but something told us some of the greatest characters still lay head, on the road[3].

We finally saddled up again on the third morning. The donuts from the motel owner - who was surprised we were actually on our way again - carried us a few miles, before the cravings were too much and we topped up again at a drive-thru donut store.

It was cloudy and cold and it was 20 miles until we were out of town. Unattractive and uninspiring urban sprawl. Every block had the same prefabricated store front, car parks, RV lots, retirement

---

[3] To know the full cast list, you'll just have to wait for the movie.

complexes and wide, uniform streets not designed for humans. I saw no walkers, no one else mad enough to cycle. Oh for the soft, mad beauty of Europe, I thought. Or at least the desert.

At one junction a truck pulled alongside us.

"Where y'all headed?"

We told them and they nodded. They pulled off as if it was nothing but suddenly the break lights flared, tyres screeched and they leant back out of the window.

"Wait! Miami, FLORIDA???"

It was like the director of our movie had whispered in his ear. 'Ok John, give it everything you got. Don't hold back. I want *total* bewilderment.' And he delivered. The reason for his reaction was that we were to pass the small town of Miami, Arizona in the mountains ahead. We stopped to pose for comedy photos of us standing confused by the 'Welcome to Miami' sign with our big paper maps as if we thought we'd made it to our final destination. Nope, this town of 1,800 people was not the end of the road. Not even close.

The road itself was rising up. Past Phoenix, the mountains that had been harsh flanks to our passage now started to ripple ahead of us, and the ascent would continue for another 350 miles. We paused to catch our breath after 35 miles and I confessed to Killer I was struggling and anxious that I had lost my strength.

"Me too, Bone. This is godawful riding," he said reassuringly. "Maybe three days of luxoire have softened us. Let's push on. What would Jonny Wilkinson say if he could see us like this?"

Was I getting sick? Or had I pushed myself too far? The little worries in my head started to grow obsessively again that I would fail because of my body. But I was getting better at addressing these mental intrusions when I saw them approaching and meeting them with action. We climbed steadily and with increasing conviction up to the 2,800 ft Gonzales Pass and, as the horizon got pulled away and the land rose around us in violent twists of rock, I started to feel the anxieties slip back down the road. I can do this. The scale of the landscape we had first acknowledged near Quartzsite now consumed us. To either side, scrubby, cactus-pricked desert, long valleys and huge, jagged mountains. We later passed between colossal red rocks; terracotta monoliths gathered together like pipe organs. Ahead of us, nestled in the foothills of the opposite range, was Superior, our intended camp for the night. The sun had been lost all day but now it broke momentarily through the mottled sky and lit up our path. The light gave the land edges, and they seemed infinitely far away.

Past Superior, the landscape only became vaster and more brutal and we relished it. We raced with Kirkendall-esque enthusiasm over a couple of 4,000 ft passes, even getting excited at the prospect of the over 8,000 ft monster pass that was just a few days ahead. One pass was an old trading post community smartly named 'The top of the world'. The riding was peaceful. So peaceful. As much as I missed the everyday attractions of the Pacific coast, I enjoyed being lost in this emptiness, unsure what lay ahead. Wasn't that why we were here? Time moved along but wasn't counted. The gears occasionally slowly shifted, but the legs just kept turning and both bike and passenger moved together onwards, upwards and then breathed out as gravity took care of the rest. Back down. Then peddle again. No people. No cars. Just the small mechanical sound of wheels and cogs and chains. Then occasionally the sharp cry of a hawk above to return you from whatever daydream you had been lost in.

Killer was being affected too. Instead of quoting, he turned temporarily to philosophising.

"Bone, I told you that grunge music was why I wanted to come to America. But I had another inspiration for coming here in this manner."

I waited for the joke.

"I had recently read Zorba the Greek."

I had not expected that.

"I had been bigly inspired by Zorba's life philosophy," he continued. "Zorba knows that there is no deeper wisdom than that which can be encountered through communion with nature and by living fully in the present moment, rather than waiting for an illusory afterlife. That is when I decided we needed to do something monumental, that we needed an absurd, torturous, surreal odyssey."

"The world is our pork chop," I replied in agreement, recalling the prophetic sign in Seattle and taking Killer's traditional, deflective role in our conversations to maintain the balance in the universe.

It felt then that we had found exactly what Killer hoped we would. I knew the feeling of ease was temporary - that pain would return at some point - and that is perhaps why I enjoyed it even more intensely, but it was with such an utter, and appropriate, calm union with the land that we crossed into the San Carlos Apache Indian Reservation. I had always loved the word Apache. When younger, my brother would dress as a cowboy, and I was always the brave Apache; not only for the fact it was much more fabulous costumery but it was just much more interesting. As we pulled up to a gas station to fill our water bottles and bags for the night, it felt like a different country. It could have been any one of the hundreds of gas stations we had stopped at. But here, the earth was dustier, the paint a little more faded. All the men loitering outside had long, black hair and groups of small children rode in the back of pickup trucks that passed by. Two Apaches came up and thanked us separately for the journey. One had breast cancer, the other had a brother with leukemia. Both said they had neither the insurance nor the money to adequately support their care.

"Welcome to our land," said one as they moved off.

There was a kind of tense silence about the place. This was indeed their land and they were deeply proud of their connection to it, but it also felt like their hope had been removed, almost totally. Fewer than half of the US' native American population of 2.5 million people still live in reservations. There are 326 of them, they are scattered across the country in small pockets but collectively size up to be bigger than Idaho. In Arizona, one-quarter of the state is made up of such reservations. San Carlos is by no means the largest but it stretches across 1.8 million acres of land and all this with a population the same as that of Sherborne; around 10,000 people. Money comes in from the casino and from hunting and fishing licenses but there are few prospects here. Half the population lives below the poverty line and a third of those who can work are unemployed. And the term 'reservation' seems more than a little loose. The land near where we were camping that night would later become subject to a legal battle that as of 2019 is at the highest offices of government to prevent Rio Tinto from mining parts of the land for copper. The disputed land is dotted with petroglyphs, as well as historic and prehistoric sites.

This was outside Peridot. Unsure of the rules and etiquette of camping on Indian land, but unable to go further due to darkness and exhaustion, we heaved our bikes over a fence by a layby and wheeled them a few metres into the desert. Thick scrub blocked us from disappearing further, to totally get out of view of the road, and we worried we were too exposed, that we may get a good old fashioned ass-whoopin' for breaking sacred rules. Or that an even worse fate might meet us.

I awoke a few times to the sound of a car pulling up, the clank of car doors and crunch of footsteps approaching, but they never came beyond the fence. Foolishly, we seemed to have made camp near an informal night-time rendez-vous. I held my penknife in my hand like a comfort blanket. I wasn't really too concerned but I preferred to be hidden away from all the humanity, my imagination having been fired by the news report I'd seen on TV in Mesa. 'More dead bodies have been found in the desert.' More? This is a thing? People getting randomly left for dead by maniacs? Or were the wild beasts to blame? It was only later that I found out it was for both of these reasons, and more. What the immigration cop we'd met patrolling near Glamis left out when he was warning us of the danger posed to us by those would-be migrant dreamers was that these people faced unimaginable terrors themselves - heat exhaustion by day, freezing nights they were unprepared for, scavenging animals, corrupt smugglers, robbers lying in wait. They call this stretch of desert 'the land of open graves' because of its harshness. A large number of illegal crossings result in death or disappearance. US immigration then plays up this danger - including on TV news reports - to deter more people from attempting the journey. Amongst all this, it seemed illogical that we had not yet been confronted by any nighttime visitors ourselves, by neither man nor beast. The only explanation was that they were intimidated by Brian, but for how much longer would he fend them off?

"What if he gets distracted by another handsome bear or gets drunk with Mr Camp Coyote and lets his guard down?" I asked Killer.

"Bone. This is Brian we're talking about," he replied. "He will protect us."

Even though we knew this was true, we both always tried to avoid leaving the tent in the thick of the night, and stir its musings, holding our pee in for as long as possible before one final, rapidly efficient exit for urination before sleep. As the batteries of the headtorch wore down, you'd focus on the small dinner-plate serving of desert you could see, trying not to concern yourself with the rustlings hiding in the expansive blackness around you.

Inside the tent, all was well. My tent was my shell. I'd lie there, happily enclosed, drifting off whilst listening to the soundtrack of the night. There was the occasional scrape of something passing nearby. But beyond that, there was just a quiet hush; the intonation of the heavy blanket of stars above arranging themselves. Little between me and the heavens and I could hear them speaking to me. I felt both vulnerable and indestructible. And then, puncturing the stillness, an 'ut ut' would fire from nearby, like a canon sneezing, and I'd be brought back to The Limey Project.

The next day was Thanksgiving and it seemed deeply ironic that we had awoken in an Indian reservation, and would pass through Geronimo that day. Thanksgiving is celebrated as the day the Pilgrims enjoyed their first harvest supper. The story purports that pilgrims and natives looked past their differences and broke bread together. For many Indians though, it is nothing short of a day of mourning, for broken promises and cultural genocide. Sorry, that got serious fast, didn't it.

When we arrived at Geronimo, we found Dr John. Out on his own, just casually cycling across three states on his time off.

"Hitting 80 miles a day until El Paso, then it's fiesta in Mexica. Man, El Paso is a crazy town. Crayyyzyyyyy. But you'll find out for yourself. Ha. Don't go fuckin' with no Mexicans though when you're there. The city over the border - Juarez - man, it's the most dangerous city in Mexico. The shit there, man. Crazy."

It was as if John had read the script. As it turns out, it was exactly as he had said it would be. Just with a little more crazy.

I noticed he only had front panniers on his bike and he confirmed he was staying in motels and hotels.

"You're missing some great desert camping," I suggested.

"For sure. But I'm also not getting killed by crazies or coyotes. I put your chances of survival at, like, *reaaaalllll* low."

Was John reading my thoughts now?

"We should be OK as long as our invisible friend Brian the Bear doesn't get distracted," I said.

John looked, understandably, confused.

"What he means is that we'll be fiiiiiiiine John," said Killer. John then looked even more confused, and it was only then we remembered John didn't know that was his name. He shook his head back to his reality.

"Anyway, gotta shoot - got to be back in San Diego for work next week." He pedaled away with a cry of "Geronimooooooooooo".

So yes, we were in Geronimo. A small plaque commemorated the last effort of the famed Indian chief and his ultimate defeat, surrendering his people to the Yankees. The surviving Apache were allowed to farm some of the lands alongside the Gila river that passes here. Their lands reduced from the infinite to an identified irrigated area. The plaque was placed at the site of Fort Thomas, where the control of the Apache was managed - I couldn't be sure then what exactly the plaque was commemorating.

To the victor go the spoils. The modest, fart-and-you-miss-it plaque was in contrast to a large Brutalist-style monument with a 50 ft spire a few miles further, dedicated to local hero Melvin Jones. He is credited with the expansion of Lions Club International into the global community service organization it is today, with 46,000 local clubs and 1.7 million members. But significantly, Jones happened to be born at Fort Thomas as his father had been a Captain there, keeping guard over the defeated Apache. I couldn't help but reflect that the name of the club, LIONS, stands for 'Liberty, Intelligence, our Nation's Safety'... just a few of the things Geronimo was also trying to progress before Jones' father and the rest got to work.

John's confusion that morning at the mention of his name led to a long discussion during the afternoon's ride about our favourite 'Johns'. This in turn - of course - led to a new game being created, 'Questions from John'. The rules were simple, much more simple than Patriot Points. We took turns to ask each other questions, posing as various famous Johns, with each John keen to understand what really took place on The Limey Project.

"Hello, yes, this is John Simpson, BBC News. I'd like to ask if either of you ever got bored of Choodle?"

"That's a great question, John. No."

John Travolta, John Mayer, John Wayne, John Craven, John Cleese, John Smith, John Suchet, Jon Bon Jovi, John Lennon, Jon Snow, John McEnroe... they all quizzed us on everything from ass chafing to how to win at Shithead, and our thoughts on the best flavoured syrups to add to gas station coffee. Some of the questions were quite flattering of our knowledge - and also went beyond the original interview scope - such as John(ny) Wilkinson asking if we had any tips for how to improve his kicking style, and John F Kennedy enquiring if we knew if Oswald had been acting alone or as part of a deep CIA conspiracy. As the game progressed - and we played it intermittently for a number of days between the usual shouts, quotes and songs - the fame of the John and the relevance of his question became increasingly distant.

"Hi, this is King John of England. You know, from *Magna Carta* fame? No? Anyway, if you had to sum up the coldness of a desert morning as a colour, what would it be and why?"

I didn't note the reasoning in my diary but the precise hue offered was 'mango mocha dream'.

And as we were now in our fourth state, another new game - admittedly only played once - was the 'Trying to name the 50 states in alphabetical order' game. I managed 33, pathetically, while Killer assailed to an all-American 43. I learned there are eight states that start with an M. (Try and name them yourself now. Impossible. Everyone forgets Maryland). We then played the 'Trying to name the 50 states in historical order game'. This was perhaps our shortest ever invented game[4].

The afternoon scenery became increasingly agrarian. Bronze, autumnal trees lined a dried out valley beside the Gila to our left. And to our right, fields of cotton flanked us all the way to our camp that night at Thatcher. Balls of cotton had blown onto the road and then been flattened by traffic, making it look like birds had been using the road for target practice. This was added to by constant scatters of glass that we were often unable to avoid. Killer was got, which made it 4-4 on the puncture count for 2,000 miles. Not too bad.

As we pulled into Thatcher we started to smell roast Turkeys and I missed home, and the coming Christmas. We found the private RV park - the old lady proprietor was just having her family dinner so said we could pay later. But she must have heard me and Killer

---

[4] If you knew the answer starts with 'Delaware' you have just won a prize. No need to make contact to claim it, as it will find its way to you.

chuckling outside about 'paying later' as she then came and found us as we pitched the tents.

"On second thoughts, boys, I better take that payment from you now. Just so I don't forget."

But I was happy to pass over $10 for a warm shower and a quiet night camping on grass after covering over 150 miles in three extraordinarily tough days. I drank my tea, cooked up some award-winning choodle and started the process of wrapping up for the evening. For it was cold. The days were cold enough - we were up at 2,900 ft at Thatcher - and the nights were now way below zero. For bed, it was full thermals (bottoms and long sleeve top) with another long sleeve T-shirt, then fleece, jeans, socks, and hat. The sleeping bag was drawn up over my shoulders, and tightened around my neck by a drawstring.

The wind that day had been exceptional. We were often pushed back again to 6 or 7 mph as even the flats felt like tough uphills. For a while, I actually relished it - I still felt the ride would be more memorable if we were pushed harder. And I was starting to feel close to finding that deeper place within myself, where I would be able to capture the big thoughts in my net. But I also knew I was reaching my limit. There was a risk I could run myself into the ground.

This was a thought that poked away at me the next day. The demands of wind and terrain just multiplied as we returned to the mountains. Our bikes were heavier here too, weighed down by extra food and water (as the ACA warned us that services were 'limited' for the next 117 miles). We turned to our Jukeboxes to help with the effort and I found myself drawing inspiration from Slavomir a couple of times to keep my legs pumping. We set ourselves mini targets to keep us going - ten miles, wee break, ten miles more, snack break, onwards...

This carried us to a seven-mile ascent. We laboured in silence, just slowly turning the wheels at walking pace. But the view from the top of the pass was the most incredible one to date. Perhaps hard work and reward really do go together. It was similar to the one by Superior but more spectacular, in every sense. The mountains were larger and the space between them more expansive. The whole scene consumed us with its enormity, and it was almost fractaled; even the canyons hid their own giant peaks and valleys. Landscapes within landscapes. There were a handful of small settlements, which pricked the land like ink dots. We felt like we had shrunk down to the size of ants. Above all this, heavy, dark clouds rolled around with intention. The whole place was alive.

By the time we descended down to Threeway - after only covering 38 miles - it was already after 3 pm. There was another camp run by the US Forest Service 15 miles further but it was all uphill to get there and the idea of riding these desert roads at night was not entirely tempting. Also - *forest service*? There would have to be some drastic change of scenery - and climate - to see how the forest service could be any more active here than offering some cactus topiary. The land was just redder and dustier than anything before it. Even the desert scrubs struggled to find anchor. The only trees that did exist lined the Gila River which was now somewhere in the middle of the vast landscape, but beyond our vision.

And we could physically go no further for the day. We were cold and exhausted, both of us were experiencing agony in our knees. Killer had been telling me of his growing knee concerns earlier that afternoon and I found myself surprisingly unhelpful, distracted by my own demons and the idea that if I thought too much about it then my own knee pain would return, which of course it did. And it felt serious this time.

Approaching Threeway, we had been unsure if we would find a town of liberal sexual adventurers where odd-numbered groups for intercourse was the most prominent pastime (this was Brian's hope), or simply a desert community where three roads met at a junction. We found the latter. There was a gas station with a store and, beside that, a Jehovah's Witness hall. There was also a ranger station atop an elevated rocky promontory that overlooked the junction like a sniper's post and where a huge stars and stripes billowed above it, looking in this empty landscape like a flag on the moon. It seemed like a nowhere town but I guess it was the only town for miles around. Even if the only common ground was a gas station store, we knew well enough that was often all you needed - a small group of men in ten-gallon hats stood outside, stamping their boots to keep warm. Our life revolved around the road and the curious ecosystem of Americana that it supported. Our second home was therefore the gas station, and the conversations we encountered at its Three Way incarnation were no more illuminating than many of the others. But the flatness of their tone did tell us something of how people here accepted a tough life.

"So you're cyclists?"

"Yeah, I guess."

"Where y'all headed?"

"Miami."

"Well, you got a ways to go."

"Uh huh."

The ACA maps had suggested we could camp for free outside the ranger's office on a scrap of dried grass. We pitched up and, before turning in for the night, I read the information boards - of course - that explained where we were. South East Arizona is a 'unique habitat', I learned. Influenced by and connected to the Rockies to the North and the Sierra Madre mountains of Mexico to the South, it has two deserts, river valleys, cactus fields, mountains and alpine forests. I still wasn't yet convinced there were forests but I could fully vouch for the deserts and mountains. The board said you can even ski in this region, at Mount Lemmon, the most southerly ski resort in the continental USA. We had passed to the north of it, through cracked rocks pierced by cactuses. It seemed impossible to imagine but, then, this land was extraordinary.

10. This is starting to hurt

Everything you can imagine is real.
Pablo Picasso

It's said that you need three things to survive an expedition - food, water, and shelter. I would add a fourth to this list - toilet. An Englishman's throne is his castle. A large part of the day is occupied in pursuit of meeting the day's complement of each of the four survival elements. And sometimes you have to improvise. Despite allowing camping at the ranger station in Threeway, there appeared to be no facilities for ablutions and we both awoke urgently needing poos. Killer set off first, in desperate haste, to see if there was something hidden behind the building. To my relief, he returned smiling a few minutes later, and passed me the loo roll.

"There you go. There are *excellent* facilities Bone - we must have just missed them."

I walked around but there was nothing, just the back wall of the ranger station and a cactus. Then I spied it, poking out of the grey gravel, a flick of white loo paper. Like a hastily abandoned crime scene, and I laughed loudly.

"Got it, thanks Killer. Lovely spot."

A car pulled up and then wisely drove off again.

The second necessity was water. The coldness of the night meant all our extra water had frozen solid. We placed our water bladders in the sunshine hoping they would thaw enough to become malleable so we could top them up and strap them on to the bikes. I found a tap and filled a pan. The water turned to an icy sludge before my eyes and I lit the gas stove to make some coffee. There is something infinitely comforting about the sound of a lit camping stove. It's a hushed growl that says 'Hey, it's alllll OK'.

And then to food. And our morning ritual now saw our bread replaced with the much more storable and less perishable, tortillas. Flat packs of ten, they could be easily shoved into panniers. We slathered them in peanut butter (which, misheard somewhere along the road, had been renamed 'penis butter', or often just 'penis'), rolled them into fat cigars and washed them down with vitamins and the essential black coffee. Our meals consisted of a lot of passing and mock agreeable helpfulness.

"Tortilla?"

"Yes please. Penis?"

"Wonderful. I love penis tortillas. And has Bone had his Hollyweird Vitamin?"

"Mmm. Just the ticket. It's just such a shame the side effects include vitamin deficiency."

We packed up the shelter and, having successfully achieved our four goals, rolled out of Threeway, setting our sights loosely on a bike and body patch-up in Silver City, two days' ride away. We had arrived at the ranger station feeling utterly broken. We felt little better as we left, but were resolved to maintain a positive intention and determination. Killer let off a ceremonial trumpet of gas as we set off. Indeed, our gas was the only consistency - as both the landscape and temperatures shifted abruptly from day to day, we had come to count on the potency and plenty of the gas. A diet of chili, trapped by lycra... well, it was a recipe for natural power.

"If only we could bottle it," remarked Killer, "we could sell it and become, literally, stinking rich."

We were right not to have pushed on the day before. The road snaked up for the first three hours of riding, taking us another 2,500 ft up to a 6,300 ft pass. The view looking back was another one to savour. We could trace the road the full 25 miles back to where we'd first spied Threeway the day before. Descending the other side, it was like a different world. The climate had been severed by the mountains like a knife. Here were the woodlands the information boards had promised - they were dry and rocky but woodlands all the same. Then through grassy ranchlands with horses and cattle. This was our welcome to New Mexico.

I went ahead and clapped Killer into the new state. We left Arizona and its 27 species of rattlesnake without having seen a single one. Thank God. We entered a land whose state bird is the road runner, a cartoon character brought to life in these coyote-stalked canyons. We hoped the dangers ahead were equally cartoon-like in their delivery. We wanted to continue to free camp and on the map we spied a cafe in a small town called Cliff. We would finally try that Love Actually charm on a cafe patron, hoping someone would let us pitch up on their porch and ply us with coffee and eggs the next day. The plan about 0% worked.

At the cafe, a sign jokingly asked customers to remove their spurs before entering.

"What about lycra?" I asked Killer.

"Mmm, I say remove, just to be on the safe side."

Inside, we were the only customers but for a heavy old man called Walter. He possessed a collection of characteristics - dribbly, doddery, a little bothersome - that we would recognise in other well-meaning faces along the road, all named Walter in the Limenagerie after this first encounter. Walter Cliff came to join our table unasked and talked at us while we ate. The waitress was a young, beautiful girl, her T-shirt tied in a knot to one side, half way up her waist. She wore sparkly reindeer antlers, the only sign here of the coming Christmas. She kept pouring me restorative, warming mugs of decaf coffee.

"I made this pot just for you," she said with a wink. I got the impression she lived off her tips.

I persisted with Walter, believing every one of us has a story to tell and sure enough here it was. And it was almost poetic. Walter had been an interpreter in the Second World War in Germany for the US Navy.

"We beat them 'cos we knew more. Knowledge is power."

He pointed to the TV in the corner, his gesture reminding me of Bill in his home in Carmel hundreds of miles and a million dollars away, and sounding like the woman who sold us La Rouche on the streets of LA, all these small voices rising up.

"Kids today don't know anything cos we don't teach them anything. We make people ignorant 'cos we want to control them. And that is not good for America."

I was about to applaud him for this observation when he leaned in again, more intently, as if about to share his final insight. But, sadly, I had overestimated the man.

"Anyway, I gotta go take a dump. Enjoy your dinner."

Walter later told us our best shot at finding a spot to camp was to head to the bridge on the other side of town and scout around by the river. "But keep outta sight. There's young kids driving around all crazy drunk on Saturday nights and you don't want them knowing you're down there."

We pitched up in the middle of a dried out river bed, hidden by some trees and bushes on the bank, our dark green tents again providing the perfect blend for the wild nature. We had no idea what weather was forecast and we just prayed we wouldn't be awoken to being washed away by the river swollen with rain, like spiders in a bath. Instead, we were awoken at dawn to a deep freeze. We'd heard the trucks driving past, horns blaring as horny teenage boys let out their testosterone but we had been untroubled. Our water bottles were frozen solid though, and the bikes and tents were covered in a cake of ice. We awaited the sun's thaw before we could get on the road.

The sun was definitely deceptive here. Arriving in Silver City later that day, it felt mild due to the 6,000 ft elevation but catching my face for the first time in many days in a mirror, I saw broken lips and my skinny face weather-blistered. Like the roads, we were starting to feel the cracks of the daily cyclical freeze and heat rhythm of the New Mexican winter. Our bikes were also suffering. They had started to groan with every tug at the handlebars as we climbed, and our bald tyres were starting to gather punctures like they were on special in Walmart. After eight punctures in the first 2,000 miles, we had gathered one every other day since then.

Silver City was our first large town since Mesa. As we pondered how it could see to all our needs, Dr (Long) John Silver pulled up on a mountain bike. He understood the legacy of his forebears and his role in this Limey play; without being questioned he offered information on where to eat - Sonic Burgers - and where to find the bike shop - "Speak to Mike at Gila Hike & Bike". He rang his bell and rode on, mission completed.

To pay for all our repairs, we needed cash but the only ATM we could find was a drive-thru. You can tell a lot about a place's attitude to walking and cycling by the number of drive-thrus it operates. After pretending to wind my window down in my invisible automobile to withdraw my money, we found Sonic Burgers was also car-only. There were no seats inside, just large menu boards placed at car window height on the forecourt, as if petrol pumps.

"How the hell do we do this?" I asked Killer.

"We must observe the native."

We watched for a while as a couple of cars pulled up to the menus, wound down their windows and placed their orders, then drove ahead into a parking bay. Minutes later a waitress emerged and clipped a tray of saturated fats on to the side of each car.

"You wait here Killer. I'll order."

"Make mine a super Sonic spicy mountain burger with sonic fries and extra sonic sauce," Killer called after me.

"Is that even a thing?"

"If it's not, tell them I'm not interested."

I pressed the 'Order here' button.

"Hello - welcome to Sonic. How may I help you this beautiful day?"

I asked for two of Killer's creations, "...and we'd like them extra sonicy."

"Certainly sir and what is your vehicle?"

"It's a Marin Muirwoods. Black. 21 speed. 2003 model. This baby's brand new."

There was a confused crackle and an even more confused look minutes later when our food arrived. We took the trays as if the most ordinary thing in the world, made the beeping sound of a reversing vehicle, and sat on the floor of the car park cross legged. Wow, after days of desert dwelling, those burgers were good.

At the supermarket we shopped for choodle (ah, beloved choodle), lip salve and suncream. Ambling about in lycra, we must have looked a little odd. At one point, I had lost Killer and became annoyed when I finally located him, calling out like a frustrated lover, "Where have you been? I've been waiting for you in the noodle aisle!"

Killer had his hands on a large tub of Vaseline that he had just pulled from the shelf.

"I was getting more lube, Bone."

We received a few odd looks.

Outside, I nearly Pelicaned myself. A colossus with a tattooed face and wearing full motorbike leather came up to me and said, "I'm sorry son but you just violated a local law."

I was in trouble.

"You know you can't park a bicycle between two Harleys." He gestured to where I had left my bike and the two shining hogs either side of it, then he roared with laughter and clapped me on the back with such force it nearly sent me back to Bremerton.

"Ha! You thought I was being serious!"

Killer and I laughed nervously.

There were more genuine glares for us at the RV park, where we pitched up. The trailer park is decidedly an American institution and some people seemed to have been living there for decades. One home had a sign on it that genuinely said 'Dun Tryin'.

The next day I lounged by the tent drinking tea and reading the newspapers - this was not something people do in RV Parks it seemed so I countered my standing-outedness by volleying a few 'Howdy's to the locals. That seemed to only have succeeded in vocalising my oddity. One teenage boy walked past in full camouflage, with a gun on his shoulder. He saw that I was momentarily looking at the fashion pages of the newspaper. On the page, a woman reclined on a beach in a designer bikini. The little assassin looked at me and then spat the words 'pervert!' before presumably then going off and shooting his sister.

I took the opportunity of time to decorate my panniers with bold writing in black marker. Killer had already penned a few short phrases on to his and it was having a clear effect on the number of people who stopped and offered a few dollars for the road. Phrases like 'Seattle to Miami', 'Cancer Research', '5,000 miles', and 'Help!'. I added similar words of clarification and supplication to my panniers alongside a map of the USA, a sketch of happy cyclists, our website in large letters and, on the largest pannier, I added a longer message.

The Limey Project is an ambitious and daring project envisaged in the minds of two men from Dorset, England. The challenge is to cycle from Seattle to Miami via San Diego. And so on 26th September 2003, Bone and Killer commenced their epic adventure. They plan to raise as much as possible for Cancer Research, and hope that wherever you meet them, in whatever foul state that may be, you will help them in their cause. Thank you.

"You forgot to mention we would like to meet some hot chicks and have everyone give us beer wherever we stop," said Killer.

"Yes it's a bit shit isn't it. I meant it to be funny."

"Not at all. I think over-exaggerated, self-heroism comedy is the precise deep layer of irony - alluding to our innate doubts over our own abilities and confidence in completing the task - that these trailer dwellers should come to appreciate."

"Thanks Killer."

"And ut. Anyway, you forgot to mention that we plan to cut out half of Texas with a train."

Killer had mentioned this before. A way to catch up and allow more time on the home stretch, and ensure our finances - and breaking bodies - would last until Miami. But I was ignoring it. For now.

Walter Cliff had said they had recently started marketing Silver City as having 'four gentle seasons' and the pensioners had started flocking here. But, seriously, gentle? I've known softer nut crackers. Then Oprah profiled it and more people came, all expecting to have their richer, more cultured tastes catered for. As Walter eloquently put it, "If you get people turning up expecting five different types of mushroom, you got to give them five different types of mushroom."

The nouveau wave was on display in a lounge cafe where we coffeed and muffined as Christmas tunes performed by Jazz greats played out. In the library, we internetted and found our latest article had come out. The West Country had been introduced to Dedric and the friendly folk of Clint's Carmel with a double page spread titled, 'The Good, The Mad and the Scary.' As I'd written the piece myself I was thrilled to have received a number of encouraging emails about it. It was all I needed to decide that I would go to the local newspaper - the Western Gazette - and ask for a trial when I got back.

At the bike shop, we chatted to famed Mike, proprietor and mechanic - he had long white hair and a wizard-length white beard.

"The beard used to be even longer - way down to my waist - but I kept getting it caught in all the bicycles," he chuckled. His smile was all-knowing and his electric eyes sparked when he told us of the bike paths he had been trying to create to get local kids cycling and make it easier for people to get around and get exploring. He was wonderful. I felt at home here, I thought of the old Mike the Bike of Sherborne and wondered if this wise soul also accepted payment in pastries.

He had a gadget that indicated our chains were 'in the red' and had to be replaced. "If you'd have left it any longer you'd have had to replace the whole rear cassette."

"Er, cassette?" We had so much to learn still.

He pointed at the rear cogs. "You get an old chain going round the cassette there, it'll wear down the mechanism and a new chain will then just jump about like a wild mustang. Costs you money. But I caught it in time."

The way he spoke it sounded venereal. I felt embarrassed.

He also explained why my tyre had a curious bulge in it - which I had been trying to ignore for a few days - and said it was lucky it had not exploded. I'd apparently got the valve trapped when I changed the tyre last, effectively creating a pneumatic timebomb.

"If it had blown while you were coming down hill at speed, then it might have been the end of your adventure," he said, with no hint of exaggeration.

I immediately thought of the Devil's pumpkin. I was unlikely to escape without injury if I lost control a second time.

Mike showed us all we were doing wrong. And this took some time. Half an hour with him was a masterclass in how extraordinarily crap we still were at looking after our bikes even after two months. He put on new tyres, told us about tyre pressure and told us about lubing, our favourite subject. He squeezed drops of oil onto the chain as he turned it around, then made a fist around the chain with a cloth and ran the chain through it.

"I always say, 'lube once, wipe five times'. Keeps it from getting gunky."

Killer and I exchanged knowing glances.

"Thanks, we'll try that," I said, infinitely grateful to the world for people like Mike.

Our bikes and bodies were now patched up to fight some more miles and we celebrated at a restaurant called El Loco Lizard, selected in honour of our new friend Larry. He was a foot-long toy rubber lizard that I'd rescued from beside the road, in the desert by

Superior. He rode along under the straps of my rear rack, or sometimes on the front if he was good.

Occasionally, Larry would hide in places to surprise me. The day before he slid under the door while I was taking a shower, having written 'UT UT' in steam in the washroom mirror. But perhaps Larry's most distinctive trait was his strong Dutch accent. His bottom jaw pointed out at an angle, reminding us of the Dutch cyclist we had met in Big Sur and Larry - perhaps naturally - affected the same timbre and tone.

"Yeshhhhhh, come on Bone, I want to ride up front today. I'll eat the flies so they don't go in your face. Yesh?"

He'd also formed a quick and solid bond with Brian, which is good, as you never know how your imaginary friends will get along.

Every civilization, settler, and prospector has carved out a stake on this landscape over the centuries. Silver City is named - you'll be shocked to learn - because of the silver mine that once existed here. Whilst the silver never lived up to early expectations, other opportunities kept surfacing. And with every new mineral murmur, more hopeful entrepreneurs and grafters would pour into town. At one point Silver City was a sea of thousands of tents and makeshift communities. Cycling out of town, the road rose up and up until we reached the main attraction for this rush, the vast Santa Rita open pit copper mine. And through a wire mesh fence we peered down to what looked like the hellscape of Mordor. The mountain had been cut away into a grey bowl, which descended in steps, with every plateau a skyscraper's length from the next. Pricks of movement far below us turned out to be industrial trucks the size of hotels. At 1.75 miles wide and 1,350 ft deep, this is one of the largest man made holes in the earth on, er, earth.

Spaniards, Mexicans, and Americans have all obtained copper from this site. The present-day open operation was begun in 1910 but mining has been going on at Santa Rita since 1800. And from its earliest days, it was plagued by Apache raids. Fur trappers, miners and military garrisons were all in the Apache's sights in this area. In one incident, it's said as many as 400 people - the entire town of Santa Rita - was killed as they tried to flee south into Mexico. The raids continued all the way until 1886, when Geronimo finally earned his small stone plaque a few miles to the West.

But the history goes back even further. From the mine, we could take a massive detour - something Kirkendall would've called a 'scenic side trip'. We had the option to loop north, adding two days ride to explore the Gila cliff dwellings. There, we could walk through the hand-cut caves of the Mogollon people, who had lived in the area for over a millennium, until the Spanish arrived and put an end to it. There, also, were hot springs, which spoke of the region's more distant past; evidencing long-gone volcanoes that had helped to form the contested copper deposits in an entirely other era. Here was something even older than Lewis and Clark. We wanted to see it all but time, money and bodily limits told us to stay on course and head straight up the mighty Emory Pass.

Through pine-covered mountains we went. Half hours would pass with not a single car passing. A cool sweetness from the woods hung in the air. Beside the road I saw a family of wild pigs scurry into the undergrowth. Ahead, Killer was making better progress and, as the final slopes rose more steeply, I saw him pass by above my head with every sharp switchbacking hairpin. Every sighting of him was a sign I had still further to climb. Then there it was - Emory Pass, and the view opened up. We'd ascended a range of peaks called the Devil's Mountains. It was hellishly tough. But oh my, it was all worth it.

The vista stretched for 180 degrees. It was like sitting in the top seats of an amphitheatre and looking down on a play that had been acted out already for millions of years. Forest to each side and, in front, the view tumbled away in jagged green steps. In the distance, we spied the Caballo Reservoir (37 miles away as the bike rides), from where the Rio Grande would guide us to El Paso; our recuperation destination for two days' time, if we could manage some 70-mile days in these conditions.

Trucks occasionally pulled into the parking lot. Retired couples and young families climbed out, arched their backs, stretching against the confines of the cars. Enthusiastic dads outlined the majesty of the place to young children who were too young to appreciate it. It was the same play you see the world over, and it felt good. Some sort of universal 'er, is this it?' we can all be part of until the curtain comes down and we look back on it all with immense fondness.

We were standing at 8,228ft. This was the highest point of The Limey Project. Our multi-day mental preparations for the 'torture' of the near 2,000 ft Leggett Hill seemed like different people on another peddally planet. This was high. This was higher than stacking Ben Nevis on top of Mount Snowdon. And we had just slipped into a low gear and spun our way to the top. It felt good. Killer caught me as I tried to secretly jump up in the air.

"Er, is Bone doing a celebratory leap?"

"Ah you got me. I was hoping you wouldn't notice and I could tell you later."

"That cycling up mountains is no longer enough exercise for you?"

"I was hoping that later today you'd say 'I can't believe we got as high as 8,228 ft today Bone' and then I would say 'Well, Killer, you may have got to 8,228 ft, but I believe I achieved at least 8,230 ft'."

"I see. That's quite a complicated plan."

"I'm a complicated person with a lot of time on my hands."

Killer nodded in the affirmative. "True, true." Then slowly he bent his knees and launched himself up.

"Damn you," I cried.

There then followed a few minutes of competitive jumping, both of us straining to lengthen our necks like eels, before even the enthusiastic dads could watch no more.

"We'll have to call it even," suggested Killer.

"Yes, I guess we will," I said walking behind him and then climbing up onto a wall.

The road snaked down through Kingston and into Hillsboro after 17 miles. It was a delicious descent but after several miles I had to pause to let the brakes cool, the hot rubber from repeated chicaning was singeing the air. Mike would not like this, I thought. Actually, Mike probably wouldn't have been applying the brakes in the first place. We made camp in a park in the centre of the community. It was a free camp but with all the facilities we could dream of, namely a shed for general toileting and - after a long absence - a picnic bench for comfortable Shithead playing. As we laid down the Law, we also started to consider the famed watercourse we would encounter a few hours' ride into the next day.

The Rio Grande had lived in my imagination since childhood. It begins in Colorado and travels almost 1,900 miles before flowing out into the Gulf of Mexico. It provides the name and setting for countless Westerns. This is where John Wayne fights off the marauding Apache. I'd pictured the deep rushes, horses being swept along as they tried to cross. Cowboys lassoing the lost. I'd been looking forward to the encounter. But since Quartzsite, I knew from Robert Duvall that I might be in for a shock.

Wow. He was right.

The most underwhelming and one of *the* most depressing things I have ever seen. What little water there was drifted lazily or gathered in pools between dried, cracked earth. As I looked closer, I saw that even the flowing water might actually be an illusion, just a stagnancy stirred by wind-blown ripples. Far from the unconquerable frontier of my dreams, this was truly an ecological nightmare. Grande? Nope, this was a disaster. This was worse than the Colorado River and, now informed by The Three, I understood what I was looking at.

The basic maths of an ecological disaster is that more is taken than is naturally replaced. Irrigation, diversions, damming, industrial extraction. You gradually eat away at it. The navigable river of old was gone. And what I was looking at wasn't even the worst of it. South of El Paso, it is known as 'the forgotten river' as there is so little water. Then, by the time it passes Presidio, a couple of hundred miles further south, there is often no water at all. It is totally barren until some of the flow is restored by small tributaries further down. I felt like this was some unmentioned but loudly clanging alarm bell, tolling for so much that we were witnessing on this journey. I felt angry.

"What the dried out piece of dicking hell kind of crap is this?"

"Let's press on, Bone. There's nothing to see here."

The route was flat from there on, as it followed the course of the 'river'. We passed Hatch - not just a great place to grow chilies, but 'chili capital of the world', of course - then along fields of Pecan groves. As the day went on our bodies started collapsing from under us again. The only comfort came from Killer's purchase of a baseball cap from a gas station that had images of chilis sewn into it and the words 'New Mexico is HOT!'

He sported it proudly. "Bone, have you heard - New Mexico *is* hot."

"Yes, I did hear that. I also heard it was a bit rubbish."

"Now, now."

"Sorry, Killer, it's just...ugh... fuck me, I don't think I have ever been in so much pain."

My left leg was really concerning me. I could no longer stand up on the pedals to take on the hills (often required to get enough leverage to push the bike forwards) and even on the flat, every effort felt like a crisis. I had had problems before but they were tolerable and ebbed away. This new wave had been building in intensity since Silver City and felt more permanent. What if my knee was like the chain on my bike. After a while, you stretch it too much and it's just gone. I applied some 'Icy Hot' lube a few times a day but I needed Mike the Bike to give me a full service (Hmmm, that sounds wrong). How can one thing go so drastically bad so quickly? The pain was a distractor from the ardour of the miles though, in so much as it gave me an obsessive focus. Every pedal stroke was examined and the pain evaluated as I made minute adjustments to leg angle, foot placement, gearage. But little seemed to help and it merely resulted in more laboured over-thinking. *Is it worse? Is it worse? Is it worse?*

And there was more. A new terror had been added to our daily labours.

Dogs.

Man's best friend was apparently the cyclist's most unbearable tormentor. As you cycle past their homes, they claw at their cages, strain at their leads, burrow under fences and rage until they are free to give chase. Even at night, when they can't see you, they sense you cycling and bark maniacally. They want you dead, and they *will* hunt you down. And the huge numbers of dogs that are left to roam free in these small, wild desert towns means there are many many dogs to give chase. Is it the sight, or the sound - a high pitched trill of the turning wheel inaudible to humans but like blood to a shark? They sense us approaching and then emerge on to the road to sight us in packs. Once targeted, they chase. And my ability to outrun them was diminishing.

On the worst occasions, one of us would be ahead on the road and make it through before the dogs could get to the battle and the next Limey would then arrive at the scene, and just see the backs of an angry pack. The dogs' ears would then prick, they'd turn and start to slather as they see their target approaching. It sounds like fun. A bit of a chase. But these dogs are total, meth-head level, nuts. Some superbreeds did get close, snarling and snapping at our heels, biting our bike bags. Killer kicked one in the head and as it yelped off I felt the warm happiness only a captor feels about their tormentor.

We could hear the canine choir as we pitched up in Radium Springs. We tried to make camp secretly in a fenced off area of nothingness but a ranger pulled up and moved us on.

We tried feigning ignorance, "Oh the campsite is a couple of miles further along is it?"

The ranger tipped his hat up and nodded his head forward a little to survey us over the top of his sunglasses.

"Uh, huh. Can't believe you missed it."

As I contemplated standing up to ride on again, I looked at this law keeper almost in hope that he would just arrest me and confiscate our bikes. I would confess to anything. Maybe potent bottom gas was illegal here?

The eventually-discovered campground was dusty and rocky. It was also covered in thorn bushes, some just poking above the soil, which pricked holes in my sleeping mat as soon as I laid it down. I tried to plug the holes with tyre puncture patches but it was a constant game of catch-up.

The campsite was almost deserted. I soon discovered one reason why. I read on an information board, 'Don't be alarmed by the taste in the water'. It then listed a number of minerals that contributed to its 'interesting' flavour, including Manganese. If anything is to cause alarm, it's a sign that says don't be afraid of the weird word you've never heard of that sounds an awful lot like something that explodes on contact with humans. The taste was like accidentally swallowing bath water infused with Victorian bath salts. Indeed, there had once been a thriving spa here. The water was once thought to cure all sorts of ills. (I think they call this quackery.) But when radium started getting a bad rep in the cold war, and it became known that radium is, like, realllllly bad for you, the spa became a prison. Maybe it still was.

We stretched out, choodled and contemplated the day. No, we contemplated everything. America was, at its best, open and infinite, but recently had been displaying its fakeness, convenience, political polarization, and the rural poverty that meant towns failed to impress even themselves. The settlements all seemed like small pieces of inconsequence, and the nature - famed on film - was now just legend. The pain was fogging my appreciation for where I was, for sure, but it had all just seemed dusty and derelict and dull. Is this what I came here for? I turned to Killer: "This was your idea, wasn't it?" But as I lay there - sating myself with radioactive isotopes - I considered that perhaps my anger was because I was struggling to accept this was the real world. A world that was bruised perhaps. Almost beyond repair, but not quite. I felt confronted by and part of the global snowball of our own overdevelopment. The Rio Grande, the scale of the open pit, the concrete towns and bright lights selling liquor and guns, the all night all day of it all. The land unchanged over millennia until it came to witness countless battles between man until just one survives to do battle with the earth itself. I thought of the gentle rolling green hills of home. I wanted to lie next to a clear stream and hear the splash of a kingfisher in a perfectly balanced ecosystem. But at the same time, I felt an almighty strength of resolve from this other land, the one that reminded me that we are all connected with responsibility to everything that is wrong, and we are all able to make it a little bit better. Everybody should be allowed to feel this confused pain, I realised. They should bus school kids up here, set up an educational visitor centre. Forget the Grand Canyon or Niagara Falls, come to the Rio Grande to experience the real great American outdoors. Set out your quadrants and jam jars and count the nothingness within. Every school child should experience and understand what is missing, so they can help us to get it back.

We urgently needed a pit stop; a hotel, a bed and a bath. We pressed on at daybreak to El Paso and arrived as the sun set. Every few yards a giant shining sign advertised motels or fast food. Looking along the length of the road, the perspective forced these myriad logos to stack up like neon dominoes, ready to tumble. At one point, following some rapid road mergers, we found ourselves in the middle of five lanes of rush hour highway. Trucks, buses, cars and other instruments of death converged on us from all sides, weaving, swearing. We had often joked that Killer would not survive the trip, as he would be terminated along the road. (It helped to assuage my own fears that he was convinced that one of us would die, and that it was to be him). I looked back as the vehicles squeezed past us and saw him, illuminated by the sun's golden descent, his eyes closed and a serene smile on his face, ready to accept what fate would deal.

We'd covered 190 miles in three days, somehow crossing mountains and creaking through frozen landscapes. It was the most painful and mentally demanding riding so far. And for this, it would later become some of the most rewarding. Some desperately needed rest awaited tantalisingly close, if we could just survive a few more miles. A car horn sounded, bringing Killer back to life. He opened his eyes and we refocused.

***

I woke up and winced. There was an unimaginable pain that weighed across my whole body. Was someone actually stabbing my head with an invisible *Topeak bicycle multi-tool*? And what was that ungodly smell? I looked over and saw Killer in the bed beside mine. I let out a muted 'ut ut?' to test his slumber.

"You passed out and then were sick on yourself," came the calm reply.

"And you?" I asked.

"I was sick and *then* passed out."

"Ah ha. Where are we?"

"El Paso still. We've been here for two nights. And I don't think we'll be leaving any time today." Killer put a hand to his mouth in caution. "Or tomorrow."

The picture started to reassemble itself in my mind. The bar, the pool table, liquor, silver teeth... a wheelie bin?

"Er, am I imagining this or did we nearly get killed by a gang of Mexicans last night?"

Killer let out a groan. "Yes, I'm sorry Bone. I think we'll be lucky if we get out of this town alive if I keep acting like that."

We had barely made it *in* alive, and now we were testing our luck further. The name *El Paso* sounds welcoming and peaceful. You could imagine trotting through El Paso on a mule, perhaps, or unpacking a box of watercolours to capture its charms. But that would probably have you shot for crimes against machismo. It's the US equivalent of the Mos Eisley spaceport in Star Wars. Bounty hunters, illicit danger, space cowboys. You know the place. This is where the heroes of the narrative get frozen in carbon or tossed to giant toad-like beasts. Texas, New Mexico and Mexico itself all converge here at this mountain gap through which the Rio Grande passes. This was where mavericks and tough bastards made their living, a melting pot for conquest, trade, enterprise and outlaws. El Paso was where Billy the Kid hung out. The El Paso jail was actually the only one he broke *in* to. El Paso had its softer side, for sure. (I hear they have a beautiful Mission, and successful universities). But we saw none of that aspect, just the mad and dangerous people you find at the frontier. Obi-Wan Kenobi describes Mos Eisley as 'a wretched hive of scum and villainy'. He might as well have been talking about our four days at the border.

Our first day was doing exactly as we had intended - enjoying the leisure of cable TV, writing home, resting limbs, and searching our bodies for the strength to head further into the desert. The night then started where it finished, in a downtown bar near the hotel. We drank thirstily, pitchers of beer repeatedly replaced in front of us by an attractive woman in a purple leather catsuit who called herself Texas. Guys at the bar started referring to us as 'Forrest Gump on wheels'. At first we thought it was intended to mock us but as every new patron entered, they'd cheer, "Check it out guys - these dudes are cycling to Miami." Cue manly slaps on the back.

We chatted to a friendly, young couple who had just moved to town from Austin, in central Texas. "It's cheaper here," they offered in defense, surveying the bar in both hope and regret. Then a

Mexican-looking guy in his late 40s entered the dark bar, wearing dark glasses. He had a dollar-bill-print tie, fat gold rings, a silver suit with shoulder pads, a slicked mullet to rival Dedric and a hands-free mobile earpiece that blinked in his ear. He sat next to us on a bar stool and introduced himself to the room.

"My name is LA. I am a promoter of music."

He gave us his card, the top corner of which displayed a treble clef, as if to authenticate his claim. This was surely the Derek Trotter of the El Paso music scene. He told us he had worked with Metallica, Bowie, U2 and The Rolling Stones. As he talked, his earpiece stayed nested in the left ear, untroubled by any phone calls. My last active memory of the night is of him agreeing to take over the US promotion for Stonegarth. He said this was exactly the opportunity he had hoped to find when he walked into the bar that night. We agreed to meet the next day to hand over a CD and discuss. It was time to celebrate.

The evening unraveled after that. We drank numerous Tequila shots provided to us by an Intoxication (that's the official collective noun) of Jessicas celebrating a 21st birthday. It was enough Tequila to even sink an Ernest. But with every shot I felt my anxiety over my bodily breakdown fading, so I drank another. We played some pool and I annoyed everyone by putting all my loose change into the jukebox and using all my credit to select one of the most annoying tunes ever invented. 'Y yo sigo aqui' by Paulina Rubio. It's catchy, candy-flavoured pop with a fast beat and an earworm chorus but, best of all - and perhaps uniquely in music hit history - it starts with a revving car engine. Listen to it once and you feel a little vexed. After the seventh time, you want to physically harm the source of your discomfort. The song would come on again and again. I grew nervous. What had I done?

"Jesus, Bone, you're going to get us killed. How many times did you choose it?"

I had no idea.

"I'm sorry, Killer."

But I was merely the warm-up annoyance. Killer took the crown. A group of loud, leather-clad Mexican men chatted by the pool table, occasionally pointing at us. Oh dear lord. Their teeth glistened in shades of silver and gold. Their necks were tattooed with what looked like the insignia of death. I think I sat down in a corner for a while. Maybe I slept. At 2am, Killer pulled me by the sleeve. "Bone, I have been wronged. Will you help defend my honour?"

"Of course."

Killer led us out of the bar and made a big deal of loudly saying 'goodbye' to Texas as we did.

"Oh. We're going back to the hotel? Goodo."

"No. That's just what we want them to think. We're going to wait, er… here," he pointed to behind a bin, "and we're going to jump them when they come out."

"Jump? *Them*?" I was sobering up.

"Yes, Bone. They refused to play pool with me. Said I was too drunk. How dare they. We must defend my honour."

'Jumping' a gang of Mexicans sounded fun. Like a dinner party game you might play after the profiteroles. Sure, there would be some punches and kicks. But hey, you can get hurt by stray limbs playing charades too. This train of thought was a new level of drunk for me. I had once talked Killer out a similar play months before back in Sherborne. But this time, I had a gallon of spirits inside me. And some strange Limey loyalty took control of my senses. We crouched there. Every few minutes exchanging thoughts on tactics. Occasionally I would forget why we were there. Killer repeated his vow for honour. There was not a sound on the street. I started to get a dead leg from cramping down. No one emerged from the bar. 30 minutes passed. We started to shiver.

"Maybe we call it a moral victory," I suggested.

He nodded.

"Well, that is one lucky gang of deadly men in there," he said. "Let's go home."

The pain of the hangover could have actually been caused by fists for all the fun it felt. Killer was right - I had been sick on myself. I stripped off my shirt only to find traces of vomit on my pillow and bed sheets. I piled them in a stinking heap in the corner of the room while I gathered the strength to move to the bathroom. This was not my proudest hour. We forced the window open the full two inches of its safety opening arc. After several episodes of Wild Boyz and Wade Robson, we then started to scour the room for reading material.

In his book *In Patagonia*, one of my literary heroes, Bruce Chatwin, says you can tell a lot about the history and culture of a place by the names in its phone book. Flicking through a copy in Buenos Aires, he said the names told a story of 'exile, desolation, disillusion. And anxiety behind lace curtains'. As the phone book happened to be the only book in our El Paso hotel room, I decided to test the theory. We had lace curtains and anxiety sure enough but in our deep, *deep* state of hungover, we had less of the other poetic discoveries.

These are the names we found:
- Maria Bastardo
- John Bollicks
- Robert Bottom
- Buddy Dick
- Robert Fuchs
- Major James Gas (Rtd.)
- Jason Git
- John Kuntz
- David Lubenow
- Luis Penegas
- Art Ponce
- Conrad Pussyman
- Up Pymps
- Wylder M. Snodgrass
- Elvira Spector
- Monica Suchoff

- Tricia Urino
- Frederick Utter
- And 27 people called Jesus Ramirez

With every new discovery, a collapse from the discoverer and a breathless utterance of the name, spoken between tears.

"He's retired, Bone. Major Gas has retired!"

Killer then vocalised a long day dream in which Buddy Dick and Conrad Pussyman ran rival El Paso strip clubs overseen by local mob boss, Up Pymps. In his excitement, Killer then started casting each of the roles for the inevitable movie of his creation, finally concluding that Harvey Keitel would play all three roles[5]. Exhaustion and alcohol poisoning were taking their toll.

Killer seemed less brutalised by the night and eventually went in search of water. He returned empty handed with a young American guy called Evan, bedecked in cycling lycra in the middle of the day. They'd started comparing routes when they chance-encountered at reception and Evan was keen to survey our ACA maps. Before long, Killer left Evan to it, in my capable hands as host, while he went to locate supplies. "I'll be back in a minute."

Evan and I watched TV in awkward silence, not speaking a word to each other. He must have been repulsed by the smell and by my appearance and yet he remained seated meekly on a small stool in the corner of the room, as if awaiting orders from Killer.

Half an hour passed before I remarked, "My friend went off to get Evian and came back with Evan. And I can't drink you."

This produced no reaction even though it had taken up all my strength to think of the joke. Worse, it actually sounded incredibly creepy. My staring at him probably didn't help. Another half hour passed before Killer returned. When he walked in and saw Evan and I still unmoved, and enveloped in a smell of decay, he

---

[5] How close we almost were. Years later, Killer trawled through Facebook for the names from El Paso and found Frederick Utter, who had listed his workplace as 'MALE STRIP CLUB' in proud capitals.

started to snigger. Evan took that as his excuse to leave. "Good luck on the road," he said sheepishly as he ran out.

Killer placed cokes, water, crisps, chocolate bars and paracetamol on the table. He wasn't planning on any more unnecessary exertion for the rest of the day.

"Don't we have to meet LA?" I asked.

"Oh I went while you and Evan were having fun. He didn't show. The dream is over, Bone."

"Damn it - and he seemed *so* genuine too."

"And ut."

In the late afternoon, we felt brave enough to go out for food. The front desk of the hotel was manned by a rotation of four almost identical men, each middle-aged, rotund, rosy-cheeked and with walrus-like whiskers. It was if they wanted to create the impression of constant reception continuity. However, they each had their 'quirks'. The most curious and questionable was Antonio. He was also quite unattractive and his fat tongue spat a little as he talked. As we passed, he leaned in and asked intently, "Are you... *sporting* gentlemen?". We weren't quite sure what he meant but we had already cycled over 2,000 miles so we figured we probably were. Maybe this was the time to put our Toseland-poked baseball knowledge to the test.

"Err, sure."

Antonio rubbed his hands with glee. "Good, good, well you'll have a great time here, a wonderful time. I can tell you the best places. Oh my, oh my." He was dizzy with excitement. He was keen to 'help us out' and we imagined he maybe had a box at the local baseball stadium. But this was not quite what he had in mind.

"Well, I can take you to the best, most wonderful..." I hope he says *ball game*, "most beautiful and giving and tender," ok please *don't* say ball game, "hardest and most loving," where the fuck is this going, "prostitutes you've ever seen."

Oh. Oh, so *that's* what sporting is. Jesus Ramirez!

"Um, actually, we're ok. Thanks."

He looked dejected but didn't give up. Maybe we just didn't know what we were missing out on, he must've thought.

"Oh these Mexican ladies, they have the softest and warmest hearts. And they're not like American whores - I mean, some of those bitches act like their *shit* don't stink. These Mexicans are the most beautiful whores around. I can take you…"

We thanked the insane blob but politely declined. This was a man selling sex from the front desk of one of the oldest hotels in town. No matter what time of day or what the conversation starter when we saw him, Antonio turned everything back to 'the sport'.

In one exchange, he told us he'd taken some guests up to see White Sands. Just a few miles away, this alluring expanse of glistening pure white dunes is famous for its soft light and still beauty, as well as for being the site of the first successful nuclear tests in 1945. It was a unique place, and a huge tourist draw.

"Wow, how was it?" I asked.

Antonio shrugged and then sighed.

"Actually, the only thing that inspires any sort of emotion in me anymore is a beautiful naked woman."

Oh well.

"I went to see my favourite Mexican whore last night," he went on, unabashed. "I took another guy with me, a cyclist staying here - American kid named Evan."

Poor Evan, traumatised everywhere he turned in this town. "Oh, did he, er, have a good time?"

"Well, he kinda just sat in the corner. Didn't say anything. It was weird."

We made our own vice-free border raid when we had sobered up the next day. There is something magically Slavomir-like about walking over a frontier that you don't get from a car or plane. The senses are awoken. The sights and smells fuse at the border singularity and then you ease into a whole other world. We walked over a bridge seemingly named by a PR man - 'the Bridge of the

Americas'. We crossed the Rio Grande, which became the Rio Bravo once we had shown our passports. Beyond the border, the road instantly became broken and pot-holed. Signs were faded. Old US school buses had been repainted long ago and were now public Mexican buses, moving people around town. The stores were now pharmacies, dentists and leather goods outlets - all at huge discounts compared to the land beyond. This was where the Americans came to stock up and get a bargain. Occasionally someone would call out offering a taxi and then, more hushed, the same man would suggest drugs and women.

This was Ciudad Juarez. At 1.2 million people, it's double the size of El Paso. Prostitution, gangs, drug cartels, organised crime... at the time of our visit, Juarez was the most violent and deadly city in the world. When we passed through, businesses were closing down, homes were being abandoned. And what Antonio had left out from his pitch was that scores of forced sex workers were going missing or being murdered. In this city, more than one person in every 1,000 is killed.

But on that day it felt like a festival. We followed the sounds of music like pied children to a beautifully-fronted Cathedral. There, we found the street full of a parade of floats and trumpeters, dancers and drummers. From the banners and T-shirts we discovered it was all to celebrate the 25th anniversary of Pope John Paul II's papacy. We weaved through narrow market streets, threading our way more keenly into Juarez. Shoe-shiners buffed the boots of men in large cowboy hats. Every man was hatted and moustached, every woman dressed in the tightest fitting clothing, whatever their size. My old GCSE Spanish found its voice as I ordered churros and warm chocolate. The market bustled. The streets had a rhythm, even away from the parade. The poverty was immediate and shocking but the place smelled more alive, whether that was tortillas or just trash. Despite the desperate danger people lived with, everyone was just busy celebrating Mexican life.

On the way back, cars formed a long, multi-lane queue at the border bridge. The gleaming bank towers, topped with massive billowing flags of stars and stripes must have looked like an advert for a whole other world. Peddlars touted, washed windscreens, sold chewing gum. We stood in line with the others. People walked the line looking for anyone that might be able to help them cross. The guards waved us through quickly, barely looking up at our ID. It must have been easy to chance an undocumented walk into a new life.

At the Big Bun Burger Joint - home to much of our El Paso sustenance - we considered our own journey. Killer again raised the idea that cutting out some of the miles was needed. Despite the days of rest in El Paso, we were both still in serious pain. Walking had made things worse, and I wasn't sure if I could cycle much further before my knee gave in completely. And continuing into the desert, with hundreds of miles until the next big town, could risk the whole project. We were running out of money and out of time. I wanted to at least try but Killer - urged by his feeling of how utterly demanding the past few days had been - suggested another option.

Killer's idea was to cut Texas in half by means of a train, and then allow time to stop and enjoy Austin, New Orleans, and of course Miami. I was still hopeful that our limbs would heal in the next few hours, and allow us to cycle on regardless of the terrain, and that we could borrow money if needed, or just camp even more wildly than we had been. I felt that to get this far, I had already crawled into some hidden corner of myself where my courage resided. And I wanted to see just what else lay more deeply buried. A lot of people asked us where we were going, very few asked why. Miami was the destination but, for both of us, the journey was the reason. I wanted to push myself as hard as I could, cycling for another few months, if that is what it took, returning with a limp and a curious stare, if required. Killer also saw this as a chance for transformation, or 'a hot-blooded exorcism of youth' as he put it, but he was perhaps not as enticed by self-destruction in its pursuit. And he was being more realistic: we had finite money and time. The idea of having to make this decision knotted at my stomach. I felt sick with the idea of failure.

"But it's not failure," said Killer. "It will still be a fucking long cycle. It will still be around 4,500 miles when we get to Miami. Look at this way - we could have taken any route from Seattle to Miami. We could have taken a straight line and saved much more distance than leaving out half of one of the ten states we are actually crossing. It's just a boost, to get us back on track, and to ensure we can get the most out of the rest of the trip, rather than rush past all the amazing bits of America ahead. That is still an awesome adventure, and much more than anyone - not least of all ourselves - thought was possible."

"He's right Bone," said Brian. "You're doing great - I guaranfrickinfuckintee it - and whatever way the dice crumbles, it will still be pretty bloody incredible." He'd not spoken to us for days but knew instinctively when I needed his counsel, even if he did mix his metaphors.

Perhaps the hardest thing was that Killer put no pressure on me - the decision would be entirely mine, he said. I contemplated the potential to not complete the challenge on my own terms. As we neared the hotel, the sky darkened and the wind swelled. A piece of tumbleweed actually rolled past with a scrape of painful irony. Killer looked up at the dark clouds.

"Viene una tormenta," he said thoughtfully.

It's a line from the final scene of *Terminator*. (Fun fact: the line is also sampled at the beginning of Stonegarth's now twice-mentioned whimsical tune, 'We will not be terrorised'). In the film, the heavens darken to suggest change, a battle even, and that decisions need to be made. A boy announces in Spanish, 'A storm is coming'.

11. Remember the Alamo

El Paso, NM to Austin, TX

One thing that cycling has taught me is that if you can achieve something without a struggle, it's not going to be satisfying.
Greg LeMond

Ultimately the decision was made for us. But the burden of guilt was no less heavy. The morning after the tormenta started, it was like all the Terminators had turned up at once. The sky was a wall of red sand. It was impossible to see the next street corner.

"You guys ain't going nowhere on those bicycles for a few days," chuckled Antonio. Indeed. But we could also not afford - financially or mentally - to stay and wait it out.

If you are going to cut some miles then the distance, really, is arbitrary and we allowed the destination of the next train heading east to lead us. The first city the train would hit was San Antonio so we set our sights on that. Was it also some subliminal decision enforced by our eagerness to escape our dribbling, pimping and bepimpled host Antonio? I hadn't even spotted the connection at the time. We needed to be near a big town and out of the sparse desert in case we needed medical help - a genuine concern right then - and the train journey was long enough to maintain progress, but short enough to keep the total mileage for the trip at 4,500 miles. I reminded myself (in my pitiful defence) that Bill Bryson very quickly decided he would not walk the entire Appalachian Trail in *A Walk in the Woods* when he realised he would gain more from completing the journey *his* way than destroying himself in the process. And Dervla

Murphy didn't cycle all the way to India, she writes in her classic, *Full Tilt*.

"What would Slavomir have done?" I asked Killer.

"Oh, he looooved trains," came the reply.

"I'm not sure if that's true. It was a train, after all, that took him to the Russian Gulag."

"Yes. But just imagine if he'd had to walk all the way there!"

Either way we slid around the train like stoways, as if not really there. I hated with a deep sickness that we would not cross the entire continent on bikes but I had to reason that this was not failure. Far from it. It was just a different route. (At least, that's what I kept telling myself.) It was a setback. But in life, I have discovered, sometimes you have to experience setbacks to be forced to consider how you can really achieve the bigger goal. And the most popular tourist attraction of Texas knew all about that. The Alamo.

San Antonio is the second most populous city in the southern United States; larger than Dallas and Houston. It's a thriving metropolis. But really, the one main reason to visit is still the Alamo. In fact, the history and identity of the state - and much of the American identity as well - is all still wrapped up in that small, unassuming building. On the outside it's modest; low-fronted, softly coloured stone, with four wooden shutters and a wooden door. In its original form as a Spanish Mission, it must have been inviting and peaceful. But it's what happened inside that matters.

In 1836, Texas was in the middle of a revolution. The last few defenders of the dream of independence from Mexico were holed up inside the Alamo. They endured wave after wave of attack for two weeks, refusing to surrender, until finally every last man inside had been killed. Perhaps as many as 200 died. The stories of their bravery and the motto 'Remember the Alamo' stirred fleeing Texans to turn back and fight on. Eventually the uprising was strong enough to turn the tide and Texas was won. From the setback, albeit a bloody big one, a motivation for victory emerged.

Amongst the heroes of the Alamo, none is more well known than Davy Crockett. My key takeaway from reading the information boards was that you could be as brave as the next man but no one would remember your name unless you wore a silly hat - made of raccoon skin and tail in Crockett's case. And since he first donned that fetid fur, his exploits have grown into bewildering, mythic proportions. Not unlike our old friend in Klamath.

"Who would win in a fight - Bunyan or Crockett?" asked Brian later that night.

Bunyan had a magic ox the size of a house. It was a pretty dumb question from Brian.

Faithful pensioners from tour buses spilled out and gawped and gasped at the Alamo as if on a pilgrimage. Some crowded round us to chat, telling us of friends they'd lost to cancer. They asked to have a group photo with us. That was a touching moment. We didn't mention the train.

They were on a pilgrimage to a myth about what America and being American stood for. This was ironic given the men at the Alamo were fighting for independence and Texas only joined the Union in desperation nine years later as they could no longer afford to defend themselves, but anyway… It was also interesting - though seemed to have been overlooked - that a slice of real estate now regarded as 'all-American' should have such a richly layered, international past. Several nations have controlled these territories. In fact, the complex changes to the whole country over time - involving Britain, France, Spain, Mexico, Canada and, of course, the *native* Americans - are often forgotten when you hear the unstoppable, amalgamous mass cheer of *USA, USA, U… S…. A...* You might think this is because they celebrate the strength of their diversity and are united in it. But even our casual observances had noted that America is still so fractured in its ideologies and identities, and certain lineages seemed to be more 'American' than others.

But they did all at least seem united by one thing; the idea of what it meant to be an American hero. And that image was perhaps born here at the Alamo. Toseland, Yarborough, Gordon and more had all learnt how to be a man and a patriot in their childhood illustrated histories of the Alamo and the John Wayne movie versions thereof. In fact, John Wayne said once that the Alamo, to him, represented 'the fight for freedom for all people.' And now Fox News was shaping an updated, modern American hero from the soldiers fighting the global War on Terror - apparently for *all* people - in the Middle East.

A few months before, the war had started, and I had watched the bombing of Baghdad live on TV. It looked like a city alight with fireworks. But every spark was a score of lives being extinguished. I watched it one evening in the school staff room with two young Iraqi boys, their father still in the city. We watched in silence. After the bombardment, 177,000 troops went on the offensive. And soon after Bush had his Maverick moment in San Diego, the Iraqi Army was dissolved. A direct consequence was that hundreds of men without employment then formed militia that would lead a multi-year insurgency that at the time we were in San Antonio was becoming increasingly led by religious factions. The recipe for a new, bolder, and unimaginably horrific terror regime for the region was emerging. The country was a mess of improvised explosives, booby traps and suicide bombers.

A year and a half later and I would be in Iraq myself, realising my ambitions as a journalist. In helicopters ironically built in Yeovil, I flew around Basra, over Saddam's upturned yacht, up the Euphrates, over flocks of flamingos and into small settlements where we were eyed up by men with raised rifles. Many of the low, dusty buildings reminded me of the Alamo.

A few days after San Antonio, in an Austin motel, we watched Oliver Stone's *JFK* on TV. Never has a national conspiracy been so convincingly explained as by the scene in which a diagram shows that, if there had just been one shooter, the bullet must have magically turned direction midway through its trajectory. We were watching it almost 40 years to the day after Kennedy was assassinated, 200 miles away in Dallas. The character of America has much owed to Texas. Was it too much to connect the myth of the Alamo to the death of JFK, then to the rise of Bush and his mission? In the film, the mysterious character 'X' is effectively speaking to us, the viewer, when he summarises the theory of conspiracy to Kevin Costner's Jim Garrison: "The organizing principle of any society, Mr. Garrison, is for war. The authority of the state over its people resides in its war powers. Kennedy wanted to end the Cold War in his second term. He wanted to call off the moon race and cooperate with the Soviets. He signed a treaty to ban nuclear testing. He refused to invade Cuba in 1962. He set out to withdraw from Vietnam. But all that ended on the 22nd of November, 1963."

When the film ended, we were inspired to play a quick game of Patriot Points, and located Saddam with our virtual missiles in a waste bin in the corner of our motel room. The very next day - which would feel like a huge coincidence if I wasn't already convinced our whole adventure had been planned out - we watched the TV again, this time the news. Saddam had been captured, for real. He was pulled out of a bunker looking bearded, bushy and bedraggled. He looked for all the world like his old friend Dedric (who I presume was watching the news at Clint's place). The news footage showed soldiers chanting *USA, USA, U...S...A...* People rejoiced like it was the end, not like it was the start of a new deeper era of global insecurity.

Austin was only 130 miles away - as it turns out - but it would take us four days to limp there. As the train had taken us off the ACA's route, we bought a large road map of Texas from a gas station and traced a direct path to Austin, to get back on track. We laughed nervously; excited to be on the road again but off piste. We even dared to feel a little optimistic. I even made up a song called ALAMO, which goes to the tune of D.I.S.C.O. But the merry mood didn't even last long enough to extend beyond the city limits. We soon realised the train had only leapfrogged us half a state, but not also transported us in time, to a place where all pain and El Paso-style frustrations had been erased.

The winds struck first - they seemed to shift to ensure they always found us head on. We thought nothing could beat the winds of the mountainous desert but occasionally we would struggle to even reach 4 mph. It would have been faster to walk. And topping 10 mph on the downhill was cause for a small, victorious, moist-eyed yelp. We would let out cries of exertion - real, deep curses to the heavens - against the fruitless peddling. On the first day we inexplicably covered over 50 miles, the last 16 of which took three hours. Late into the evening, we collapsed into Blanco State Park, where the ever-present wind carried my tent away into the trees and various men in large hats had to help me retrieve it. They did so one-handed, the other appendage forcing down their ten-gallon stetsons. As we raced and grabbed, the wind would snatch the tent from our grasp, or blow it back, wrapping it around someone's face, so the men then knocked into each other. At one point I just stopped to watch and played the Benny Hill theme tune in my head.

"They're very friendly. But they're all hat and no cattle," I said to Killer.

"Um, come again, Bone."

I had found a leaflet on Texan sayings. And I intended to pepper my speech with as many of them as possible while I was a guest of the State. But that would have to wait - as we set up camp we realised we had left Larry at Radium Springs. When I broke the news to Killer, his face fell.

"No one should have to live in that hellhole. For God's sake man, he's only got radioactive water to drink!"

Our cycling computers (a very flattering term for a speedo and milometer that you can't read in glaring sunshine) had found new functions as intercoms to the Limenagerie so I called Larry the next day to see how he was doing.

"Oh yesh, don't worry about me. It's very nice here. I have a smart ranger's uniform and…"

252

"You have a what? What happened to the old ranger?" I asked, incredulous.

"Oh yesh, I ate him. Well he was annoying and I was hungry. I am the ranger now. Oh, and I grew a little since I saw you."

"Grew??"

"Yesh. Grew. I'm now about, er let's see, I'm about 50 ft long now."

Perhaps the legend of his actions was behind his growth spurt - expanding with every new heroic deed like Bunyan - as he went on to explain how he had implemented new laws like 'naked Wednesdays' and how he now threw a karaoke night that was the talk of the New Mexico geothermal reserves community. His go-to tune? Backstreet Boys, just like his Limey uncles. I felt proud.

If anything, the wind picked up the next day. Added to this, finding a place to camp seemed impossible. After 25 miles of slow toil it was already late afternoon, but the only campground indicated on the map - at Wimberley - was closed. In an echo to Manzanita, a sign simply read, 'Closed, see y'all in April.' I asked the owner of the RV park opposite if we could camp there, gesturing to his inviting expanse of empty grass.

"No. If you want to camp, y'all have to try the campsite opposite."

"It's closed until April."

"Well try the other one."

"Oh, there's another one? Where?"

"I dunno. Down the road I s'pose."

I pretended to doff my cap and gave a short, cold bow. "Good day to you, sir."

The road ahead threaded its way through nice country; gentle rolling hills, beautiful pasture land, quiet roads. But it taunted us from behind miles and miles of barbed wire fence, almost calling out, '*Yes, isn't it lovely... WELL YOU AIN'T HAVING IT.*' We didn't fancy jumping the fence only to be shot by the owner of one of the romantically named ranches: Rocky Ridge, River Mountain, Wood Creek, Dickhead Canyon. I might have misread the last one. Many of the postboxes beside the road looked like they'd been attacked by baseball bats by passing teen drivers, a la *Stand By Me*. These were the backroads. Or, as my leaflet said, the place where the buses don't run.

More specifically, we were in the Texas Hill Country, also known as Lance Armstrong country. This association was proudly volunteered to us by Dr John Spring Break, Dr John Blanco and Dr John wherethehellarewe, amongst others. Armstrong had also been one of the inspirations for our Limey trip. Cycling, raising money for cancer projects… we hoped to bump into him and enthuse him with our aligned missions. My hero would then shower *us* with praise. The summer before, I had sold Livestrong yellow wrist bracelets to help the cause. He had just won his fifth Tour de France on the trot after recovering from advanced cancer himself. Was he some kind of superhuman? I drew strength in those days from the achievements that he didn't even achieve.

Armstrong also owned a ranch in the area, not far from our path, in a place called Deadman's Hole. And this was actually very tame by Texan naming standards. There's a town in Texas called Cut and Shoot. A few miles down the road from Security. The list goes on - there's Lovelady, Bacon, Noodle, Rainbow, Salty, Earth, Venus, Happy, and Tarzan. There's a Ding dong (that one's in Bell County) and, in a sign of united America, there's even a place called White Settlement. How these people were allowed to buy guns was beyond me.

The only other buildings on this road seemed to be churches. We spied one with a welcoming sign and a wide driveway. And it's only fair to share the name of this institution with you: St Stephen's Episcopal Church on Old Kyle Road. We pulled into the large grounds. There was even a school and something called - and I shit you not - 'the gymnatorium'. Surely a place that liked made up

254

words as much as we did would provide a home for the night. The plan was simple: meekly enter the office and rely on their good Christian kindness, and as it involved feigning servility, the job fell to me.

"Hello, I'm from England. Ever so sorry to trouble you," I said to the retiring receptionist. "My friend and I are cycling across America to raise money for Cancer Research, and we're having a spot of trouble finding a place to camp…" I continued to affect my heightened Hugh Grantular vernacular, hoping it might carry some currency. I said we'd be clean and would be gone by morning.

"I'll go ask the priest."

Oh good. In *Les Miserables*, the priest welcomes our heroic traveller in and even loads his sack with silver. I anticipated this Texan priest walking orchestrally through the doors, singing his line softly, "Come in sirs, for you are weary…" Instead, there was muffled conversation from the back office - the inner sanctum - and then the lady returned.

"I'm sorry. We can't help," she said, the priest seemingly not able to even show us his face. "You see, we're not so well lit so we couldn't be sure about safety." She was wringing her hands awkwardly.

"You're safety or ours?" I asked bluntly.

She blushed and opened her palms up, as if to say sorry.

"But there's a gas station a few miles down the road - they have a well lit area of grass. You should try there." It was no point explaining that 'well lit' was the complete opposite of what we needed. Outside, I told Killer the news. "Not even God will help us now."

We pressed on and found Hays City Store, essentially a small gas station with a very small convenience store attached. Hays City itself had long gone. Outside there was a patch of scrub and a picnic table under a street light, right next to the forecourt and parking lot. I repeated my story of woe, exhausted, to the cashier who then telephoned the owner and I repeated it all again, while customers lined up behind me.

The owner said yes.

I had never been so happy to camp on top of a reservoir of fuel in my life.

As we pitched up, a guy told us he'd heard me talk inside and asked if we had everything we needed. We insisted we did but he vowed to return later with beer, and skidded off in his truck. I was too tired to tell him I didn't want any beer. I just wanted sleep.

But sleep, as expected, was sporadic. Trucks pulling in late into the night lit up the insides of our tents with their headlights. At one point I thought the beer man had returned, as I heard Killer's tent zips flying open and then rushed footsteps.

"Killer, are you having a beer party?" I asked.

But there was no response. Just groans from the bushes nearby. Oh fuck. Was this the Bundycize we had been promised at the roll-necked parties of LA?

In the morning I realised Killer had not been used to form a human skin suit but - only slightly better - had vomited four times. His face was ashen. He looked beaten. We tried to cycle on but the road had become shoulderless and every driver seemed to have graduated from the Tom Toseland school of driving; brushing past us, squeezing us onto verges, laughing like loons.

We took refuge in a cafe, and took in coffee and Tex Mex breakfast tacos. In the corner sat three cops, actually eating donuts, watching the big screen TV. The channel was showing Pro Bull Riding, PBR, Harrison's favourite. Cowboys were getting shaken around like rag dolls and then showered in cash. Outside, I spied a large water tower emblazoned in various messages. At the top, 'Kyle, Texas - Welcome Home' was written on it. But we were very very far from home. We thought we were still at least 60 miles from Austin but lower on the tower it said 'Austin 21 miles'. I unfurled the road atlas and saw that, sure enough, the Interstate ran straight from Kyle up to Austin. We'd intended to take quiet roads, and thereby give our chances of extended survival a boost but if we could last a few hours of I-35 then we would make it to the city early. In Killer's condition, maybe this was a risk we had to take. As if hearing our thoughts (or more likely our words because we did discuss this out loud), one of the cops came over to us, hitching up his gun belt and spitting on the floor. The crumbs of his breakfast fell from his belly like celebratory ticker tape. I mimed getting out my 'American cliché-spotters notebook' and ticked him off with satisfaction.

"If you take the Interstate into Austin, be sure to stay on the right. I seen plenty people get hit. And I ain't in the job of cleanin'."

We discovered that 'on the right' meant the spur road, a quiet access road that ran parallel to the motorway. We pedaled on, the wind now seemingly emanating impossibly from Austin itself. Killer stopped a couple of times to vomit up his burritos and desperately started cursing the spirit of Kirkendall, reaching for anyone to blame. Truly, these winds were harder than any mountains we had crossed. Just a few miles out of town, Killer raised an arm and slumped over his handlebars.

"I'm done Bone. Bury me here or ask Brian to carry me home."

We bunkered up in the aforementioned JFK-watching motel and then slowly completed the journey to Austin in the morning. We arrived at our hostel as waves with white tops, whipped up by the wind, crashed about in the small lake outside. The manager asked where we'd cycled up from. I didn't want to say, 'the red barn motel a few miles south, off the interstate, do you know it?' I mean, who shouts about a transcontinental challenge on their panniers and then cycles eight miles? I reached for a name.

"Er, Blanco."

"Blanco? Shit that's a looooooong way."

Oh yes. I'd overreached.

"In this wind? And all before lunch? Jeez."

I nodded. In fairness, I didn't say *when* we'd left Blanco, that it was two days ago.

"I'd better make you boys a nice cup of British tea. Take a seat."

Ah, tea. We'd arrived in civilisation again. Willie Nelson said you feel yourself becoming more free the closer you get to Austin. Its official slogan is 'The Live Music Capital of the World'; it has more music venues per capita than any other US city, and over 150 acts perform every night. It was also an attractive city. The State Capitol - slightly taller than, but of similar design to, the one in Washington - is constructed of a soft granite that glows red at dusk and when built in 1880 it was the seventh largest building in the world. On our arrival, it was also reflecting the merry lights of a colossal Christmas tree. But for Killer, one of the main attractions was the presence of the University of Texas, also known as... the UT. These two letters, holding magical powers to me and - especially - Killer, could be found on sweatshirts, mugs, bumper stickers… and there is even an UT bar.

"Extraordinary to think they have named a whole higher education establishment and its associated watering holes after one Stonegarth song," remarked Killer, shaking his head in dizzy disbelief. He happily yelped 'UT UT' periodically but it was a short respite between bouts of vomiting.

And even the UT was not enough to revive Killer. He was at an all time low. He looked like he'd just heard the world had run out of choodle. The doubts in El Paso now needed to be resolved for good.

"Would it be so terrible if we headed home, Bone?" he asked me in all seriousness.

Both our bodies were battered, our joints rattled in pain and, on top of this, Killer was listless with sickness. I saw that I could talk him into a decision in either direction.

The dark thoughts started to affect me too. I found a photo in my diary of me and the girl. I looked so carefree, I was short-haired and fresh-faced. I shaved my beard off, as if trying to recreate my mood, then called her. It was a slow, stilted chat to start, as if we were both trying to show we had moved on, but it fell back into laughter and reminiscing. My feelings were still unclear - so were hers - and we understood that meant it had been right to let each other go, and that understanding relaxed both of us. There must be no greater feeling than a confidence of love, I reasoned. Now I know that to be true. But right then I needed someone to help me get past the painful uncertainty of the trip itself. I turned again to Brian.

"What would you do, Bone, if Killer couldn't carry on? You've already done over 2,700 miles - not bad for two alarmingly inexperienced and unlikely kale deniers."

It was the first time the question had even been contemplated. The challenge was getting tougher than I had ever anticipated. But I knew I could not quit.

"What if we fail and this is just another curious unconcluded incident in my life? If I step back from this, what other life challenges will I baulk at, what example would I be to others, how could I justify the sponsorship we had already received, how could I deal with the loss of potential future sponsor money to help with cancer research? To tell you the truth, Brian, the idea of not doing this depresses the hell out of me."

"Well I think you have your answer then."

"I came on this trip partly to prove to myself that I am capable of more. This Limey Project is giving me a good thrashing, for sure, but it won't beat me. Goonies never say die."

"Sometimes you have to take a hit before you can be a hit."

"I don't think that one works so well."

My main worry all along had been that we would fail, and in that moment I realised that failure was not possible. I'd be limping into Miami in a year's time if that's what it took. And once I had realised that, I stopped worrying about how tough it was, and how hard it could become. My whole body relaxed. Brian smiled, satisfied. The happiness of the realisation threaded through every fibre of my being. Whatever hardship was ahead, it was nothing compared to the pain of not facing it. From that moment, I appreciated every strain and grimace, because it meant we were still doing it. And I knew I could give Killer this feeling too. He didn't want to go home. He just needed to find his belief again. But right then he needed rest. We'd sit it out in Austin for a few days while he got his strength back and while we waited, I'd enjoy some old school, old fashioned, old time fun.

The city's unofficial slogan is 'Keep Austin Weird' and I had no intention of letting anyone down. I headed off to Sixth Street - the centre of weird - solo. Whereas in El Paso, we drank heavily to drown out our nagging fears, here I drank lightly, to celebrate my hopes. And something happened to me that night. In my happiness I became such an exaggerated version of myself that I appeared to morph into a modern day Count of Monte Cristo. This transmogrification manifested itself in a heightenedly posh British accent and made up stories of my travels around the casinos of Europe. The Americans adored this Count. I bowled up confidently to groups of exquisitely beautiful people. They were both confused and charmed by this stranger. I was bought drinks, introduced to models, invited to parties. I had to turn them down, "No, I must find Mercedes."

At the last bar, I spied a blackjack table and I took a seat.

"Wonderful to make your acquaintance. I am here on a light expeditionary mission," I said to the other players.

"Er, hey, I'm a student, er, here at the UT," came one reply.

"I believe it is actually pronounced *UT*," I chastised[6].

Waitresses would bring me drinks. I'd tell them "Surprise me", then give them a few dollars. If I'd seen anyone else behaving like I did that night, I would have truly thought them an utter wanker.

The dealer was a leather-clad Jessica. She dealt me a 5 and 6, making 11. I looked at her. "I'll stay, my dear."

---

[6] I assume this comes across as clearly in type as it does in my head.

Everyone around me contorted. "What? Twist!"

I held Jessica's gaze. "Trust me, I learned these card skills at the Chateau d'If."

Jessica dealt her card and was bust and I made 50 dollars. The process was repeated, and more people crowded around this eccentric oddity. I twisted on a 17 and got a 4 - 21. I twisted on a 19 and got a 2. The crowd was getting ecstatic.

"That's the weirdest thing I have ever seen," remarked one girl.

I stood up and announced I was leaving.

"But you are on a roll," said Jessica.

"You must always leave a place knowing you could have stayed a little longer," I said, and nodded to her politely before walking out slowly but purposefully.

The next day I returned to myself. I felt that if the Count and I didn't part ways then he might take over entirely. And what was wrong with being plain old made-up-name Bone. I set off again late in the evening, heading to the Warehouse district this time, for some slower, more cultured fun. I wandered a little aimlessly until a hotdog seller grabbed me by the elbow.

"Listen - if you want great music, Wendy Colonna is playing across the street. Check it out."

I entered a small, bare-brick-walled bar. Wendy played guitar and sang, accompanied by one other guy, Reese, also on the guitar. The sound was transportative, soft, sumptuous, velvety. Every song a story. She was performing numbers from her debut album, Red. The song titles were a little heavy, including 'Everyone dies alone', 'Dirty wife' and 'Sodom'... but the tunes were genuinely beautiful.

On a silent TV above the bar, PBR was on. I imagined Harrison in his millionaire apartment eating artichokes and those donut-gobbling cops, all reclining right now in front of the same spectacle as me. My hard-learned knowledge of baseball would not help me down here in Texas.

Beside me was a young guy, forearms rippling with sinew and muscle like a steroided Toseland. He introduced himself as Tyler and I pulled back a limp, rubbery hand. And in the grand, unfolding coincidence chest that is The Limey Project he said he used to be a pro bull rider.

"What, like these crazy guys?" I pointed at the TV.

"Yes sir."

"But it looks sooooooo painful."

"Can be."

"Did you ever break anything?"

"Yeah, I broke a arm a few times. Broke my back too. Spent three months in a wheelchair. Oh, and I gone and lost my sight in my left eye." He then pointed at his right eye.

"Oh," I thought for a while. "Perhaps you weren't very good."

He quietly held my gaze. I was unsure if I was about to be ripped apart or if it was just his glass eye lingering unintentionally but as I didn't know which one that was I decided to make my excuses and go and speak to the band.

"I really like your musicality," I said to Wendy and Reese. (Was I saying it right?)

"Thanks, that's so nice to hear."

They invited me to sit with them and we chatted until we were the last ones in the bar. I told Wendy how I'd found out about her.

"Oh from Carl? He has *the* best hotdogs in Austin. Come on."

A queue was now forming at Carl's cart. Everyone knew his name and he knew them all back. He was a big guy, with a bushy handlebar moustache and thick leather jacket. He seemed to own this dark street corner like a city guardian. Wendy said she sometimes liked to just sit and watch the people who come by and see how Carl lights up their night. Communities are built around people like Carl. He leaned in and told me Wendy had the most awesome talent but not enough self belief and I was inclined to agree, back then anyway. It must be hard though - to keep funding her ambition, Wendy had to supplement her musical income, she did this through teaching yoga and waitressing. She was also a trained physio, so in the next bar I told her about my knee, and she seemed to have the answer.

"Have you heard about these shoes you can clip into your pedals? It ensures your knees come down straight and means you can pull on the pedals when pushing is too much. It might help out."

I thought immediately of the German cyclists, Mikhail and Anke. Damn the bloody Germans and their efficiency. I thought about it but I remained unconvinced. I told Killer this all later and he wisely pointed out that, "if a continent can't be crossed in old trainers, then it's not worth crossing."

"Yeah well we sure showed them, eh." I said.

"Yeah, never mind the fact you'd probably be further down the road, wouldn't have such bad injuries and might not have needed the train," added Brian unhelpfully, hardly looking up from an extended preening session.

I thought about Wendy's life. She was drawn to Austin to get noticed, but whilst the microscope was turned on the talent in the town, perhaps it was harder to stand out in the melee of similar ambitions.

Reese said that might be true. "We'll just keep on going till we make it, but - really - we just love doing what we do."

Maybe that was the difference with LA - there they all wanted to be famous, here they just wanted a bigger stage for their art. But like LA, everyone in Austin seemed to be in the business. The barman at Wendy's gig was also a well-regarded blues harmonica player. And he introduced me to Clifford Antone. Clifford was not only a local club owner but also one of the main drivers behind the city's 'live music capital' tagline. Naturally he just happened to be in the bar when I was there, sitting near me. Oh,

The Limey Project. Clifford had come specifically to hear Wendy play.

"She'll be big one day," he said.

"She's big today," I replied.

Naturally I told him about Stonegarth. But I fancied her chances of future success were just marginally higher.

Killer had recovered enough strength by the next afternoon for us to hit up Austin's weirdly-named (of course) Armadillo Christmas Bazaar. It was $5 to enter, to walk around craft and gift stalls, enjoy live music and food and drink. And Jeff Goldblum was there, just walking around, although he seemed not to recognise us. Killer and I bought each other $10 gifts that we would exchange a couple of weeks later on Christmas Day. I also bought a baseball cap to finally rival Killer's 'New Mexico is HOT' hat. It had a bull, throwing a cowboy off its back and the phrase '7 seconds' above it, indicating that - like Tyler - the rider had failed to make the grade of 8 seconds. The cap was a dull beige and the scene of bull and rider was a mix of browns and oranges - it was quite unattractive. I loved it.

"You see what happened to Davy Crockett after he started wearing a funny hat. He was *nothing* before. Imagine what this hat will do for me," I told Killer.

"Yes, I expect you are more likely to be attacked and killed now, that's true," Killer concluded.

Either way, I was keen to find out what the next chapter held in store. We still had half of Texas to cross and I couldn't bloody wait. My enthusiasm had also buoyed Killer. The next morning, we fell back into being the relaxed, wide-eyed discoverers that had rolled out of Seattle, just with a load more resolve, confidence and calf-power. We also had a new mantra to power us. In San Antonio, I had absentmindedly muttered the phrase that had been presented to us in a hundred scripts and fonts, *Remember the Alamo*, as I tucked my right trouser leg into my socks to stop it from flapping into my chain (yes, we still did not wear the most ergonomic of cycling clothes). Killer must have noticed this as he then performed the same combined manoeuvre, simultaneously tucking the trouser and muttering the words. We nodded to each other. A new daily routine had been formed, with the one physical act providing a visible homage to the expression. But what were we really remembering? As we prepared to leave Austin, I realised that for us, the lesson was not about blind machismo and battle. It was about pulling your socks up after a setback - or just a night's sleep - and pressing on to fulfil the mission. That day and every day from then on, whenever it was trouser weather, we were reminded by a simple tuck that defeat was not possible.

We mounted the bikes.

"Remember the Alamo, Killer."

"And ut, Bone, and bloody ut."

12. Never-ending Texas

If I can bicycle, I bicycle.
David Attenborough

Texas is famous for many curiosities, and it has put its name to many things - Texas barbecue, Texas longhorns (what they put on the barbecue and on great hats), Texas Hold'em (my style of cards)... but many people when asked to complete a phrase that starts 'Texas...' will offer 'chainsaw massacre'. The film - or, rather, franchise - involves a cordial chap called Leatherface and his penchant for tortuous murder and then wearing his victim's skin as a mask. It has something of a fanatic following. Many of the scenes for the original film are located around the eastern fringes of Austin. And you'll see the odd chainsaw tourist cruising the area looking for the film locations of the garage, cemetery and other happy haunts.

It's said one of the inspirations for the role was Ted Bundy, who killed over 30 women in the 1970s, winning over many of his victims initially with charm, even establishing something of a fanbase while he was still denying everything. In another odd Limey journey symmetry, it is said that Bundy's first murder took place in Seattle and his final killings took place in Florida.

Many of the Chainsaw Massacre scenes were filmed around Bastrop, a small town 40 miles east of Austin and where we camped in the State Park. It was a tranquil setting and we had the place to ourselves. There was one lone caravan in a far corner, half hidden by some trees. Was this home to one of the more than 2,500 serial killers that have been recorded in the US? We did occasionally hear some muffled cries, but they sensibly decided it was too cold to do any massacring our way. Indeed, the cold desert nights we had experienced in New Mexico were back. And to get past darkness and ice it was now common for it to reach 10am before the camp was packed up, the bikes loaded and we were on the road.

But the scenery post-Bastrop was more innocent and idyllic. Park roads, farm tracks, pockets of woodland, quaintly shabby little communities and grazing lands for cattle and horses. Our first sight of people didn't really come until we then stopped at Winchester after two hours riding, merely to warm up. We found a cafe in the form of a battered wooden shack that resembled a half completed game of Jenga. Inside, two cowboys drank Budweisers at midday. On the counter, a jar of pickled eggs and a box of pop tarts. Behind the counter, an extraordinary woman. Her white hair permed, her glasses held on a pearled chain around her neck, sparkly brooches on her chest, her face - and entire frame - sagging with the weight of time like a half-burned candle. You imagined that if she hitched up the hem of her skirt you'd catch sight of a nipple.

"Jesus, she must be at least 103," suggested Killer.

And yet, she knew just what we needed. For $1.50 she cut up a plate of cheese, sausages and crackers and tottered over with it all laid out on a huge plate.

"Ok darlins - you lit me know if ya need s'mowor."

On the TV, a soap opera was playing. It seemed that some smart Hollywood exec had got wind of our idea for the show *Carmel*, modeled on Bill and Patsy's wonderful coastal life. Beautiful characters, highly fluffed and bronzed. Opulent sets, long stares, high tension. One of the characters had the exceptionally Carmelesque name Alcazar and he was presently embroiled in determining the progeny of his lover Sindy's baby. As it transpired, he wasn't her only admirer. "I'm sorry Alcazar, I just don't know who's child this is!"

The old lady at the bar tutted loudly. "I bet ya dont ya bitch."

At least I'm pretty sure she said that. It was very hard to work out these East Texas accents. That evening we met Wayne, the owner of the La Grange RV Park. He came over to our picnic bench once our tents were assembled, accompanied by his small, white, fuzzy-haired dog, Skipper. He asked where we hailed from and then nodded knowingly at hearing 'England'.

"Oh interesting. Yeah, we had these Norwegians stay here recently and they took lots of wildlife photos." The words hung there as if waiting for the bit that connected his thoughts to mine, but apparently relevance was a mere accessory to conversation here.

And of course that's not what he actually said. I translated it from the East Texas sound cloud of *NorWAYshuns* and *WAAD-laaf* so you could read it. He liked to stretch words with extra syllables and squeeze at least three tonal shifts into each sentence. When his dog climbed up on to the bench, he employed a particularly complicated assemblage of noises.

"Hey, Skiyippperrrrr, git dowun frum theyerer."

But perhaps the most extraordinary thing - but obvious when you really think it through - was that he found my standard British accent as indecipherable as I might a Martian mumble. When checking in, he asked for my name for the registry. I kept repeating 'Stones' but he wasn't getting it. I said it slowly, stressing the 'o' but he would say it back or write it down with e's, r's and even a 'y'. "Oh, Steyernes? No? Oh I got it - Strainez." He seemed reluctant to let me write it down myself though, so after a few minutes he just sighed, scribbled something and then closed his book.

In a complex scene of imaginational wondering, we later pictured a sheriff still hunting us down from the runner at Pelican Point, asking Wayne if he had seen us. Wayne ponders the enquiry. "Two fellas, camping together, probably gay you say? Let me check the books. Hmmm, no we had two guys here but the name was Sterneyperkel."

Wayne walked everywhere with a full mug of coffee in his hand. Amongst his many quirks, a favourite of mine was the way he would use his mug to point at things as he talked. It had the effect of making otherwise inconsequential ideas appear to carry the utmost importance, with the coffee prod gesture evidencing their significance. At times, this theatrical gesturing made it feel as if he was presenting a case to a suspicious courtroom.

"I see you have set up your camp [point to Evidence A - two Vango Phantom tents]. You picked a great spot. [Let's just look at Evidence A again, your honour]. Funny - you are right next to where the Norwegians chose to camp [point to Evidence B - a patch of empty grass]. Interesting. And yet you say you don't know them? [Big sip - I rest my case, whatever that case may be...]"

As we left Wayne in the morning, we had no idea that on TLP 82 we were embarking on the greatest EVER Limey day. An extraordinarily wonderful limificent day that started in unassuming fashion with ice on the tents, cold Wayne-brewed coffee and Skipper yapping at our heels, but soon warmed enough for both shortage and shirtage, and was so merry that it was sountracked by us loudly singing Christmas carols.

The first stop was Round Top. A sign on the town's outskirts declared the population to be 77, precisely. There was an abundance of low wooden homes, some on stilts, and each surrounded by pasture, rustic wooden fences and a whiff of old time charm. We made straight for the post office to send postcards and packages back home. The building was covered in bunting and balloons and, inside, festooned with tables laid out with cakes, crisps and fizzy drinks. Beaming middle aged women implored us to help ourselves.

"Welcome, welcome. Oh yes, you're so welcome. Come on, tuck iiiiiiin dears."

"I am unsettled by this change in our fortunes and the friendliness of these people," I said to Killer.

Killer shrugged, unable to speak with two muffins in his mouth and a cup of cola in each hand. I followed his lead.

"Oh yes, please enjoy yourselves," said another enthused postmistress. "We've put out a few treats because it's our annual customer appreciation day."

I sighed with relief that the madness of the friendliness at least did not have murderous intentions. It was simply Americans being American.

"Ah, what a coincidence," I said. "Today happens to be *our* annual *post office* appreciation day."

The women dropped their smiles. Silent confusion. I had not only forgotten not to attempt such subtle comedy on Texans, but I had omitted to underline my statement with the cup prod, a la Wayne.

"Don't. Forget. To. Use. The. Cup," coached Killer in my ear. "It's the only language these people understand."

As we gorged on salted and sugary treats, we leafed through leaflets (I was as big a fan of leaflets as I was of information boards) to discover more about this curious town. In one, we discovered that Round Top is listed as one of America's top small towns (although it failed to say what it was top of. Weirdity?). In another, we read it even has a Shakespearean Theatre where UT students come to practice their thees and thous. Killer practically skipped at the sight of the word, UT. One particular flyer really caught our attention - it stated boldly, 'Come to Round Top if you like…' There then followed an extensive list of precisely 100 activities - many of which we had never heard of. Round Top was *the* place to come, it said, if you liked goose plucking and German plays, as well as quilt making, fence fixing, yarn spinning and even fragrant woodland walks.

"Anyone who says Round Top is not the place for them is clearly lying", I summarised loudly. "There's something for everyone here." I pointed my cup to the evidence on the leaflet, and the postmistresses nodded happily at my words.

The next stop was another contender for freakishly friendly town of the year, Burton. As we entered a cafe, all the diners simultaneously stopped their conversations and looked up to take in this sweaty, grubby duo. There was a pained silence. We turned back to the door but there was now someone in front of it, blocking our passage. We smiled desperately and took a seat, hastily ordering chilli and sodas.

A diner left and soon re-entered having read about the mission on our panniers. The ensuing vocal scene, which included the whole restaurant, would never ever have happened in England.

"Hey, everyone. Listen up y'all. These two guys here are from Ingerlund and they're all cycling to Miami. Can you believe that? Isn't that awesome!"

The united puntery of the restaurant cheered and the woman who'd made the announcement pressed $20 into Killer's hands. The waiter then said he was waving the cost of the lunch and as we left we received such an enthusiastic mob-like cheer that I'm sure that if someone had said, 'Hey, let's *carry* them to Miami!' they would have surely hauled us skyward.

It was just ten miles to the next town and we sang merrily the whole way, for it was a place that had been in our minds since we first got to know Brian - we were about to pass through a town called Gay Hill. This was the location of America's annual gay bear convention and Brian was beyond excited about attending for the first time, to meet bears like him with pride.

"Look at these rolling hills and meadows Bone," said Killer. "No wonder Brian wanted to come here - it's beautiful."

"I didn't fucking come here for the fucking hills," added Brian, catching us off guard. Not only did we not know he was behind us, we also didn't know he swore so energetically. Regardless we left him to it.

"See you at the next fucking camp," he shouted after us.

In a field just past Gay Hill, there was then a group of bulls - all entirely male - but it seemed more of a gathering than a convention. Either way, we then received a call on the Limey communicators from a certain Bernard the Bull - he said he'd just seen us pass by. He told us about his former life on the PBR circuit, before he started modeling for hat designs and other paraphernalia. As soon as the telephone had cut out at the end of the conversation, I found a small plastic, bendy Father Christmas on the road and wrapped it around one of the straps of my handlebar bag.

"Hello," I said. "You must be Santos. Would you like to join our Limenagerie?"

"YESH!" he declared, curiously in the same strong Dutch accent as Larry. "My friend the ranger told me allll about thish great band of beings on the road to Miami. Count me in."

"I can't quite work out what's real and what isn't," I declared to Killer.

"Oh, it's all real," punctuated Killer, putting an end to that line of thought.

The final stop of the day, of the greatest ever Limey day, was the greatest little town, Independence. We had agreed I should use my charm - so far entirely unsuccessfully applied - to ask in the 'General Store' if we could camp for free somewhere, anywhere. The owner, Mike, pointed to the overgrown small field over the road, which was framed by some rundown tin sheds.

"That's all my land. You can camp there, next to the shacks, no problem at all" he said.

Our eyes lit up as if polished by a psychotic taxidermist (oh, sorry, we haven't got there yet, have we). We set up camp and immediately started cooking. I tucked into some delicious choodle while Killer ate soup and bread rolls. Killer was still suffering from the psychological trauma of his epic chundering episodes and could still not take choodle. His inability to eat the sacred dish was so strange and disturbing that we decided we should not discuss it, ever, and instead should simply rejoice when he returned to the fold.

Mike came over as the pans were being rinsed out. He said he'd been thinking and would like to pay the $30 required for us to stay in the B&B he knew a few doors down. We instantly refused, despite Mike pushing the issue hard. Mike eventually left looking desperately sad - and confused - at the refusal to accommodate his generosity.

"I must surely be an Englishman," I reasoned, "for I would sooner perish with frozen testicles in this tent than accept such generosity from a stranger."

Killer agreed with a sharp nod.

"Having said that," I continued, "if I hadn't already set up my tent and wasn't convinced the owner of the B&B was probably murderous, then I would have jumped at the offer in a jiffy."

Despite the refusal of the lodging, we were very pleased to accept Mike's offer to join him in the store for some warmth. The outside of the store consisted of a low stone facade, designed to resemble the Alamo and to honour its Texan pride. It was constructed in 1939 by then owner W. C. Lueckemeyer who's name still appears in the stonework. Lueckemeyer had wanted to create a place to not only cater for the community, but also to create a community. He offered slot machines, bootlegged whiskey and a pot-bellied stove for locals to gather around on seats resurrected from old airplanes.

Inside, when we visited, the idea of a community hub was still very much alive. The slot machines had gone, but beyond the usual aisles of essentials, there was now the added facility of a spacious back room where the stove and salvaged seating had been replaced by a large TV and plastic chairs. Mike pressed non-bootlegged beers into our hands and we relaxed in the back, watching Seinfeld. In the episode, the character George - the hapless misanthrope - discovers he can create a great, lasting impression if he leaves the room immediately after he makes a joke. People are always stuck with that final thought of him; they are left wanting more.

"This is something I will do as soon as I make my next joke," said Killer.

"We may be waiting in this room for some time then," I suggested.

Killer laughed at this so I immediately stood and walked out.

"You're amazing," Killer called out after me. "I'm going where you go."

In the front of the store, a few locals had gathered to celebrate the 60th birthday of one of the regulars and Mike insisted on us joining the fun, passing us another beer. He stood at his post behind the counter. Next to the till was a large jar of pickled gherkins and a multi-tiered stand of cigarette lighters. Nothing else. I imagined the number of times Mike must have said to his customers, "Anything else I can help you with today... A pickle? Some fire?"

The store patrons - six of them - stood in a semi circle around Mike. There was an old bearded 'vet', a big bear of a man in workman overalls, the birthday boy proudly leaning against the counter, and a woman with a glint in her eye, all in their 50s and 60s. They were a curious ensemble but, by Texan standards, the most normal gathering of folk we had or would come across. And they were the most welcoming of them also, the sort of people we had hoped to meet when we rolled out of Seattle.

"If I'd known you were coming, I'd have cleaned out my spare room," said one.

"Here's my address. You boys need anything - laundry, internet... anything - you come on over tomorrow," said another.

"It's no use," said Mike, still hurt. "I tried paying for the lodging but they refused."

An hour or so into the merriment, the locals reflected with nostalgia on the last time people had cycled through town and stopped at the store.

"It was about a year ago I suppose," said Mike. "Three people on one bike - quite a sight. Nice people - a brother and two sisters. Went by the name of Campbell, I believe." He pulled out a notebook from under the counter and flipped to the most recent entry, which was indeed over a year before.

Killer's face contorted into a question mark.

"What? The Campbells? They cycled through here?" asked Killer, gasping out the words. He looked at the notebook entry and sure enough, the three Campbells had written their names, including the elder girl, Caroline, and their home town - the same as ours, Sherborne.

Killer looked up and spoke to the room, his finger now pressed to the page.

"I used to date this girl."

The entire gathering drew in their breath as Killer went on to explain how they had met at school eight years before, and they had both played the lead roles in the school's major production of Hamlet, staged in a genuine medieval castle. The last person to cycle through the town, which was far from being a frequent occurrence, also happened to be Killer's first girlfriend. Even my chin was beyond my belly button.

"I knew she had done some cycling in America but didn't know she had come through this place. I mean, what are the chances - this road, then stopping in this town. We stopped here because it was getting dark. We might otherwise have just cycled past and never…" His words drifted off as he comprehended the enormity of the coincidence.

"Well ain't that the darndest thing," summed up Mike.

"We still talk about the Campbells. We'll probably still be talking about you in years to come," said the randy old woman, winking at Killer.

"Well, we're pretty tired, we might actually still *be* here for years to come," I added. The laughter at this was enough for us to take our cue to bid goodnight. It was time to leave our Seinfeldian mark.

As it turns out, Independence wasn't just any old Texan town. It had once been a thriving, burgeoning hub with Universities. It was the wealthiest community in Texas in the mid 19th Century. But its fortunes changed when the town said they didn't want to be troubled by this new fangled railway invention and the Santa Fe Railroad routed to the north and soon the students, businesses and townsfolk moved out and left behind a quaint, friendly community. One of the best in fact. Whilst many people must have really kicked themselves over that railway dodge, something told me Mike and his chums were quite pleased with that. Well, we already knew trains were nothing but trouble. The town had a free-spirited atmosphere becoming of its name, a name borne from the deeds of one of its most famous sons.

I never could quite work out how Davy Crockett fought at the Alamo, lost and died and yet Sam Houston, as General, led the army on the retaliatory battle at San Jacinto - that ultimately won Texas its *independence* - and is not bathed in such rich folklore. But Houston lives on in other ways. As well as having the state's capital city named after him, his legacy is also honoured in the title of scores of forests, libraries, medical facilities, educational institutions, parks and, of course, towns across Texas. It seems Houston also knew something of what the myth of the Alamo and Crockett might become. "All histories," he said, "have been made by white men, and a man who tells his own story is always right until the adversary's tale is told." Houston had lived in Independence and I think he would have liked Mike and the gang.

Independence was also a thriving Baptist community and small white chapels beautifully dotted the soft, rolling landscape as we continued to cycle on, arriving after a hard, windy 40 miles at Richards. In fact, we saw an increasing frequency of churches as we pressed eastwards. Even now, with the growing secularisation of the west, 80% of Americans say they are Christian - the largest group of which are Evangelical Protestants. The numbers of churchgoers are highest in Mississippi and Alabama - which both lay ahead on our path - but across the whole USA the numbers are high by European standards; a third of people attend a weekly church service.

However, we didn't see any such dedication in Richards. Instead, we were back in Terminator territory. More specifically, we seemed to have arrived in a town that had just experienced the nuclear winds of the *tormenta*. In the centre of Richards was a small family park. It was overgrown with shrubs and long grass. There was a merry-go-round off its hinges, three broken seesaws and a fractured slab of concrete under a rusted basketball hoop. We decided to see if we could pull off the same camping trick twice and asked in a small store where we might put up a tent. Sure enough the owner, Deborah, pointed back to the park.

"Why don't you just camp there. Don't s'pose no folk will mind."

"No, I guess no one will mind if we camp, er, on that." I agreed.

We cooked dinner on a stone table that must have been quite ornate at one time, but was now fractured in two with weeds growing through it. We waved politely to the locals who slowed in their trucks as they passed to catch a glimpse of their eccentric interlopers. After Shithead and once dark, we found our way into our sleeping bags. I was just drifting off when I heard what sounded exactly like what I imagined a flamethrower to sound like. After a few minutes of confused head scratching I looked out and saw that the end of the park furthest from us was, indeed, on fire. About 20 or 30 metres from us flames as tall as a man were burning almost the entire width of the park. And they were moving towards us as they worked through the dry grass. Maybe this was the work of Skynet.

"Er, Killer. Can you just look at something and tell me I am not imagining it."

Killer poked his head out. "Hmmm, now that is interesting."

As we contemplated our next move, which most likely would involve actually moving, a small fire truck pulled up. A man got out, unrolled a long hose and he then started dowsing the fire with water. Once the fire was extinguished the man jumped back into his truck and drove off.

It was still not late so I walked over to the store on the pretext of needing water (for drinking).

"I say, funny thing… someone just set fire to the park and then later put it out. Is that, er, unusual in your town?"

Deborah laughed and shook her head. "Oh dear. That'll be our fire chief, Trevor. He likes to practice so he's, you know, ready for when he's needed. He's not the shiniest turnip on the truck."

That one wasn't even in my obscure phrases leaflet but, even so, it was a satisfactory enough response to confirm that this was some sort of professional arson rather than a Texas flamethrower massacre. I returned to my cocoon. An hour later though, the fire was started up again. The sound of the flames was strangely quite soothing and I closed my eyes. I'll probably wake up, I reasoned, if my tent catches fire.

The eccentricities of Texas continued the next evening at Pumpkin, where we found Walter again. He looked a little different from when we last saw him at Cliff but we recognised him as Walter Pumpkin through his bumbling mood. Here, he had taken up the role of camp host, a sort of perennial camper that gets free accomodation for keeping the place running and for talking at the guests. He wandered over as we pitched up and said something we couldn't decipher about 'Ohio' and 'good sleeping bags'. Then he nodded and said, "yeah, ok" before walking away. After a few paces, he suddenly turned and strode purposely back as if he'd forgotten something important. But it was irrelevant. "…last year it rained pretty bad but not this year…". He did this seven or eight times, each time with intent. "Oh, one more thing…" But each time with no valuable exchange. On the last turn, Killer let out an exasperated, "Oh Jesus, man." But Walter continued.

But he was also charming and was kind enough to take an interest in our adventure, so we accepted his offer to eat our choodle with him and his wife in the camp kitchen. I am not sure I understood a word they said but their abundance of herbs, spices and hot sauces - that they allowed us to make use of - was enough excitement to even lure Killer back into the choodle fold. This was the first time ever that the choodle was cooked on a real stove and not on a small burner propped up with sand and rocks (or on a loo). It gave us an excited sense of what life might be like in the busy UT bar, as braying, hungry customers roared desperately at the chefs for more choodle. One day, one day...

We then washed. Everything. We cleaned our pans properly for the first time in weeks - with actual soap and not a wet hand. We washed clothes thanks to a kindly camp neighbour donating some soap powder. We cleaned our water bottles, removing some of the black mould that was regrowing threateningly at the bottom (the first such cleanse since the indulgence at Harrison's in San Fran). And we washed ourselves, lengthily in (rare) hot showers. It was heaven. In fact, the state of being so clean in every way was so enjoyable and so rare at Pumpkin that it took up several lines of my diary.

The cycling in those days was slow but superb. The mindset switch I'd activated in Austin meant that even the pain in my knee - which meant I could still not stand on the pedals to go up the hills - didn't often occupy my thoughts. And Killer was also restored. We were averaging 40 or 50 miles everyday, which was decent enough in these cold, short days, and we had stopped worrying or even thinking much about our 'pace'. We were just enjoying ourselves. We spent the next night at a caravan resort called Chain O' Lakes, then camped at Silsbee. The leaves had mostly fallen from the trees, but still a few drifted lazily down to us, and the woodland around us was becoming more flooded as we headed east. This also brought more bird life to our path and on a few occasions, huge cranes appeared and flew beside us at eye level.

We talked happily, riding side by side, and our telecommunication devices were busy fielding calls from Larry, Brian, Santos, Bernard, Mr Randy Rattlesnake, Mr Camp Coyote and others. The frequency of the communication and the extent of its comically complicated nature was a marker of the relaxed mood. At one point Killer interviewed me for a *Desert Island Discs* special, the special aspect being that each of the ten songs I was allowed had to be taken from Stonegarth's collection, of which there were only ten. Killer then received a call from Mick Jagger who wanted to enquire as to the possibility of a joint Stones - Stonegarth tour.

"Speak to my agent," he said. "His name is LA, he is a promoter of music."

Larry, particularly, had a lot to say. Over the course of just a few days, we learnt he had grown in size again, now to an unrivaled-on-earth 400 ft. The true reason for this, he hypothesized, was that the Radium in the water was causing his gene sequence to mutate. That and the fact he had just discovered his mother was the moon. Not even I could keep up when he let that secret out. He had also been nominated for Ranger of the Year in Ranger's Wives magazine. I told him that I suspected the magazine was not quite what he thought it was. Regardless, we received a number of calls from famous Dutch people wanting to pass on their good wishes to Larry via us. That is to say, we received a lot of calls from the footballer Ruud Gullit, because we didn't know that many famous Dutch people.

Meanwhile, the people around us - we discovered in the gas stations and stores we rested at and stocked up in - were starting to reflect more of a confederacy feel. Tight jeans, big belt buckles, bulging bellies, military haircuts and huge handlebar moustaches were the norm for the white guys. And they were joined by an increasing number of black people as we neared the very end of Texas. "Where y'all headed?" once again became a favourite line of enquiry. And we were either "heading the wrong way" - always met with gales of laughter - or "could get there faster in a car."

Indeed, this was not a land for cyclists. Our last day in Texas included a 15 mile stretch of highway where construction works had narrowed each lane, meaning we were again nudged off into the verge by Toselandian trucks keen to make their presence known. It was not even a place for pedestrians - a fact that was on clear display at our last Texan town, Kirbyville. The main road - US96 in this case - rolled through the middle. People pulled up in trucks in front of a store then got back in to drive to the other side of the street. We paused under a black sky and found a cafe.

"How y'all doing today?" the waitress asked in an accent so thick I was forced to ask her to repeat herself after every sentence.

She must have sensed we needed nourishment and vitamins, as she took out her notepad and asked, "Would y'all like the super salad?"

"Well yes, we would!" I beamed in reply after her second time of asking.

"Indeed we would!" agreed Killer. I don't even need to know what is in it. It sounds super. We'll take the SUPER salad."

The waitress screwed up her face and shifted her weight to the other foot. She looked around to see if her colleagues were witnessing this.

"No, sirs. It's not a *super* salad. We have two choices. Would you like the soup... or salad."

"Ah..." said Killer, looking sheepish but laughing. "Then for me, the soup."

"And for me the super soup too," I concluded.

The waitress frowned and walked away.

"You shouldn't tease them, Bone."

Outside the window the clouds grew darker and reflected the grim, grey hue of the surrounding buildings.

"It's towns like this that make the OK towns look amazing," I said after a while.

"Go on..." suggested Killer.

"Well no offense to Kirbyville, it has a great name but it is just another town straddling a main road. In all these towns you have big roads and big trucks. No actual *human* activity. How do they put up with this crap? Don't they want something better for themselves?"

"Now, now, you're just tired and hungry," said Killer. "I think you'll feel better when we get out of Texas. We have been here for several years now."

"Texas, I don't mind. It just has so much potential to be amazing here but no one is even trying."

Just then the waitress returned with a particularly enjoyable linguistic trick, timed as if to purposefully buoy me.

"Y'all 'bout ready for y'all soups y'all?" she asked, placing the dishes in front of us.

Three y'alls in a single sentence. A new record. My eyes lit up. I was starting to come round.

"Indeed w'all are y'all!" I declared.

She sighed again but then told us the soups were already paid for. Someone had read our panniers and said they'd pay for whatever we ordered. I was charged by this human spirit in this inhuman place. But, as it was a free lunch, I also slightly regretted not ordering soup *and* salad.

Beyond town, the clouds loomed but never broke, save for a few refreshing specks. We neared the Sabine River. The afternoon sun breaking through the clouds cast a glow across the autumnal trees, and wide sandy river banks. Across the bridge stood the state sign, lit by a single sunbeam, like an invitation to finally leave Texas. 'Welcome to Louisiana. Bienvenue en Louisiane,' it read. Ah, but what are those other things on the sign, I thought. Oh yes, I see, just a scattering of friendly bullet holes. Well, at least we haven't met a serial killer. Yet.

13. Let the good times roll

Sabine River, LA to New Orleans, LA

The will must be stronger than the skill.
Muhammad Ali

Seeing the state sign in both English and French was the closest we had got to a cultural indulgence since spotting a light goose plucking in Round Top. As I clapped Killer in, he gave a regal wave and a round of 'merci, merci'. I then noticed another, smaller official sign beneath the state sign that had clearly just been nailed up. 'Louisiana 1803 - 2003', it stated, 'Louisiana Purchase Bicentennial'. Under the words, it displayed a small map of the USA with a large swathe of the country highlighted to indicate said 'purchase', made precisely 200 years before we arrived. Napoleon gave up his aspirations for an extension of the empire in North America by flogging the whole of the middle of the current US (instantly doubling its size) to fund his war against the bloody limeys. I think I could hear Thomas Jefferson still chuckling about the bargain all the way from Mount Rushmore. This was the deal that led to Lewis and Clark, and the association that many Americans feel towards the spirit of pioneering into the wilderness, or simply into other people's land.

The name Louisiana had once signified the entire territory but after the purchase remained only in the name of this state, our seventh. It felt like the toughest riding was behind us, but perhaps only geographically. I found a list of the '7 deadliest things in Louisiana', which not only suggested deadly spiders and snakes were still very much on our prowl but also listed 'the roads' as having murderous intentions. Bad road surfaces and crazy drivers lay ahead, it said, describing the highlights of the Ronald Reagan Highway.

Despite the two languages on the sign, there has never been an 'official' language here. The rich soup of French, Spanish, British, Native American and African cultures led to the state constitution enumerating 'the right of the people to preserve, foster, and promote their respective historic, linguistic, and cultural origins.' Perhaps strange then that in Louisiana we would meet people in public office who clearly had different views on equality of people. But certainly, the locals seemed to enjoy their right to freedom of expression. And this did not hold the highest standards of comprehension as we entered the new land. A number of people in Bleakwood sat simply drooling beside the road, nodding as we passed. A toothless man in a store in Bon Wier got hysterically excited about a tin of beans, holding it to my face and laughing. (Although, I must admit I also do really like beans). Whenever we told people, "We are from England", it was met with blankness and confusion rather than incredulity or a Yarboroughesque search for connection. And people would line up to say things, just for the joy of saying words, no matter how pointless. And so it was with a little nervousness and caution that we arrived in Merryville.

We had planned to camp on the grass outside the town museum. The maps had said this was allowed for free and that there was even a toilet and shower we could use. All we had to do was call up the Town Hall to say we had arrived - they'd then send someone to come and unlock the facilities and show us precisely where to camp. While we waited, we rested outside the museum's main attraction - the historic Burks House - a log cabin which dated back to the 1890s and which had raised four generations of locals. I read the information boards, of course. Merryville, it seems, had followed a similar path to Aberdeen in Washington - its population had once been significantly larger, and its industry alive with saw mills, until the entire local timber land had been used up, and the town nearly collapsed. One character that stood out in these times was the outlaw Leather Britches Smith. He didn't sound too bad (I was especially confused by the intended fearsomeness of his nickname. Leather britches was not quite on a level with Leather face) - he roamed around drunk, waving his pistols menacingly, and once shot the head off a chicken before demanding the owner cook it for him. But this behaviour was too much for the people of Merryville. Several young men formed a posse, ambushed him and killed him. I was just contemplating how this might reflect local hospitality when I noticed we had attracted the interest of one of said locals ourselves.

The woman must have just been in her 30s but with matted hair and lesions, and a stoop as crooked as a question mark, she looked like she'd been wandering that corner since Burks' day. She looked a little like what Cher might if you left her to soak in a swamp for a year or two. She walked slowly towards us as if she'd been expecting us, or perhaps hoping.

"Y'all camping tonight?" She laboured over the words and looked intensely at us as she spoke.

We nodded silently.

"Oh, it's gonna be a cold one. Yes boys. A real cold one. Down in the 30s. 32 I think. Uh huh."

I didn't know much about converting fahrenheit to celsius but I knew 32 was zero. We'd had much worse but that was certainly cold. She stepped closer. Her face was now almost pressed against mine. She smiled, her teeth jutted at odd angles or were entirely missing, like tombstones in an abandoned graveyard.

"My. You got perty blue eyes." She pronounced 'eyes' as 'aahs', and the word seemed to exist without end in her mouth. Aaaaaaahs.

I flinched and she turned abruptly to Killer, moving into his face.

"And you! You got perty green aaaaahs."

We slightly pelicaned ourselves, said thank you and shifted backwards.

"Y'all should come over. We live next door, just around the corner there."

She nodded slowly to us as if suggesting we didn't have a choice.

"Yes that's right. We just like to sit on the porch at night and drink a beer. You're welcome to join us. My boyfriend is the town taxidermist."

She said this final morsel as if a proud declaration and as if to reassure us that he was of some standing. We were unsure if we were more terrified by the fact that a taxidermist wanted to drink beer with us on a moonless night, or that by virtue of being the *town* taxidermist, it was suggested that in every community for miles around you will find a professional dead animal stuffer, as surely as you'll find a baker or butcher. And that every one of them would like to store your aahs in jars.

As the museum keeper arrived with the timely keys, the woman - Amy - walked off, only to return minutes later with two cans of Coke. She pushed her message again - *come over, save your gas, relax, have fun.* We politely turned down the offer of food but said we would go over later if we didn't feel too tired.

"I feel like we should go," I said later. "It'll be… fun?"

"You are ridiculous," said Killer. "You know she intends to kill us then place our heads on wooden mounts for their wall."

I thought this was a strong possibility, and yet I felt compelled by politeness. I was also slightly curious as to what poses they might choose for our embalmed eternity.

"But we are merry Englishmen in Merryville. Would you rather be gutted and stuffed or be rude?"

Killer contemplated this.

"Oh, I think I am quite happy with being rude, Bone, especially when murdering is afoot."

The kindness of strangers was exactly what we had asked for and I fully intended to welcome it. Ultimately though, as soon as the choodle had been consumed, the draw of the tent was too much. In the morning, Amy walked past, paused, shook her head at us and then walked on again, presumably waiting for the next visitors. We had survived, but for how long? It was just to get weirder the deeper we went into Louisiana.

We had our sights set on a camp the next night at what the map indicated was an RV park but what our eyes suggested was Ted Bundy's house after a fight with a tornado. There was a run down family home, a couple of trucks 'parked' in the garden and throughout the long grass were rusted kids bikes and broken toys, as well as a scattering of odd chairs and upturned tables. The only RV we spied seemed to have a small woodland growing through its windshield. Images of a dark pit and a human sacrifice came quickly to mind. On one side of the terrain was a large catfish pond, presumably where the 'remains' got deposited. I turned to Killer, but he already knew what I was thinking. More than that, by spending so much time together, we had moved beyond mind reading to another level of mental acuity.

"Well, I think we should be safe here, Killer[7]," I suggested.

"My thoughts entirely. But, er, did you just insert a footnote into your *spoken* speech?"

"Er, no[8]."

A woman staggered out, looking as surprised to see us as we were her.

"You want to camp? Oh, er, sure. We don't get so many… well, why don't you find a spot and wait for my husband."

"Is he by any chance the town taxidermist?" I asked.

It was getting dark so we had to make do. There were no formal 'plots' marked out, so we found a patch that had the least detritus and pitched up. We played Shithead and a cat came and sat with us for a while. We called him 'Cat'. He was entertaining, until he started to claw holes in my tent and I chased him away. This was soon replaced by an inquisitive dog who seemed to have stored all its piss and shit up for the visit.

---

[7] "This is a death trap."
[8] "How the hell did Killer hear that?!"

"Tomorrow, we enjoy the luxury," Killer and I reminded ourselves, almost in meditation, picturing the motel break we had planned.

For the next day was Christmas Eve. Perhaps it was the cold weather, that was continuing to drop in degrees daily, or the proximity of eye collectors, or more likely the draw of a bath and some festive face stuffing, but we set a blistering pace from Merryville to Oberlin (and by blistering I mean 'not terrible'). It was possibly the fastest day yet, faster than those summer Dorset days a few months before, riding the back roads to Yeovil, when seven miles with a light rucksack and a tail wind was quite a journey.

Beyond the scrappy little towns, the scenery was spectacular - it had rained mightily in the night, freshening up the woodlands beside our path. The greenery found itself on fat trees with thick mosses. We started to seek out our motel treat once we hit Mamou, 25 miles down the road. As we chugged back our coffees on the gas station forecourt, we asked a woman for her recommendations for our luxurious (i.e. any motel will do) Christmas break. She weighed up the options but really wasn't sure where the nearest one was. She seemed to still be thinking helpfully when a large middle-aged man with a goatee called over to us.

"You boys need help? Come on over."

His name was Greg - no relation. "OK, well first of all you're on the wrong road. So first I'm going to put your bikes in my truck and drive you to get some lunch then we can get you back on course. Sound good? Let's go."

Greg had decided everything and we were very happy to be led. His truck was the standard behemoth that everyone drives in these parts. Four wheels but about 40 square metres inside. He was sitting in what looked like an armchair, with large arm rests. I could stretch my legs out and barely reach the back of his seat. When people walked in front of his bonnet you could hardly see the tops of their heads. Human scale had been removed in this land of cars.

He was chewing tobacco and occasionally would spit it into a cup that was now half full of thick, black liquid. He had a sticker on his dashboard that read 'God bless these United States of America.' He was the chief of the local volunteer-run fire station. When he told us this, I thought of the fire chief in the town of Richards and wondered if Greg intended to set fire to our motel that night.

"You boys tried boudin before? No? Oh, well we're gonna fix you a real nice treat back at the fire station. Yeah I'm gonna pull in here and buy the boudin then we'll head to the fire station and I'll call the boys to come meet us and we'll enjoy the boudin."

"This is all very kind of you Greg," I said hesitantly, again suspicious of kindness, and slightly concerned by the word 'boudin'. There must be a catch, I thought.

At the fire station, he laid out a plate of the boudin - which turned out to be a spiced Louisianan sausage - and soon his volunteer buddies turned up, including a farmer who wanted us to try his crawfish. We'd cycled past a number of flooded fields that day, wondering what they were - the farmer said that for half the year they cultivate rice in these 'ponds' and then they let the crawfish mature.

I had read somewhere that crawfish - a sort of mini lobster - was the 'State crustacean'. The state had awarded official stately titles to all manner of the living and dead. State fossil - that would be petrified palmwood. State vegetable plant (oh, the list gets quite specific) - the Creole tomato. State mammal - Mr Black Bear. I imagined all the stately flora and fauna of Louisiana - which also includes the Catahoula leopard dog, the Brown Pelican and the Mayhaw jellyfish - all gathering at the Mamou fire station to sing the state song, *You are my Sunshine*, and then washing it down with a nice cold glass of state beverage, milk.

Greg seemed more articulate and aware than many others we had met recently - but maybe that's more a reflection of the people you meet beside the road than an indictment of the State. Either way, I could see by the way he led his friends why he was the chief. It struck me as even more alarming then that someone who otherwise displayed all the signs of intelligence and hospitality should have such strong racial prejudices. And there was the catch.

"Well, I knew these two British boys needed my help when I saw them asking for directions from a *black* woman at the gas station. Ha ha, right?" He laughed gently and his friends shook their heads in the enjoyment of our mistake.

OK, so not an arsonist, perhaps, just your average friendly racist, chucking out slurs like it was a how do you do. The ease of their discrimination was terrifying. Killer and I exchanged confused glances. What should we do? I genuinely thought America had moved on. We bit our tongues, silently agreeing not to stay longer than was necessary to finish our lunch.

Amongst those proud, red-blooded white men the conversation quickly turned to fear-fueled patriotism. The farmer was keen to get into it.

"So what do you boys think of Bush and the war in I-raq? I'm glad they caught that son of a bitch Saddam."

We were truly amongst the Republicans, hungry for an even harder line.

In my head I was screaming, *It is ridiculous. It's not right on any level - can't you see that you have been conned by this kakistocracy? Can't you see the enemy is an illusion to consolidate power? Aren't you concerned this phoney safety they seek 'for you' will destabilize the Middle East with growing sectarianism and will lead to increasing polarisation of the United States itself?*

I took a breath. All eyes were on me. "Well," I said, trying to measure my words, "I'm not sure I agree with Bush's reasoning for the war, if I'm honest. I don't feel his stated intentions for this conflict are entirely, er, genuine or backed by evidence, and it seems to have been rushed through, without, er, the appropriate international consensus?" I spoke cautiously.

Greg sort of shook and nodded his head as if to say he didn't agree but he welcomed my opinion. But my answer had really riled the farmer, who leaned into me.

"Oh yeah, well what would you think if you had relatives in the twin towers? You might think different, I'd say."

And here was Bush's America. Conflating Bin Laden with Saddam and everything anti-American to justify a war in the Middle East; more specifically a war in one of the world's most oil-rich nations. They'd bought the need for a War on Terror at all costs, every Bushy bit of it. It didn't matter if the facts didn't add up; the story was too rich for it not to make sense to their hearts. America was leaving truth behind, in favour of stories.

But I had no intention of insulting the farmer further in his own home, and I knew there was little point trying to change his mind.

"I suppose then my feelings would be different," I said, not elaborating on what those feelings might be. He seemed satisfied and slid me over another crawfish tail, as if to conclude the affair.

Greg patted me on the shoulder and said we could stay the night in the fire station. "It's got all the facilities you could need and you are more than welcome to use them." Beyond the desire to escape, we had our hearts set on motel luxuries. We were preparing to leave when Greg's ten year old son turned up with his friend on their BMXs. They probed us about the trip in awe and asked to have their photos taken with us. It felt good. I wondered at what age these bike toys would get dumped for real transport; living rooms on motorised wheels.

Ten miles later and we were at the Best Western Motel in Ville Platte. It was an excruciating $80 but it was the only motel for miles and, well, it was Christmas. We drowned in the site of the mini fridge, TV, microwave, bath… but our enjoyment had to wait until we had done our Christmas snack shopping, so we walked over to the Walmart Supercentre. This involved crossing a small highway, of course, running across the traffic. But the discovery of a whole aisle of Louisianan hot sauces to pep up our choodle was worth it. They stood like proud soldiers, in angry red uniforms, with names like

Kickassin' Nuclear Mule and Badass Bitches from Hell - it was almost worth cancelling Christmas and getting back on the road so we could try out new choodle mixes.

When we finally returned to the motel, we took turns in the bath, whilst drinking cold beers, smoking cigars, and shouting out Arnie quotes. The bathroom mirror provided an opportunity to assess our curious bodies for the first time in some weeks. I looked at mine as if it was someone else's in a museum. It was not Mr Universe. The biceps and chest were losing their definition, the waist was flat and toned and the legs rippled with muscles and sinews in strange places. Painted on top of this, of course, was the strange, neat tan lines which were growing excessively in the southern sunshine. But I liked that; it made us look like we knew a little bit about what we were doing, some sort of adventurer's badge and a marker that, yep, we had been on the road for a bloody long time. We had come 450 miles since Austin without a break. We stank, ached and were exhausted but we had also truly rediscovered the love for the ride, even if on this day our thoughts were of home.

Over the past few days and weeks, we had heard Christmas songs in the stores and we saw the pleasing, shiny decorations that said it was the season to be joyously tacky. I thought romantically of Sherborne - the main street would be lined with mini Christmas trees bedecked in white lights and the manger scene at the bottom of the road, still the same as when I was a child, would be welcoming a new generation to reach up and thread a few pennies into the collection tin. I was reminded of why it was such a hard town to leave. We called our folks and luxuriated in their warm laughter and pride.

The relaxing continued through Christmas Day. Pharrel sang, Wade danced, the Wild Boyz chased wild beasts, and we discovered a new TV marvel, Newlyweds. Cameras followed around singers Jessica Simpson (that was her real name but presumably it was no coincidence that she was also pretty, like her Limenagerie namesakes) and Nick Lachey in their newly married life. It was really a vehicle to show off the comically dumb moments of Simpson.

Often the camera would pause on Lachey's face as he reacted to her latest frederick utterance, his expression clearly suggesting, 'Hmmm, maybe we rushed into this whole marriage thing.' In one scene she opens a tin of tuna from a brand that had been named 'Chicken of the Sea' to express the mass popular appeal of this fish.

"I'm confused," Simpson says, assessing the distinct flavour, "Is this Chicken or Tuna?"

It would be funnier if it hadn't been obvious that the more shows they made like this, the more Jessica Simpsons there would be in America. And, as we had witnessed and been told by everyone from Bill to Walter, this was truly on its way.

But the best Christmassy TV was a Bond movie marathon - known as a Bondage - and Killer revelled in Roger Moore's abundant delight in the use of blue screens to perform his tricks.

"Look Bone, I'm skiing whilst winking at girls whilst being shot at by baddies while trees whiz by. Oh watch out - a baddie with a gun! No problem. Judo chop. And oh look now I am driving, the mountain roads behind zig zagging around in no apparent connection to the random jerks of the steering wheel I pull while eyeing up this cute young thing. Hello? Have we met? Now I'm running over alligators. Is that Larry? It is great to be Bond. It's bloody brilliant to be me, Roger Moore. Now be a darling and get me my DAMNED BLUE SCREEN!"

We hoovered up crisps, chocolates, hot dogs, and random supermarket snacks. In many ways, this was just an exaggerated version of our continuing high-calorie and low-nutrient road diet. And we exchanged gifts. I had bought Killer a small carved blob at the Austin Armadillo Bazaar that I told him was called 'Ed Wind, reasoning that if he owned the headwind then he was less likely to be troubled by it. He thought this very sensible indeed and glued it to his handlebars. In return, he'd bought me a combined bike bell and compass.

"All we need to do," he said, "is follow the dial eastwards until we hit the bit of Florida that looks like a flaccid penis, then it's due south to victory. I suspect we won't even need maps anymore. Remember Greg and his rocket-like recumbent? He had a bell. Need I say more?"

The discussion of Greg (original, recumbent Greg not racist Greg) then led to a particularly complicated new creative imagining from Killer and I. We decided that what America needed was not a show called Carmel, but that The Limey Project should manifest itself next in the form of its own TV show and that this show should largely be filmed in front of a Roger Mooresque blue screen. Rather than allow the Americans to put up with mind-numbing shit TV, we would create something wonderful for them. It would be a cultural counter to Newlyweds. It started simply enough - we'd pedal our bikes whilst the scenery would whizz by and characters like Dr John, Gordon and Greve would enter the scene. It was also a way to provide a more fitting stage to our daily random sequence of Limey impressions.

"YOU! I like the way you dance," said the Governator to Wade. After a while it became incredibly convoluted, with the side characters having their own story arcs that were racing away from us. One scene involved Steve (who now has a slow, baritone gravelly voice) catching Greg (who now sounded like a high pitched excited schoolboy) writing a letter to his then girlfriend Jessica, as he had been doing when we first met him. In the letter Greg starts to explain that he has met someone. Steve sees this.

"Do I know this person you have 'met' Greg?"

"Uh ha ha uh yes you do Steve."

"Is it me Greg?"

"Uh, would you like it to be you Steve? Oh my Steve."

Steve shrugs. "Oh, sure Greg."

"Oh Steve - I love you - you are my Steve. You are so beautiful. Sopapilla?"

Later, Steve leaves Greg and we see Greg writing another letter to Jessica, explaining he's made a terrible mistake and he wants her back. We then cut to Jessica and see her reading the letter out loud. The camera pans back to reveal Steve, naked, covered to the waist with a silk sheet, sipping Darjeeling from a bone china cup. He shakes his head as he listens, then says reflectively, "Damn near breaks my heart."

There was also a scene that involved Steve being told by the Green Flash to *stop fucking telling people about it*... I can only conclude that the wild imaginings we were experiencing were testament to our positive frames of mind. The dark days felt well and truly left behind in Texas. Even though there was still over 1,000 miles to go, we felt close enough to the finish to know we would limp past the chequered flag, if we had to.

But first, more merriment. One of the films enjoyed in our Bondage was Live and Let Die. Not only was it Moore's first, it is also, significantly, set in New Orleans. From our Louisianan motel beds we were plotting our own expedition to the city of voodoo. It was hugely off our route but we were determined to have our own Bond moment. The death roads into the city looked impossible on the map - massive motorways for miles and miles - so the only other options were more cheating (no longer actually an option for me) or getting a bus in and out. I rang all the Greyhound bus stations in the surrounding area and finally found one in Opelousas, 20 miles away, that would store our bikes if we took a bus from there. So we did precisely that. It was six long hours in the bus to New Orleans but as we neared it and spied the glowing skyscrapers we itched at the idea of a night of revelry, Bond-style.

We really should be more careful what we wish for.

***

I wake up. I'm pretty sure I'm in New Orleans. I'm alone in bed, fully clothed. I'm in what appears to be a hotel room and there are two women with their backs to me in the next bed. Where am I? Who are they? Why am I not in bed with them? And where is Killer? I lie still for a while as if the answer will come to me in the fog but nothing. This painful confusion is all feeling a little too like El Paso for my liking (and in my defense, this had not been my plan). I reach over and find a hotel manual that tells me I am in some swanky place near the bars of the French Quarter. OK, I remember being in the French Quarter. I am desperate for the loo. In the bathroom, I see a glittery cowboy hat that I remember a woman wearing at a bar. A woman on holiday with her daughter? They opened a restaurant in Texas? I think that was it. There's a used tampon in the loo. I flush it and then undertake a gassitas. I try to be silent but all this flushing and puffing I must've woken them? No. Still no movement and still with their backs to me.

I stand there for a while, very confused. Maybe I should just take a shower and see if they join me? Jeez, I am still drunk. Hang on, what if I have caused these people incredible offence, what if I have been sick on them? After all, there's none on me. I realise I need to leave quickly and I make my exit. I have no idea what time it is but it is light so must be morning. Suddenly some nauseating hunger takes over me and I grab fists of food from the half eaten room service breakfast trays left outside a few of the suites. Someone comes out of their room and sees me - poised like an animal - and then sensibly retreats. I'd be disgusted with myself if it wasn't so delicious, as well as being the most balanced arrangement of food groups on one plate that I have had in some weeks. I suddenly realise it's not half eaten breakfasts but stale dinners from the night before that I am picking at. I inspect the gymnasium and pool and consider waking myself with a swim in my pants. But thankfully decide against it.

I call for the lift. I have no idea what floor I am on. The lift pings and doors open. It's full of respectable people, even families, no doubt on their way down to the sort of breakfast enjoyed with knives and forks. In my drunk confusion I stand there facing them all instead of turning to face the lift doors. The group finds this unsettling and they start to shift in their loafers. I must look a fetid, messy state. One man looks at me and says loudly, and angrily, "Do up your fly." Oh God. I reach down and raise my zip but keep facing them, making it even more weird. The lift doors open on the ground floor and I stand there, still confused, until the man speaks again to tell me to 'get out'.

I walk conspicuously through the marble and bronze lobby and out of the revolving doors onto the main street. Yes, I know where I am - I'm near the streetcar stop that we got off at the day before. I don't know the name of our hostel but I do know that I can take a streetcar to the Garden District and perhaps I will recognize it when we pass. I settle in and realise the journey and buildings are actually beautiful. Everything feels so emotionally charged in this delirium. I hope that Killer is still alive and is at the hostel. My god, where is the sodding hostel?

I get out and ask around. I ring on doorbells. "Er, have you seen a hostel near here? What, you have??" Energised by the hotel's cold slices of beef in gravy, I almost jog into the dorm we are staying in. There's a killer-shaped lump in the top bunk and I recognise the hue of his sleeping bag. Without having to announce my presence Killer bursts into laughter.

"Oh dear Bone, oh dear. That was quite a night. Roger would be proud."

We slowly started to piece it together.

"I woke up in bed *next to* but not *with* that mother and daughter combo I think."

"Yes, we put you there. You were lucky we managed as you were a dead weight. I wasn't sure if you'd still be alive today or if they'd take you back to Texas and barbecue you. That was just before I got drugged and punched a guy. Anyway, what did you do this morning?"

"Oh I think I did what most people would do. I took a shit and left."

This was too much for Killer and he was almost crying with laughter now, before pressing a hand to his alcohol-pained head.

I suspected we would not venture too far beyond the hostel that day.

Our time in the city had started innocently enough. After the bus, we had an early night, then headed into town the next morning. We had barely stepped into the French Quarter when our unexpected city guide introduced himself.

We heard his soft southern lilt behind us. "Oh yessss, it looks like Santa has come to town."

We turned and saw a tall, thin, older man with one hand clutched at his heart as if in love and the other pointing at Santos, who was clinging to my handlebar bag (which I took everywhere with me and whose form demanded it be sported like a handbag).

"Oh that is wonderful. Where are y'all from? My name is Billy and I MUST buy you breakfast."

It seemed more than a little sudden but we weren't in the habit of turning down free food. Billy took us to Cafe de la Madeleine for the eponymous small pastries and a hearty French feast, with the instruction to eat as much as we pleased.

"My daughter is called Madeleine so I like to come here when I'm in town."

"Oh you have a daughter?" asked Killer, surprised.

Billy was from Mississippi, a retired teacher, and apparently had a wife and family but there was something about his expressive gestures, his friendliness, soft voice and his penchant for a caressing arm touch as he talked that suggested he was not entirely convinced by his situation. This was soon confirmed when we passed a row of gay bars, recogniseable for their rainbow flags, and Billy held me tightly by the elbow.

"Oh, I've seen a few things in there," he said, holding one hand to his mouth and chuckling lightly. "You should really go there later."

Ah yes, another person assuming we were a gay couple. Perhaps he had felt safe confiding in us the feelings that in

Mississippi were never allowed to be expressed. Maybe he just enjoyed the friendly energy of the gay scene. It mattered not to us, but we did wonder what reception the rednecks of the deep south, a little down the road, would give us if they followed the same assumptions. More than that, I wondered what it must be like to have to hide your identity in these places out of fear to just be yourself.

"Now, I don't want to take up too much of your time. I just want to show you a few things. I am having so much fun with y'all."

Billy was generous and harmless, but I did find his attention - and constant arm holding - a little trying. Killer had stronger thoughts.

"How do we lose this old nutter? He's wearing out the fabric of my sleeve."

We took our leave in Virgin Megastore - chosen by Killer because it had 'gas' hidden in its title - when we sought new diaries to buy. There was an awkward hug goodbye where Billy held us each longer and closer than is socially comfortable.

"If we keep hugging, one of us is going to have to start charging," Killer said to Billy.

He laughed and waved goodbye.

"Promise you'll call me if you get into any trouble!" he said with a wink.

It was a sunny Saturday two days after Christmas and the city was incredibly busy. Everywhere people queued for the must have snacks and sights. We sipped cafe au lait and gorged on beignets smothered in powdered sugar at Cafe du Monde, as we allowed the sounds of jazz, zydeco and blues to wash over us, the tunes meandering through the city from various bars and street performers. Groups of ragtag musicians stood under wrought iron balconies weeping with plants and the thump thump of the double bass caused passers by to shimmy a little in their stride. It was coming alive.

"Do you know any Stonegarth?" asked Killer to one performer between songs, "No? Oh you're missing out."

Artists and tarot readers busied themselves outside the Cathedral. Small boys tap danced for coins on street corners. And we took a deliciously romantic horse and cart tour, befitting two bearded lovers, where we learnt the city was pronounced N'awlins and its motto was 'Laissez les bons temps rouler' - let the good times roll. I really liked this city. If Louisiana was the state where cultural expression was celebrated, it seemed to all be focused here in N'awlins.

We had dinner on a balcony overlooking the famous Bourbon Street - this really was where the good times got going. Although still early, only about 6.30 pm, the streets were already filling up with revellers, drinking in the street and festooning themselves in colourful beaded necklaces like it was Mardi Gras. The table next to us was crowded with frat guys with bulging arms, laughs like apes and heads like lego blocks. They were highly lubricated and occasionally howled at passing girls or simply yelled 'Show us your tits!" They saw us flinch at this.

"Hey, relax. It's Bourbon Street tradition."

On the next table, a man spoke loudly into his phone. "Listen Jimmy. Just forget it. I know you won't pay me back so just keep the money. I lent you that 50,000 in good faith. I worked hard for that money and lent it as a friend. I don't want to hear it, Jimmy. Forget it."

Presumably Jimmy had used the money to buy the truck off Dedric.

In one bar, we stood by a fountain that had flames coming from the water. Jessicas came round and sold us shots of bright, glowing spirits in test tubes that they carried in science class-style wooden racks. When you bought one, they held the test tube in their mouth and tipped it into yours so you got close to kissing. After a few weeks on the road, this was intoxicating and, in my drunkenness, I confused this for affection. One of them, particularly skilled at cunning me out of cash, had a husky voice and called me 'baby'. I offered to take her for lunch and then - quickly escalating my offer - to marry her at Sherborne Castle.

"I have a young child at home," she said.

"I don't mind," I replied, whilst thinking 'I'm in wayyyyyy too deep'. She wrote her number in my Lonely Planet.

We had to leave to get to the House of Blues, the music venue owned by the actor Dan Aykroyd. In one of the more extraordinary Limey coincidences, the headliner that night was a certain musician by the name of... Dr John. After three months of bumping into him in various forms on the road, including potentially in person in Tillamook, we didn't want to miss him on stage.

"Extraordinary, simply extraordinary," I kept saying to Killer while looking at our tickets with his face on them.

"I think if I contemplated it too much my head might actually explode," said Killer.

"Well, let's see," I suggested.

As we awaited the Dr's famed musical soup of blues, pop, jazz, boogie-woogie and rock and roll, we stood by the bar drinking and smoking fat cigars that we had seen being rolled the traditional way that afternoon by some pleasingly Cuban looking gentlemen. As Killer started introducing himself to the mother and daughter combo, I got into some heavy drinking with a Marine, a guy just a little older than me. He bought Tequila shots for us both and we cheersed. I remember wincing slightly at the knowledge that this would be my undoing.

"What are we drinking to?" I asked after a couple of eye-melters.

"Death," he said blankly.

I half laughed but he looked serious.

"I have seen too much shit man. It's fucked up."

He'd just come back from Iraq and seen first hand the result of those stories of American freedom. When the boys in Mamou celebrated war they forgot about the human cost of it.

"And do you know what - now it's going to just get worse. I've had enough man. I'm not angry, I'm just ready to die and I plan to do it with this."

He held up his shot glass and ordered two more. As he did, I managed enough clarity to think of my oldest friend from home, who was at that time in the Middle East for the British forces. I worried about him. I looped my arm over the Marine's shoulder. Come on, I said. I tried to persuade him it was all still to play for, that there was so much to live for. I tried to persuade him to harness what he had learnt - the discipline, strength and skills - and focus himself on the future. But he just said, "No, man - I'm going to die." And he'd order more drinks for us, and then more and more… for some reason I thought that if I drank when he drank, he wouldn't be able to kill himself as I was a lightweight drinker so he'd have to stop when I keeled over. Never mind the fact I'd likely die first. In my drunk imaginings, I wondered if all these Dr Johns had led us here to save this man. As my eyes started to cloud over, Dr John finally took to the stage in a top hat and brightly coloured shirt, and my last conscious thought was, 'He looks different.' That's my last memory. In one of the Dr's songs, he croons, 'You wanna do some living before you die, do it then in New Orleans.' I sometimes wonder what that Marine must've been exposed to - and then not given professional support to deal with it - that led him to that point. I wonder where he is now.

Killer and the Texans soon realised I could no longer stand and they took me back to their hotel so they could all continue to enjoy the good times. They were quite the classy ladies these two. At one point Killer heard the mum say to the daughter, "Why don't you take him to the toilets and fuck him."

"I can't," she replied, "I'm on my period."[9]

Killer lost the girls along the way and was still wandering the streets at 5 am, still drinking Buds and shots. At one point some guys

---

[9] I nearly deleted this exchange. It's not pleasant. But I decided not to sanitise our experience.

offered him a drink and his view went fuzzy. They tried to drag him into a car but - suspecting they planned to rob him or worse - he refused. They insisted and started pulling at his clothes. In a lightbulb moment, he thought 'What would Roger Moore do right now?' so he punched one of them in the face, ran off, and then jumped into a moving cab. No blue screen needed.

In our hungover state, we progressed *The Limey Project: the TV show*, before eventually mustering the strength to get to the cinema for Tom Cruise in *The Last Samurai*. We delighted in Tom repeatedly shouting a Japanese word 'Utay, utay' at random moments.

"What do you think it means?" I asked Killer.

"Well, it can mean anything you please, Bone."

The following day, we walked more than was good for our knees. We surveyed book shops and museums and galleries. In the public bathrooms of a mall, a man clung to a railing as if about to be swept away by some force. He pointed at the cubicles fearfully.

"Man, can you smell that? That guy's *ill*, he must have a *disease*." Then he called to the man directly, "Hey buddy - send it down the river!"

The ever-cleansing Mississippi was out of sight but was known to be able to wash away all manner of sins. And that day it must have been washing a lot. It was raining so hard it was impossible to make out the tops of buildings. I remember thinking then this must have been the most rain the city had ever seen. This was two years before Katrina flooded 80 percent of the city and claimed the lives of more than 1,800 people. It completely reorientated the city, affecting the poorest communities worse and forcing many to leave, never to return. When we passed through New Orleans, the population was over 450,000. After Katrina, it fell to a little more than 200,000, with the black population seeing the sharpest decline. It is still recovering.

We dodged the rain at the Voodoo Museum, where we discovered voodoo is not the witchcraft I had been led to believe by

Bond but was an explosively interesting mix of traditional African beliefs colliding with Catholic Saints and practices. As much as 15 percent of New Orleanians still practice voodoo in some way and many others drip a little occasional Voodoo into their lives, just to be on the safe side. In the museum, hundreds of visitors had draped beaded necklaces over statues of the Virgin Mary and wooden voodoo carvings, or pinned up photos of troubled loved ones. A large area was dedicated to the most famous of all the Voodoo Queens, Marie Laveau. Thousands went to see her in her lifetime for voodoo dolls, potions, advice and charms. And not just everyday folk but politicians, lawyers and businessmen too. People still lay offerings by her burial site and still shout her name when throwing dice at the gambling table.

And who was the most famous Voodoo King? Well, a guy by the name of Dr John. I would have been surprised if it hadn't made so much sense; the Dr's ability to take on various different forms and the way he would appear when we most needed his advice. He really was watching over The Limey Project.

That was a fitting way to conclude our visit to N'awlins. It was time to get back in the saddle. With a little less Tequila and a little more of the Dr's black magic we could be in Florida in a week.

14. Hunting Graceland

__The mind of man is capable of anything – because__
__everything is in it, all the past as well as all the future.__
Joseph Conrad, Heart of Darkness

The Mississippi delta was shining like a National guitar. So goes the line
from *Graceland* by Paul Simon. It's a song I must have listened to a
hundred times or more. You probably have too because, quite
frankly, it is awesome. You are probably singing it your head right
now[10]. The line refers to the old National brand of music makers,
known for their reflective metal construction, that seem to emanate
light as they move. I had long wanted to see this shining landscape,
the second largest river basin in the world after the Amazon. And
certainly, in every corner of the land as we cycled onwards we saw
flooded woods, lakes, rivers, marshes and rivers that all mirrored the
bright blue winter sky and shone, almost blazed.

But the song has deeper meanings of course. The National
brand was popular with African American musicians, who down
here in the South were planting the seeds of rock n' roll and inspiring
the likes of Elvis Presley and his successors. We'd heard some of
those tunes on the streets of New Orleans. And we'd seen a National
on display at the Experience Music Project in Seattle, sparkling
alongside a bashed up Fender guitar used by Kurt Cobain. Even Bill
Hagen's slide guitar and shuffle found its heritage here. Paul Simon
is making the point that the Mississippi delta is the birthplace of

---

[10] I sit down in a cafe to work on this chapter, wondering if it is too much to start
with Paul Simon. As I open my laptop the Graceland album starts to play on the
cafe's speakers. I have my answer.

today's American musical culture. And that much of this was built on battle and blood. The next line in the song: *I am following the river, down the highway, through the cradle of the Civil War.* And this was our route too, through the delta, across the river and down through the southern slaves states of Mississippi and Alabama to see yet another aspect of America, before hopefully finding the sea again at the Gulf of Mexico. That would be our Graceland. And we hoped there would be slightly saner, less murderous people on the next leg. Sadly, that ambition would have to wait a little longer.

The first four days beyond N'awlins merely took us just past N'awlins, having started in a long bus-shaped dawnular retreat back to the north west to retrieve the bikes at Opelousas.

"Was wondering if you'd ever come back," said the man in the storeroom.

"Oh. There's no stopping The Limey Project," declared Killer. "Not even a Marine bent on destruction, a spiked test tube or a drunk Texan mother and her horny daughter can stand in its way."

The man looked confused, and slightly scared. He pointed to the bikes as if to say to hurry the hell away. We pressed our pinky fingers together and rode off. We had the ACA maps to help us but we had also been advised to carry a road map in case of road works, detours or if simply the feeling overcame us to make up our own route. Sure enough, the temptation to accelerate our return to the longitude of N'awlins was not long in coming - a quick comparison of the maps indicated quick gains could be made over the coming days, cutting out handfuls of miles here and there, by taking more direct roads.

"I don't mind doing fewer miles on our bikes as long as all miles are now covered on our bikes," I suggested confusingly. "Ah, yes, it looks like we can shave off a few miles today and still be further along the way. If we go... *here*...'. I jabbed a penis butter, bike grease, Vaseline and general grime-smeared finger at the page, "we can cut out this 14 mile-section, meaning we can be seven miles further along the road, having cycled seven fewer miles than we would have done otherwise."

Killer blinked away his confusion and nodded. As the aches and pains continued to gather in our limbs, 'shaving miles' was always welcome. But, really, the miles didn't worry us, the main reason for taking the small number of shortcuts that we did was for the exhilaration of being totally in the unknown after many, many miles of following a plotted course.

"There must be a reason the ACA has us on this drunken zig zag though," Killer suggested, on our first such off-piste attempt. "Remember Dr John Geronimo's warning. He did say we would be tempted to cut across country here but insisted it was dangerous on the back roads."

The Dr's spectre appeared momentarily before us. His gnarled face leaned in and let out a ghoulish exhalation, 'Them roads are baaaaaaaaaaaad'.

"Well this ain't no holiday, John," I declared out loud to our conjoined imaginations. "If there's shortcuts to be made on these strange backroads, we will be cutting them, er, short."

Soon onto said cut of dirt track and my front tyre started to make its own deathly hiss. Instead of the usual 'damn and blast its' though, I let out a squeak of joy as the puncture meant I could put on the new tyre I had bought in New Orleans. Rolling on after deploying it, the bike felt infinitely more lively and I, too, more eager to take on even more obscure roads marked in the faintest ink on our maps.

We had started the day with the intention of charming a friendly local into accommodating us. But there appeared to be none. Indeed, at Melville they simply stared at us and growled or glared as if we were an invasive foreign species.

"So much for the southern hospitality," I observed.

We pressed ahead and on to a small tugboat ferry, which carried us over a wide river.

"I have always wanted to see the Mississippi," beamed Killer as he delighted in the crossing.

"And so you will. Tomorrow," I said, unraveling the map before him and pointing at the waterway we were actually on, a tributary called the Atchafalaya River.

"I know, I know," said Killer, who then raised a purposeful finger and strode to the other side of the ferry, as if recalling he was due at some important meeting that meant any further questions over his misgeography would have to wait.

Our next back-country shortcut found us on a ten mile gravel road bedecked with bumps and hidden dangers that caused our bikes to bounce and groan and our bottoms to bruise. Soon, we were surrounded in the wild abandonment of nature. The forest either side of the track was dense, huge trees swamped in thick tufts of weeping Spanish Moss that provided a shifting wall of green. And with little traffic we could better hear the mechanical sounds of the bikes, which made their own percussive rhythm inspired by the landscape. But we were far from being alone.

Occasionally we would pass an abandoned car with its wheels removed and windscreen smashed out near a sign saying 'No Trespassers'. The few cars we saw that did have occupants were filled with angry men in camouflage, holding rifles, ready to kill anything that moved. Bullet holes hung on every road sign like decorative necklaces, as if the state sign itself had been a design quirk to show off a little of the statular appreciation for shooting.

So this is what we were being warned about by Dr John - hunters.

And over the coming days we would see them everywhere - outside every store, trucks and ATVs were parked up, guns poking from every half open window. The abundance of men in camouflage led me to form a collective noun for this new breed of American - a 'discomfort'. Inside the stores it was no better - hunting gear in every deathly shape for sale and adverts for Budweiser-sponsored hunting competitions. The spirit of conquering the land and everything within it, a la Lewis and Clark, was very much alive and a fully ingrained strain of American geneticular identity down in the swampy Deep South.

It was with no sense of exaggeration that I suggested to Killer, "I think we are going to die."

But Killer shook his head and invited me to consider the lesson of Arnie's often-overlooked 1987 masterpiece, *The Running Man*. In the film, Arnie is selected as prey for a live televised hunting competition in a dystopian future (that now didn't seem so far off). Whilst all the other participants are picked off, Arnie realises that to survive, he must himself hunt the hunters. Killer quoted a line where the exasperated TV show host tells Arnie to "Drop dead". Arnie replies, "I don't do requests." Arnie then annihilates everyone in sight. "It's showtime."

Killer suggested we now needed to take on the same position, to become hunters ourselves. He said this was the thinking behind the other gift he had presented to me at Christmas, a toy cap gun. It was resting in my handlebar bag, ready.

"You'll know when it is time to deploy your weapon, Bone," Killer suggested sagely.

My mind turned to the two cyclists on a tandem we had passed earlier that day heading in the opposite direction. Their ashen faces looked haunted.

"We're heading to San Diego from New Orleans," they said. "Does it get any easier?" We laughed at this and shook our heads as if to say they had no idea what was to come, until we realised the implications of their question and our faces fell a little. Perhaps we weren't out of the woods just yet. But that just excited me even more.

Half way along the next secret alley and a dry path was spied into the woods. We lifted the bikes down and pulled them through the bush and into a wide clearing. Tree stumps were covered in thick autumnal leaf litter like goblin houses and the evening glow painted the browns of the wood a magical golden hue. And so we spent a safe and happy night camping in what became known as the fairy forest.

"Every deathly cloud eh," I suggested.

The Mississippi River appeared through the trees the next morning. It was quite a sight to mark the last day of 2003. It was vast, perhaps almost a mile wide. Its banks and reaches ever-shifting. Its blue-brown waters slowly swept through the land as if an unstoppable, timeless force. It was magnificent. The trees beside the water had lost their leaves, the ground was a muted colour, and yet the water of the river somehow did shimmer and shine. After the Colorado and the Grande, this was finally a river to float a showboat on, or simply to float a turd away, as our friend in N'awlins would put it.

"I thought it would be larger," said Killer who then, immediately sensing my anger at his disappreciation for natural wonders, quickly raised his hands. "Joking, joking. Hey, send that shitty frown down the river."

In its effort to push towards the gulf of Mexico, the river has ever-jumped across land to find the shortest and steepest route. Most of the modern day state of Louisiana was formed by deposits of sand and silt as the Missisppi moved its channel to and fro in a 200 mile arc, its erratic jumps likened by one writer to someone playing a piano with one hand. When the Indians lived on its banks they would just move their teepees when the waters moved closer. But you can't move N'awlins. In the 1720s they started constructing levees to hold back the floods - they thought 3 feet should do it. But the floods continued regularly until the levees were over 30 feet high by the 1930s and it was finally decided that a more comprehensive system was required. This included rerouting some of the river's flow along the other watercourse we had crossed recently, the Atchafalaya. Before Katrina, the Army Corps of Engineers said the mighty Mississippi was now under man's control.

The only other passenger on our crossing was a woman who exited her car to press a ten-dollar bill into my grubby gloves.

"You boys look like you could do with some food," she said before hastily retreating to safety.

As it was, we *were* eating, just very badly. The carbs and sugars were powering our legs but it was apparent the lack of protein, vitamins and minerals was not saving them from aches and injuries.

In the first town post-crossing, St Francisville, we sought out a cafe to purchase some home-cooked nutrition. Named 'the town two miles long and two yards wide' because it sits atop a narrow ridge above the river, St Francisville still houses a number of historic buildings from its establishment nearly 200 years before. It must have been one of the first 'American' towns built in this land.

As we relaxed over super salads, we reflected on how strenuous the morning had been. The days of busting out 40 miles by 'lunch' seemed to be behind us. The problems in my right knee were now being met by similar levels of pain in the left, which had been working overtime to compensate. I had purchased an elasticated knee brace in New Orleans but it seemed to have no effect. I was back echoing Oreon, testing minute shifts in foot placement to see if any relief was forthcoming. It was not. Killer was faring little better. But I knew enough about my body by then to understand that I could accept and tolerate whatever pain that was to come my way.

"I think I am falling apart," I declared emphatically. "I believe by the time we get home my knee will be completely unfunctionable."

"If this happens," soothed Killer, "we will get you the finest cane like the good Dr. And we'll fashion you a shimmering cape that will unfurl behind you like a goddamn superhero."

I nodded in excitement.

"Of course, you'll have to be extremely eccentric to pull this off. No more mild oddities. You'll have to go full out peculiar and your breath should always smell of the most exotic brandy," Killer concluded.

I relaxed into the picture and waved over the waitress.

"Another cup of your finest coffee my dear," I said, standing and tipping my cap.

I was still rehearsing my role when we arrived a few miles later at Oakley House. There are many old plantation houses in the delta, but we must have chanced upon surely the most splendid and significant. The house dates back to the early 19th Century. A long drive approached through thick Louisianan jungle to the pristine white-washed wooden-slatted house which was topped by a large red brick chimney. With white peacocks proudly parading the lawns, it was the sort of house where caped Bone felt truly at home.

In every room we found exquisite wooden chairs, finely upholstered chaise longues, ornate mirrors, decorative sheets, brass candlesticks, paintings. It was quite a life for the plantation owners, the Pirrie family. We were escorted around by a toothy, whispering tour guide who insisted on us trying candy made from cloves and drinking tea made from tea bricks (which I assume were in turn made from actual tea…). As Killer commented, "This plantation was obviously not wealthy on the back of sweets and drinks." No, the money came from somewhere else. At the far end of the 100 acre grounds, to ensure it didn't spoil the view from the main house, were the slave huts. Small, closely huddled wooden cabins that formed the cradle of the civil war.

There are many reasons to go to Oakley - many go to experience America's past and understand how that established the culture of today, but by far the biggest draw is because in the summer of 1821, one of the world's most notable naturalists and artists, John James Audubon, had lived here.

Precisely 200 years before, Audubon - who was born in the French colony that is now Haiti - secured a fake passport from his father to escape conscription into the Napoleonic army, the very same army that was being funded by the sale of the Louisiana he was destined for. He worked at Oakley teaching the Pirrie daughter drawing, a job that allowed him time to conduct his own studies on the surrounding fauna. But instead of the talking, flatulent bears and ever-expanding lizards of our America, he set his sights on the birds. It was at Oakley that he started to amass a collection of bird paintings that would eventually form one of the greatest ornithological works of all time, *The Birds of America*, containing 435 hand-coloured, life-size prints. It is a masterpiece. (And considering one of his first jobs was as a taxidermist, perhaps we should have been more open to mad Amy in Merryville).

The flooded landscape we cycled through, enriched over millennia by the Mississippi, had certainly added a variety of sexy storks, erotic egrets and horny herons (as they were noted in our diaries) to our daily distractions but back in Audubon's day the bird life was even more profound. Further reflections on the state of the natural world around us were in evidence by the fact that Audubon had painted six species of bird that have since become extinct. This includes the passenger pigeon. There were an estimated 3 billion passenger pigeons in Audubon's day - making up about one in every three birds in North America at the time. Their flocks were so large that it took hours, sometimes even days, for them to pass. Audubon described them moving overhead like thunder. 100 years later, they were all dead. Hunted and stripped of their habitats until extinction. Silence. WH Auden had said a culture is no better than its woods. I'd add birds to that, of course, as well as insects and mammals too. And it was by then my strong belief that all of these would be better preserved with more investment in bike paths. With that, we'd have more human communities, that were also more connected to - and invested in protecting - our natural world.

Audubon hadn't had an easy ride to success. He understood the true lesson of the Alamo. It was while in prison for debt that he reassessed and formulated the idea for his complete bird catalogue. In another strange twist of our story, at precisely the time we were touring Oakley, two other young men were considering how to create their own formative experiences. Two college students from Kentucky were forming their plans to steal an original edition of *The Birds of America*, not just for the money but also for the uniqueness of it. Later, whilst in prison for that crime, one of these young men would also turn to painting birds, perhaps in penance for his crimes against Audubon.

"When you said you wanted to tour an old house, I thought you had finally lost it Bone," said Killer as we left. "But that was really rather bloody good."

Killer was interested. Something must be looking up. But that may also have been due to the fact one patron pressed $30 into his hand as we left, 'for your journey'. A matter of minutes later, some of this cash was handed over to the patron of the nearby Peaceful Pines RV park. Having over indulged financially and aesthetically in N'awlins, 'peaceful' would be perfect for us to see in the new year. We settled into our tents, set alarms for 11.59 pm so we could wish each other well and drifted off to the sound of a group of men gathered around a trailer listening to Celine Dion songs. When the alarm went off there was no sound outside and the celebration was quick.

"Happy New Year, Bone."
"Happy New Year, Killer."
"Happy New Year Bone and Killer."
"Oh, Happy New Year Brian. Glad you could join us."
"Yes, Happy New Year Brian."
"Happy New Year Brian, Bone and Killer."
"Oh, who's that?"

As soon as said, and the year turned, sleep was found once more, but only temporarily. The Celine Dion fans marked the New Year with a loud countdown at precisely 12.32am. We had long stopped being surprised by such actions.

2004 started as any other day, by 'talking to David', the phrase now given to the daily mixed-pleasure that was applying a cake of Vaseline - or lube - to one's grundle. The otherwise hopefully forgettable task now being chronicled with its new moniker thanks to the discovery of 'David Lubenow' in the El Paso telephone directory.

As the days between showers built up, this daily task became less pleasant as the hand smeared the lube onto existing application layers, stirring an unpleasant scent into the air. In a complete opposite of Mike the Bike's advice, we were wiping once and lubing five times... Normally this routine was reserved for the privacy of the tent. But as we happened to have campsite facilities, and assuming no one else would be up so early on New Year's Day, I stood in the communal area of the bathroom and pulled my trousers and shorts down. As I scooped out a thick wad of lube, a large man with checked hunting shirt and camo hunting cap and an all-round generally very obvious enthusiasm for hunting walked in and spotted me. A fist full of Vaseline in a public loo while your cock is on display is rarely a signal of republican values. He took one look at me and turned on his heels, probably to retrieve his gun.

But there was a deeper unpleasantness in those days. We had run out of gas before Christmas and whilst we were getting used to life without our cooker, we were far from enjoying it. We asked desperately in stores but camping gas was just not something that existed down here.

"Oh, you mean like meths for a Trangia stove? No? Oh, then no."

The lack of a morning coffee was played out against our mourning for the beloved nightly choodle. Our evening meals now consisted largely of some muesli bars, a banana and tins of beans. Lots of beans. Whilst we were missing one kind of gas, the other kind was still in full and free abundance. It was a common sight to witness your companion lean slightly off the saddle while riding along, to relieve the painful build-up of vapours. Occasionally I would also see Killer frown in concentration and I could tell he was still trying to work out how he could bottle this lucrative, tax-free, 'natural' power supply.

One thing was pleasant, however - the sun was shining enough for us to declare both shortage and shirtage.

"Forget the Alamo," I declared, discarding the long trousers.

We cycled on through more watery and wooded landscapes, which now had the added attraction of more of the white chapels we'd first seen past Independence, and which shone brightly like adverts for worship. And where no chapels had been seen for some miles, real adverts would bedeck billboards for telephone pastors. 'Call me if you want to talk to Jesus', said one. We had truly reached the Bible Belt. In the restroom of one gas station a sign stated plainly: 'No graffiti - this wall is dedicated to God.' It might be the only public loo in the world that doesn't have at least one phallus sketched up.

But beyond this Baptist backdrop, the more urban stops were unspectacular. This was most noticeable at Franklinton, where again it seemed you couldn't even cross the street without a car. And at Tangipahoa, where we found an exceedingly odd assembly of run-down houses. There were no discernible boundaries between properties and every yard was littered with a myriad of miscellany, a few also contained burnt-out cars and one even displayed a burnt-out railway carriage. We weren't even anywhere near a railway track. There was the odd lone cow, untethered and aimless. Groups of men stood beside the road in silence and stared at us as we passed. Perhaps it was a desire to escape these towns that led to the global search for stardom for Britney Spears who grew up just four miles from Tangipahoa, in Kentwood. I wondered if Kirkendall would have suggested a scenic side trip to go there to visit 'The Britney Spears Museum'.

The humidity at night during our journey through the delta was beyond anything I had yet experienced, forcing me out of my sleeping bag to lie on my mat in my pants. That night in Tangipahoa I thought it must have reached maximum levels of discomfort and annoyance, but it just got worse the next day. The morning started cool enough. And there was a dawn chorus of birds that even Audubon would have admired. As the sun warmed, the sky developed into an English-style greyness, before mottling and giving way to cool blue and sunshine. As it did, the humidity ascended again and not even a late torrential downpour calmed it. At every stop, fat drops of sweat weapt from our brows.

Still keen to save money, we pressed on through the town of Bogalusa and, at the sight of a quiet path, we ducked into the woods. We knew that hiding out in the woods was not the safest with a disharmony of hapless hunters on parade, not to mention psychos and serial killers, but in fact all that had little on our new nemesis, mosquitoes. In these swamps they existed in enumerate, ravenous legions and they were mightily excited to see us. They seemed to be drawn to the fortitude of our foulness.

We stretched our clothes and towels out on the tree branches like vagrants, hoping to air them, but the humidity just made them damp and smell worse. Then, once the sun had gone in, the mosquitoes formed a fog that seemed to seep into our lungs, so our cold, tinned dinner was 'enjoyed' in our tents.

"We need to find gas soon," said Killer.

"Yes, I long for choodle," I agreed.

"Sure, but I was thinking more so we could set a light to these fucking bugs."

Whilst the insect orchestra provided such a womb-like hum it was enough to tip me into sleep, their presence made the morning ablutions the most unpleasant of the trip. Every footstep in the leaf litter stirred the mosquitoes' search for blood, and my front and rear apparatus were both exposed to the feast. I spared a thought for Brian and the obvious issues his kind must suffer when undertaking such affairs in assemblages of trees, which is where I presume they do it, right?

We made a fast exit and hurried over the Pearl River, where Killer went ahead to welcome me into Mississippi. We applied the new state flag onto our steeds, noting the top left corner was made up of a small confederate flag - the symbol of the pro-slavery side of the Civil War. The flag design had existed for over 120 years. Two years before our visit, a proposal to update the flag, to make it more inclusive of the current world, was defeated with a significant majority. This despite the fact that a third of the population of Mississippi is black, and they actually make up the majority in the former plantation lands. What chance of equality for people here if tradition is favoured over progress? A pledge of allegiance to the current flag is taught in every school in the state.

There was no option but to pay for a campsite the next night. On arrival, the old owner insisted on talking incessantly in outbursts of non-sequiturs and random noises. Everyone around these parts had impossibly indecipherable accents (well, I have been saying that since Texas I guess…), so I picked little comprehension from the conversation. He kept infuriatingly returning to the point that we were going the wrong way - *that*, I could hear - despite never having asked our route. I stood there half asleep as the words washed over me. The conversation attracted the attention of a kid who came over and hovered, listening. Having heard our tale, the youngster seemingly took pity on us as, having rummaged in his pockets, he placed all his spare coins - a total of 43 cents - (and a few balls of fluff) into my hand. He nodded in punctuation to the proceedings and walked off.

As our general aroma now resembled the bowels of Satan in these God-fearing parts, we luxuriated longly in the showers. But we were unable to turn the water temperature above 'tepid' without troubling the bites and rashes of our Netherlands or without provoking more sweat outbursts.

One of the most wonderful things about the campsite was that not only did it have a laundry but that said facility was deliciously named the 'Washeteria'. Anyone who can make up words with such wonder can't be all bad and this was proven when the owner later tottered down to us - finding us pressing our clean clothes into our nostrils dreamily. I didn't make out exactly what he said but he passed bowls of chili into our happily shaking hands. It was as if he knew about our longing. It was a welcome, small act of kindness, or as Killer put it, "a small, unsatisfactory and unpleasant meal."

In my tent I was reading Joseph Conrad's *Heart of Darkness*, purchased with three other books - in cocky disregard for the added weight - from the exceptional Faulkner House Books in N'awlins. It wasn't too hard to find the parallels. The main character Marlowe - turned into the Martin Sheen character in *Apocalypse Now* - heads off on a journey to complete a mission, but in the process, his real discovery is to find what lies inside him, in his core. Conrad describes Marlowe as not needing a break from activity, but from his imagination. And so it was for us often. There was so much time for the mind to work away - on the bike, in the tent, every day, every night. Slavomir made the same observation about long journeys. 'There was time and to spare for a powerful amount of individual thinking.' There are too many thoughts. Jobs, lovers, friends, futures. I had been willing to go all the way into these thoughts on this journey, to see what lay in my own core. But, to my surprise, I was discovering that it wasn't so dark any more. Lying sweaty in that tent, I realised that where they had once been suffocating me, the vapours of ideas were now starting to take more recognisable forms; clearer visions of the road ahead that I wanted for myself, rather than intangible worries. I felt things more intensely than many people - and my mind was busier than most - but I now realised that when I could control those things, I experienced life much more richly than many also. And where dark clouds did gather, I had Killer's quotes, Shithead and Brian's big furry embraces to keep them at bay.

Indeed, as we felt increasingly alienated from the communities around us, it was perhaps unsurprising that our Limey telecommunication devices were busy fielding calls from our old, trusted friends during these days. Sometimes with important updates, but mostly just happily twattling. Brian checked in with us regularly. I said I suspected we'd be friends forever. "Even longer," he corrected. I remarked to him that the next day was TLP 100 - we were now 100 days into the challenge; something worth celebrating for its achievement, of course, but also something that caused us to reflect on how long the journey had already taken. Brian told us not to worry about the time though.

"Just ask the rivers," he said. "They cut through rock, not because of their power but because of their persistence."

It felt like an appropriate motto with which to carry us on, and it became even more apt on the hundredth day itself. The destination we aimed for was Vancleave, a 50-mile ride away. But before we could get there, we found our path blocked by hefty barriers, bedecked with flashing signs announcing 'Road Closed'. In fact, it was more than closed - the road just ended. A wide track of churned, orange earth extended ahead of us and continued over the brow of the next hill. Colossal diggers and trucks were parked up across the scene, waiting to fill it in with tarmac, but as it was a Sunday there was no one around. Was this obstacle a test? We didn't even check the maps to see how long the detour would take. We lifted our bikes over the fences, then pushed them forward. As we did, our shoes and wheels became caked in heavy clay. It was a couple of kilometers before we found our way to a road again. As we cycled on and gained speed the wet earth started to fall away from our tyres. It felt like any remaining metaphorical obstruction was being left behind as well.

"Nothing gets in the way of The Limey Project," I said to Killer.

At Vancleave we typed up and sent the next installment of the Limey diaries to the newspaper. It was very hard to convey the longing for choodle or the abundance of ammunition in these parts within the limited word count. The road continued beyond Vancleave through pine woods flush with the usual gunslingers. Only one person was devoid of camouflage and he was the only to talk to us. He told us he was thinking of building a camp especially for cyclists, as if an endangered species found only in the paintings of Audubon.

"It's too dangerous round here for cyclists right now." he said. "They're likely get themselves killed so I want to make them a place they can call home."

He said it as if oblivious to the modes of transport we were at that very moment astride and Killer gestured to his bike with wild theatrical sweeps of his arms.

The fearful sentiment was echoed more directly by an excited lady in a gas station. She sided up to us as if making a secret rendez-vous.

"I got to tell yous boys something," she whispered nervously. "You're heading into some bad lands now. You be best off carrying a gun for protection. Watch out boys, watch out." Her voice trailed off spookily. She held her handbag close to her chest.

"I think you'd better reassure her," said Killer.

I reached into my hand(lebar) bag and pulled out my plastic cap gun (which looked *incredibly* plasticy), brandishing it confidently, and then looked her straight in the eye. "Oh, I think we'll be just fine, thanks ma'am." She seemed a little confused but also strangely reassured, so backed away nodding to herself.

I was too far beyond worrying about things like that. I'm not sure bullets could have even pierced the odour armour I was wearing. But it did remind me that I needed some actual caps for my gun. I went in the store and laid my gun on the counter.

"Do you have any ammo for this bad boy?" I asked. It turned out they had quite an arsenal available so Killer took the opportunity to also 'arm-up' and purchased a very handsome cap gun called 'The Enforcer'. We were like Starsky and Hutch, or perhaps the Wild Boyz, or maybe more like the two Ronnies. Either way, we both finally had the 'light guns' that *Bicycling 1874* had suggested we carry for such an expedition. We celebrated with a round of Russian Roulette at the next rest stop; a bridge over a lush, peaceful creek. As we feigned death, turtles slipped into the watery woodlands and long-legged birds escaped from the tops of tall trees, as if being blown away like dandelion seeds.

And it wasn't long before the guns were put into live combat use with our old foe, the murderous dogs. In Louisiana the dogs had lost their enthusiasm for the chase and we had even rung our bells out of morbid curiosity, to try and awaken their interest, but here they were back in force. Our only means of survival was the fact dogs really didn't like the sound of guns, even very cheap, toy cap guns. At one point I had fallen a few hundred metres behind Killer. I could see him ahead and heard the excited barks and yelps as a community of canines rushed out of every corner of a small neighbourhood and chased him. I heard a few 'cracks' as The Enforcer delivered its message left and right, and Killer was gone. The dogs, however, remained. They stood in a line watching him disappear, still slathering. Then their ears pricked and they angled their heads around as they tuned in to the sound of my approach. There then followed an almighty sound as the creatures roared with excited bloodlust. I headed straight for them, charging and ringing my compass-bell. *Fuck you, fuck you,* I shouted as the adrenaline took over. (These were some seriously large and angry-looking dogs!) I took aim and fired. Bang, bang. A few scurried away but a few stuck with me. In the ensuing fast-paced battle, I dropped all my caps. I tried to stop and go back for them but the dogs were regrouping for a further charge, and behind them I spotted one dog owner on his porch stand up and hurriedly head indoors, no doubt to fetch his own - real - gun.

I moved on, caught Killer and - somehow energised - we increased the pace to around 18 mph until the state line where I went ahead to clap Killer in. Killer had long said that he had never liked the idea of Mississippi. He would say the word 'Alabama' sometimes, slowly, luxuriating in the soporific sequence of syllables, and then shake his head as if he'd just enjoyed some damn fine Irish whisky. I was more suspicious - the state flag was merely a large red cross as if to say 'best avoided'. But lo and behold, he was right - at the border, there was a clear line where the surface of the road smoothed and the grass greened. There's an old joke that there are numerous unsolved murders in Mississippi for the one reason that there are no dental records. Perhaps their dental hygiene wasn't quite that bad, but their highways could definitely do with a brush-up.

We had covered Mississippi in two days and hoped we would only need two to get across Alabama also. It was only a short ride to the coast and as we paused to plan our path there, we noticed a small lizard resting happily on Killer's pannier, and was it our imagination or was its bottom jaw slightly jutting to the side.

"Larry?" asked Killer.

The lizard didn't move and we took this as a sign of confirmation. Killer lifted Larry and kissed him on the mouth before settling him into the long grass.

"I'm glad you survived those maniac hunters, Larry. See you in Miami old friend."

Like the rest of the Limenagerie, he was on his way to celebrate the completion of our journey at the finish line. Neither of us thought to ask how Larry had shrunk down from his previously recorded 400 ft length. We were too pleased just to see him again.

As we neared the sea, the weather cooled and the humidity dropped. The woodlands eventually gave way to more open land and then the horizon opened up completely. It had been a little over 50 days since we last saw the sea and in our excitement, we joked, sang and rang our bells all the way to the Gulf of Mexico, with cries of "Utay, utay." And there it was. It looked fairly grey but it was the sea nonetheless. The road went straight into it, along a concrete causeway on stilts, which then raised impossibly into the sky. From our angle of approach, not being able to see it was the ascent of a bridge that allowed ships underneath, it looked like an Evel Knievel-style stunt ramp. But atop the arc, the view then revealed Dauphin Island beyond and we freewheeled down towards it.

"Ocean in view. O! The joy!" I happily declared, channeling Lewis and Clark.

"Who's idea was this? It was mine," Killer replied.

15. Damn the torpedoes, full steam ahead!!

Dauphin Island, AL to Homosassa Springs, FL

You're braver than you believe, stronger than you seem and smarter than you think.
Winnie the Pooh

From Dauphin Island we were to take the ferry straight across Mobile Bay to be within a few miles of the border of our final state, Florida. But not that day. "Ferry's cancelled. Bad weather. Who knows if it'll run tomorrow, or even this week." That was all we were told. If it didn't run it was 140 miles or more to cycle all the way around the bay to rejoin the route on the other side. And we were eager to press on - we were expected in a few days a little up the road. But we could see why the ferry wasn't running - the wind was frantic and it was churning up the waves, making even sturdy tankers bob about like bath toys. We'd have to wait it out the night, at least.

On the southern side of the island, we took in the full pleasure of the sea's return. That fat, fresh salty air. The beach was wild, lined with driftwood and stubborn bushes. The sands were white and stood out against the near black sky. At the far end was an old stone fort and beside it the most wonderful sign I had read on the whole expedition. It commemorated the Battle of Mobile. It displayed in huge, bold letters, "Damn the torpedoes – full speed ahead!!' With two exclamation marks (understandably). The words had been spoken in August 1864 by Captain David Farragut when the Navy ship he led was slowing, under attack from the Confederate forces that were occupying the island. This was his command to his timid crew - don't let a few torpedoes get in the way of smashing those rebels. We liked this guy's style and the words became another instant motto for The Limey Project, to be repeated repeatedly and at any opportunity, in increasingly surreal and barrelous voices, hurled at any physical or mental obstacle in our path. And for that day, it seemed an appropriate message to volley at the once again hazardous seas.

As Killer set off back to the campground, I took a detour through the adjoining large 'Audubon Wildlife Sanctuary'. A thick abundance of trees, dotted with small lakes and with walkways snaking through. I took out my binoculars (much untroubled in use since the first puncture in California!!) to see the birds and stopped at every information plaque to find out more. It was soon dusk and it became hard to read but I distinctly made out the last sign, 'Welcome to Alligator Lake'. Oh fuck. And beneath it the words, 'Please watch out for alligators and water snakes.' Oh fuckity fuck. I then realised I was now totally alone in this place - all other sensible sentients had long left. I tried to trace my way back in haste, back to the campsite, but escaping a 160-acre wildlife area, whose pathways are thrown down in mad loops and 'dead' ends, takes some time. Along the way, bushes rustled and the undergrowth moved, strange hissings came from beside my feet. It was almost pitch black as I moved through the woodland and waterways. I was totally Pelicaning myself. Where was Captain Farragut and his massive balls?

"Damn the torpedoes?" asked Killer when I eventually returned, deftly turning our new phrase into a question over the state of my obvious distress.

"Alligators," I simply replied.

Killer amused himself at what long fable might sit behind that word, opting to settle on my having snacked on them.

"Well I hope you saved some appetite for cold beans. And join me in reading the newspaper you kindly purchased."

"Oh I thought you paid for it," I said.

"Ah ha, well I guess we stole it then. Oh well, it's barely worth the paper it's printed on anyway."

I had to agree there. In the camp communal lounge area, we passed each other sections of contraband USA Today whilst the high octane, flashy graphics news also played out on TV. 2004 was only six days old and yet already a rover had landed on Mars, a Boeing 737 had crashed into the Red Sea killing all 148 people on board, it was announced the Orangutan may be extinct within 20 years, and a new 'social media' website called MySpace was launched. As Killer said, "why don't they just check out The Limey Project website - it has all you need to know." In Iraq, US helicopters had been shot down, suicide bombers had attacked civilians, and Iraqis protesting unemployment in the new era had come under machine gun fire by their compatriots. It seems Saddam's capture hadn't quite had the peacekeeping effect that very few people thought it would. And yet the US was sending in more men, and at huge cost. The news said the US National Debt had just passed US$7 trillion. Meanwhile, the domestic policy in the US in the past few days had included launching a scheme to monitor visitors to the country and another to tighten regulations around foreign working rights. 'No, don't come to us, we'll come to you', was the message from the US to the world.

"Oh my god - have you read this Bone?"

"Yes, it's all pretty heavy isn't it."

"I know. It says here our friend Britney Spears got married yesterday morning, and then divorced later the very same day. Isn't that incredible?"

Killer knew how to stop my mind getting too dark.

"Bloody Louisianianians," he added chuckling, "mad bunch."

Speaking of which - a group of six guys, at least in their 60s, sat around playing cards and swearing loudly. They all wore baseball hats that marked them as veterans of various conflicts. Even a deaf eavesdropper with fingers in their ears would have picked out they had just been on a hunting expedition into the woods we had just passed. Amongst the men we recognised Walter, who chatted to us for a while.

"Yeah, I went to England once. Yeah, 20 years ago. Yeah, I had this drink called 'bitter', it's a kind of beer. It's not like American beer, it's more, well, bitter. It's brown and they serve it in… what is that.. pints? Yes. Bitter. Yeah, I drank bitter. It's a nice beer, bitter…"

He went on and on. Apparently it's nice to drink bitter with nuts. We tried to interject and assure him that we knew this concoction of which he spoke well, but it was to no avail.

"Imagine if we met as many hot young women in these campsites as we do rambling old men," said Killer. The man continued, undisturbed by the comment, and told us more about that magical day.

"Imagine if the weather never improves and we have to listen to this story forever." I suggested.

Killer buried his head in his hands. "I always knew Alabama would be my undoing."

The delay did provide an opportunity, however, to get online - once we had extricated ourselves from Walter - and check up on our aforementioned website. As well as static information on the adventure and a few photo uploads, it had an online guestbook. It seemed that both real and Limenagerie guests had been busy leaving comments, and it was now impossible to tell the two camps apart. But the message was clear - we had a lot of incredible support.

Name: *Lance Armstrong*
From: *America*
Comment: *Wow guys - sure puts the Tour to shame. Keep peddlin, you're doing awesome - Lance*

Name: *James*
From: *James and Sharon*

Comment: *wish i could afford to make a gigantic contribution for a great cause like what you all are working on, however im not in that position presantly. so i guess a hamburger is it for now hope your stay in the U.S.A. is a good one*

Name: *Killer*
From: *The Limey Project*
Comment: *Hi Killer, Killer here. Just to let you know you are doing well. Killer*

Name: Arnold S
From: California
Comment: *Hey guys, thanks for all your help with my campaign - couldn't have done it without you. We sure showed those democrats a thing or two xxx*

Name: *Chris Martin*
From: *Sherborne School*
Comment: *Keep on truckin'*

Name: *Redsleeve*
From: *Odessa, Texas*
Comment: *glad yall lurv my state george dubya luvs ya!!!!!*

Name: *Janie & Megan*
From: *Texas*
Comment*: Had a great time in new orleans, hope that nasty illness you had in the French Quarter is better*

Name: *Natasha*
From: *Moscow*
Comment: *Hi 'Killer', remember me?*

Name: *Martin*

From: *The Abbey Friar, fish & chips, Sherborne*
Comment: *We're all supporting you both. Good luck guys!*

Name: *Beverly & Chrissy*
From: *Manhattan Beach, CA*
Comment: *We're so happy that you made a stop in Manhattan Beach!! Good Luck!! xoxo*

Name: *Mr S. Hussein*
From: *Iraq*
Comment: *If it wasn't for you pesky kids I'd still be free, damn you!!!! P.S. Good effort on the cycling though!*

Name: *George W Bush*
From: *USA*
Comment: *I think I speak for the nation when I say… ut ut*

We were rattled through the night by a savage wind so I had few expectations of escaping the island ever, let alone the next day. But I woke up early to check anyway and wandered over to the dock. There seemed to be activity. There seemed to be cars driving on to a small ferry, similar to the one that took us across the Mississippi. Surely that little fairground ride wasn't going to attempt the crossing?

"Yep, this ferry's heading over to Fort Morgan on the other side, probably the only one going for the next few days - leaves in 25 minutes."

I ran back to the camp, my knee burning with the effort. *Killerrrrrrrr. Get upppppppppp!* There was no time to change into cycling clothes - we just rolled up the tents, loaded the bikes and raced onto the boat just before the rear ramp was raised.

We soon discovered just how huge Mobile Bay is. It's actually an estuary and it's the fourth largest in the US. The crossing took about 40 minutes and halfway into the journey the only sight of land were the two headlands the ferry passed between. Large tankers drifted past. Countless oil platforms scattered the horizon. Hundreds of gulls rode in the sky behind us for a mile or more. Browny grey waves rocked us enthusiastically and we were cut to our bones by a bitingly cold wind.

My God it was cold. The rest of the passengers were safely stowed in their vehicles. We tried to escape the wind by sheltering behind a car, and then behind the life jacket store. Huddling and shivering like miscreants. And as we cycled on, our eyes even started to feel pained as the wind pushed against our faces like iced daggers. At the first gas station we raced inside for coffee and to buy thick winter gloves.

We entered Florida, our final state and our fourth state in just a week. Killer excitedly clapped me in, his hands nearly fracturing like brittle salt water taffies.

"Welcome to Flow-rider," he spluttered through chattering teeth.

After 20 miles we arrived at a bike store to grab some essential provisions. The owner took in the contrast of the pan-continental crossing advertised on our panniers with these two gaunt men, dressed in jeans, fleeces, woolly hats and gloves.

"You guys really come all the way from Seattle?"

"Of course. Now do you have any PowerBars?" asked Killer. "Oh, and some David Lube-now."

"Oh, I don't think they call it that," I reminded Killer.

The scenery started to look reassuringly, expectedly Floridian. Grassy wetlands to one side, duney beach to the other, flanked by colourful houses on stilts. As we went further, it became more urban with condo projects and building works, but these were always punctuated by the occasional lagoon or shady, tree-lined avenue or vast tracts of orange trees. And even the sea had suddenly, away from the estuary and the Mississippi, become blue. A gorgeous, encouraging blue. It was a blue that said, 'You're nearly there boys -

just don't screw it up in this last State.' We might well have been in our last state, but Miami was incredibly still 800 miles away.

Things continued on their positive trajectory the next day when we were finally reunited like merry fools with the life-giving canisters of cooking gas. After a three-mile bridge that rose into the sky once more, like at Dauphin, the roads approaching Pensacola - naturally renamed *Penis-cola* by Killer - started to frustrate us with heavy traffic, and then rain. We ducked into a gas station for coffee. We asked to borrow the phone directory with the hope it would help us to find a camping store, which piqued the interest of Double Dr John Penis, our first double Johnular encounter. They were vocally in both awe and confusion about our trip and insisted on telling everyone who walked into the store about it. The common response to this was always the same: "Man, you guys are crazy," they'd say, then shake their heads and walk off. Yeah, we've heard that a few times. And this was ironic because, by then, we had started to realise that - by nature of our riding bicycles - we might be the most sane ones around. Depressingly, we hadn't seen a single other person on a bike - not even a kid on a backstreet - for several weeks.

Drs John offered to drive us the eight miles to the camping store we'd found so we threw our bikes into the back of their Dodge pickup truck and Killer road along with them. The truck had two stickers on it, both of a cartoon man peeing - in one he was pissing on the word 'Ford'. In the other, he was pissing on the word 'ex-wife'. I sat in the cab fielding questions on England.

"You guys have different beer over there, right?"

I changed the subject immediately and we settled on Harley Davidsons - they assumed that if we were riding bikes then we enjoyed all two-wheeled forms of transportation.

Perhaps it was my giddy joy at finding the gas in the camping store, but I then also got lured into buying a 'compact travel towel'; a kind of lightweight, quick-drying squeegee for the body. My actual towel never seemed to dry and always smelled of damp. It had probably been cultivating small civilizations of bacteria for the past three months. The new towel was the sort of space age tech ze germans probably used. Or rather, it was probably the sort of very simple thing I should have bought in REI in Seattle, not on the home stretch.

"Why don't you treat yourself to some nice clip-in cycling shoes when we get to Miami," chirped Killer, mocking my late acceptance of professional equipment.

The gas was put to work on choodle that evening, and after a few weeks away from its soul-nourishing richness, the resulting thespionic contorted facial expressions performed as we displayed our appreciation for the flavours were worthy of a scene from Carmel.

"My sincere and Frederick Utter compliments to a most talented chef," beamed KIller.

It was also comfort food against the shock of extortionate camping prices. We had wondered if Florida might be able to topple California off the top spot of US States Top Trumps but not a chance. In California, we had enjoyed peaceful near-wilderness camping with simple facilities especially for bikers for $2. In Florida, even the state parks cost a small mortgage - making no differentiation between a simple tent and a family hotel on wheels - and they came complete with a suite of all-inclusive luxurious facilities we had no need for.

The first stop in Florida had been $17 and the second night was $28. I commented to Killer, "I neither want nor need a children's playground or a chilled coke machine or an electric multi-socket or a hot shower or a dump station - whatever the dump that is - or a boardwalk to a fishing pier or a wash area for my stinking fish guts. I just need two square metres of fairly even ground to put up a sodding tent and I will fuck off in the morning."

Instead, we rolled our eyes and paid, furious for not having found a free alternative, but it seemed every square inch of this land was occupied or fenced. We'd have to be more creative. As we chastised ourselves, two guys sided up to us. One stout, one skinny, both wearing matching oriental-styled silk dressing gowns that were unfastened, revealing black speedos beneath.

"Hello there. You two coming to the spa? No? Well you should pop by for burgers in our RV later. You'll be able to recognise it, it's the…"

"The one with the big satellite dish?" I suggested.

Had we really exhausted the playbook of the Americans? Burgers, RVs, speedos... It was Chris and Jus and James and Sharon all rolled into one. It was the same people in different forms. It was cyclical. We declined - we had already met these people before. Instead, we conserved our efforts at civility for the next day's super-hosts.

Aunt Valorie is my dad's half sister. Her husband is Uncle Howard. So of course, combined, they were 'Aunt Howard'. They emigrated from the UK to Canada in the 60s. Val was some sort of spy but the details are vague; any inquisition is met with a light chuckle. In retirement - and they were in their early 70s when we saw them - they left the freezing snows of Ottawa every winter and headed south to Florida for three months. In a sort of generational timeshare, they leave again just before the college kids invade the very same accommodations for the famously debauched Spring Break parties. As Killer observed, "It's a stroke of luck Aunt Howard are on our path, just a bloody shame their very presence indicates a profound absence of young sex parties in the vicinity."

The migration of these self-styled 'wrinklies' is so numerous that they even have their own collective noun, Snowbirds. But most importantly for us, Aunt Howard's winter HQ was directly on our route - a seaside motel outside the town of Panama City Beach, and they had booked us a room there for two nights. I had called them from the campsite to say that - given the 60 miles to get there and a large thunderstorm overhead - we would see them the next day.

"Nonsense, we'll see you later," said Howard. "There's a mini bar in your room with beer in it," he added by means of encouragement, "and you can't miss the motel - there's a big sign outside with your name on it."

I wasn't sure what that meant but it gave us something to look out for. We stopped a few times for hot chocolates, warm sustenance and to dry out. I imagined Ottawa must consist of one solid ice block if they felt this was worth escaping to. The coldness lingered. When the rain cleared, the sky remained dark and threatening, and yet this only framed and accentuated the beauty of the place - the sea had now turned an intoxicating other-worldly emerald, flicked by the white whisks of small waves. We rested at one point on the beach to just take it in and - devoid of any dogs larger than a handbag in these manicured towns - Killer chased seagulls with The Enforcer.

Eventually we spied our names. They were on a giant, 30 ft high board, in front of the motel. It was the kind of board that lights up and you can change the letters like outside an old-style cinema; presumably it was normally used to advertise key motel facilities to lure passing tourists. Howard had obviously given the proprietors a nice phrase to put up and they had kindly done this, but they had also left in the rest of a previous marketing message at the end. The result had a curious but very pleasing effect.

WELCOME
ADAM & NICK
BIKING USA
HOT TUB

Aunt Howard were generous, warm and wonderful. They took us for dinner, opting to eat at 5pm so we could benefit from the 'early bird specials'. It was a cheap and cheerful BBQ 'family restaurant' with American Football on a big screen TV and food served in mini plastic baskets. The waitresses were large-breasted women in low cut tops with smiles as broad as Mobile Bay. As the rest of the diners were also - entirely - discount-seeking seniors, presumably the waitresses made their tips from a later-arriving clientele, and yet they maintained a sincere enthusiasm.

"I hope you have a *wonderful* meal with us," our server declared.

I was surprised by the choice of restaurant, imagining Aunt Howard would find such scenes immensely tacky but, like us, they found something fascinating in it all. Val held me by the wrist and leaned in.

"Aren't these Americans so wonderfully eccentric," she said, chuckling.

I hadn't seen Val in a decade and was struck by how much she had now come to look like my grandmother - her mother. And she had inherited the same sharp wit. Spying Killer was wearing a cap at the table, she said calmly, "Oh, I think they fixed the roof dear. You can take that thing off."

The sun broke through the next day and Howard suggested we truly immerse ourselves in some quintessential Floridian activity. Golf. You may have already noticed but older people like to play golf, and there are a lot of older people in Florida. People aged over 60 make up around a quarter of the population of the state, and there are 1,250 golf courses there to cater for their needs. This of course means thousands and thousands of golf carts, which in many parts can be ridden on local roads. In fact, we saw far better infrastructure and signage for golf carts in Florida than we did for cycling. Golf has even imposed itself on the state costumery. There is a uniform that all old Floridians must wear at all times or face imprisonment, regardless of whether they intend to play a hole or not: pastel-coloured trousers, diamond-patterned sleeveless jumpers, flat caps, white shoes, walnut-hued skin.

We saw many of these identi-retirees at the driving range where we blasted balls as far as we could, enjoying the stretch in parts of our bodies that had been untroubled by the millions of pedal rotations. Afterwards, Aunt Howard drove us along the route we were to cycle the next day through Panama City Beach itself so we could orientate ourselves. Killer and I found this painful - the journey was long and we hated the idea of having to travel back along a road we were already familiar with but at a much slower pace. No doubt, they didn't enjoy it either, but they took us out of kindness and we were grateful for that. How funny, I thought, that none of us want to do this but we are all going along as we want to be polite. Better for no one to enjoy it and to give each other the happiness of having felt they had done a good deed than for any one of us to protest. How very British we still all are.

As we waved Aunt Howard off the next day, I watched the large motel sign drift away in my mirror. I liked its simple descriptor of our trip, 'Biking USA'. It was exactly what we were doing. We were often referred to as 'cyclists' or, more often, as 'two fucking crazy cyclists', but even after 4,000 miles we still didn't feel this was accurate. I've used the word extensively in this book as a shorthand for anyone on a bike but you might as well label us for any one of our daily activities; calling us breathers, or farters (well, maybe there was a case for that one given our near professionalism of it…) Why was cycling singled out semantically, as if we were fused with the machines to form a new, distinct species, Homo Pedalus? The label 'cyclists' made all those who enjoy riding a bike sound either like professionals or activists, rather than just normal people doing normal things. As far as we were concerned, we were just two guys on a journey, and we were doing this on bikes. We were 'biking the USA' and the emphasis should not be on classifying *us* but on normalising our activity, shining the spotlight on the humble bicycle that carried us forward and connected us to what we passed through. The bicycle broke down barriers and allowed us to get closer to the country and its people. Biking is the great leveller. It forces us to meet each other as equals. In that regard, it's like sitting in a hot tub, I guess. Perhaps 'Biking USA Hot Tub' - the extended descriptor on the motel sign - summed it all up perfectly, actually.

And perhaps we had finally cracked this biking malarkey as we started to turn the corner of the panhandle and head south, getting closer to the finish line. I can only describe the next phase of cycling as 'colossal'. We would cover the final 720 miles without taking a single day off, averaging around 60 miles (100 km) a day in the final two weeks. The next four nights specifically each consisted of free camps in the most exquisite of locations, with us gathering foul odours and cakes of grundle lube happily as we went.

The first camp was on a pocket of deserted beach, hidden behind a small dune. The sea was only a few metres away from the long grass but it was calm. We noted the high tide line from a scratch of shells and seaweed and pitched our tents on the sand above it. The two green tents nestled there looked staged, as if for their own brochure. Or maybe that would be the picture used to advertise choodle; a promise of a peaceful but heroic lifestyle with every dish. Mmmmm. I considered this dreamily and the potential world domination we were about to unleash on the, er, world when we brought our discovery back from the Americas like Sir Walter 'smoking' Raleigh, or Sir Francis 'dysentery' Drake. I role-played my pitch to the Queen. She chokes a little and holds a hand to her mouth, then puts the bowl down for the corgis. "A little too much *Badass Bitches* hot sauce, Ma'am?"

Sleep was deep, rocked off by the gentlest of gently lapping waves. I could have recorded the noise and sold it as a hypno sleeping tape. As it was, the sound inspired lucid water-themed dreams for both Killer and I. Infuriatingly, he dreamt that he drank champagne in a bubble bath with Beyoncé and then made passionate love to her. Whereas I dreamt that a killer whale (a metaphor for my companion?) beached itself purposefully to steal my jerky and then flapped back into the sea. But at least it had the decency to say sorry.

The cloudless night was cold and in the morning we brushed a thick cake of ice from the tent. The sunrise was all soft pinks and blues, reflected perfectly in the pond-still sea. As Killer stood ankle-deep, washing the pans in the salt water, he was mirrored perfectly. It was like he was reaching out to hold hands with himself in another world. How was this place free and the shithole with the fish guts and RVs and loud speedophiles cost a week's supply of choodle? Well, it's true what they say about the best things in life.

We pulled the same voodooish magic trick again that night. We followed the 98 round the coast, passing a cop car parked next to a phone box that had a sign painted on it saying 'World's smallest police station'. It was the first time I had seen anything in America celebrated for being small. We then ducked off onto a quiet road flanked by beachside properties and land plots, we noticed many had 'For sale' signs in the yard. It was perhaps a new development alongside this until-recently untouched stretch of American coastline. More mudflats than sand here. We found one plot that hadn't been built on yet, just boggy ground in a wooded area, with a boardwalk extending through the reedbeds about 20 feet to sea to allow for docking in the deeper water. It was the last unclaimed slice of wilderness and we sat with our feet in the warm sea, waiting for the sun to go down. We pitched up in the blackness of the tree canopy, and read in our beds. It was then I noticed in small letters on the map that we were at, what was it, ah yes, 'Alligator Point'.

Surprised to wake up alive the next morning, we set our sights for the third free camp on a riverside 'rest area' marked on the map. There, we found yet another idyll; a quiet spot consisting of a picnic bench next to a bend in a narrow, dark river, all backdropped by a wall of moss-draped trees. It looked like the land that time forgot. A small group of guys working for a government water test centre had all sorts of apparatus out, taking samples from the stream. They seemed almost Californian with their plaid shirts, neat beards and big smiles. They knew why we were hanging around, waiting for dark, but didn't seem to mind, even if it did mean their water quality readings would probably be inaccurate in a few hours. Instead, they chatted to us about our route and imparted some wise, Dr Johnular, advice.

We'd well and truly left the ACA route behind at Penis-cola. It was heading further east, destined to hit the coast in the north of the state at St Augustine, but we needed to go south to reach Miami. So we had started making our own route each day using local road maps, not really knowing what was best from the entanglement of options we were presented with. And so advice from locals to steer our general approach in this huge state was invaluable. With the help of the water testers we started to sketch some provisional checkpoints to the checkered flag: we would stay closer to the west coast as we headed down through Florida to avoid the worst of the traffic, just looping inland a couple of times to avoid the Disneys and other big tourist attractions. Then we would cut straight across to Miami through the Everglades. It was a rough outline of a route and that was all we needed to get hugely excited about the final experiences ahead.

The relaxed nature of the route was echoed across our general approach to the ride. The self-inflicted stress of El Paso and the days before Austin had totally given way to a confident ease. Not every day was easy cycling necessarily, but it was all enjoyed rather than examined. We stopped interrogating our progress, and just felt happy with the very art of riding a bike every day. We were not worried about our camp being discovered, or really of wild animals. We were just going through our daily motions. Camping, cycling, laughing, living. There didn't seem to be anything else.

This unexpected retreat from stress made for stronger, faster cycling. My knee was not cured but I also did not notice it. My cycling computer / speedometer thingy had completely given up and so I no longer obsessively looked as the miles rolled over. For a while I used my watch to make estimates on the passing miles but eventually I just let the time pass. At one point I was cycling along, listening to the Rolling Stones on my Archos brick and I realised I just had a big smile on my face, a feeling of total contentment. *'You can't always get what you want, but if you try sometime you find you get what you need'*. It was one of the moments when you just feel everything is and will be alright.

Maybe it was the weather too though. The sun was out and it had warmed to be like late spring in the UK, meaning it would be shortage and shirtage all the way to Miami. The roads were fairly flat and not too heavy with traffic outside the towns. A pattern of long days punctuated with breaks every 20 miles or so (as identified by Killer's computer) at gas stations was to become the routine for Florida. It was efficient and cheap, giving us more time in the day to make the sort of side trips Kirkendall would have been proud of, or to pause in one of the state's many lush, verdant pockets of wildlife. And, of course, it gave us plenty more opportunity to examine the last cohort of Americans.

Even though many of the conversations were loud and senseless, at least the Floridians welcomed us and engaged with us, some actually taking an interest in the journey and the decision to ride bikes rather than drive a big car. Not everyone told us we were going the wrong way and then laughed loudly. Killer and I considered the fate of an American if the roles were reversed. He'd be sitting alone, confounded, on the forecourt of a BP garage, drinking a coffee, devoid of any company. He'd occasionally offer a friendly wave to the people trying to avoid eye contact and rushing past him to the safety of the shop. "Don't look at him dear, he might try and talk to you."

At the gas station at the end of the fourth day past Aunt Howard, we saw our new friend Rehab. We'd named him this as he had the look of someone who had been enjoying various forms of alcoholic and drug stimulation for many years. For three days we had leapfrogged him as he hitchhiked beside the road, including passing him twice in one day. Every sighting produced a euphoric cheer from us, but seeing him one last time so close up was too much and we couldn't hide our delight. We pointed and laughed, only a few metres away from him. But Rehab also seemed pleased to see us and pressed himself into our faces.

"Did you know you are standing by one of the most beautiful spots in Florida?" he asked, bouncing happily at the thought. "You are at the Suwannee River. You must have heard of it, heard the song, right? No? NOOOO??"

Rehab then broke into said song, throwing his arms out like he was performing a Rodgers and Hammerstein number, thus exposing the full trampishness of his attire.

Way down upon the Suwannee River
Far, Far Away
That's where my heart is yearning

After he'd caused himself to almost well up with the beauty of his own voice, he asked us where we were from.

"The UK? Well I'll be. I got relatives from Germany! Anyway, gotta go." He looked around, almost to check he hadn't been followed, then hobbled away.

"Totally standard gas station conversation," I concluded to Killer.

We were down upon the Suwannee River because we were trying to find a spot to free camp after an epic 80-mile day. And we were specifically hanging out at that gas station as it was near the entrance to the state park we intended to camp in. As it was a day-use park only, we were waiting for the ranger to lock up and go home so we could sneak back in and pitch up. But he was taking forever and it was already dark. So, instead, we settled on the field opposite. We couldn't make anything out in the dark, but we threaded our way to the far end of the field until we found the riverbank and set up camp. We had no idea what was around us but we became more excited the further we moved out of our comfort zone.

Our mental wellbeing was being charged with every day that we pushed ourselves further. But we were also finally giving our *bodies* more opportunity to grow. Whilst we still enjoyed the daily choodle, penis tortillas, occasional Snickers and gallons of coffee, we had also started to introduce some beneficial ingredients to our diet. I took the occasional vegetable juice drink, we selected 'Good for You' labelled foods when we saw them in the store, and it reached the point where we became those people that turn supermarket tins in their hands to check the nutritional makeup on the reverse of the label, even if we weren't sure what to look for.

"Oh look Killer - let's try this one, it only has 2g of fat but 17g of protein. Oh and it's low in salt. Wait, it's high in fiber, is that good?"

"Well done Bone. If only Greve could see us now."

"Yes, but we aren't going to ever be kale people though, right?"

"Well we can't. We don't even know what it is. It might be a sex toy for all I know. Greve's sex toy. Yes, that's actually probably what it is. Damn near breaks my heart."

We were still pretty clueless but we were trying. In fact our most frequent 'healthy' meals were still Subway rolls, loaded with extra salad, and we felt our bodies sigh with contentment as they got drunk on the vitamins, enjoying some rest from processed beef. But why oh why had we waited over 4,000 miles before we attempted to even vaguely resemble the 'cyclists' people said we were?

16. Race across the Everglades

***Ride as much, or as little,
or as long, or as short as you feel.
But ride.***
Eddy Merckx

Before the final push, we set our sights on one last motel, to refresh and prepare for a week of fast riding and wildlife pursuing. We felt you always knew where you were with a motel - across the country they had had the same layout, the same peeling wallpaper, the same shitty bathrooms and small wobbly side tables, and the big TVs were always pressed right up to the foot of the bed. They even all had the same proprietor; an errant, maudlin soul with skeletons in the closet, as well as the basement. Staying in a motel was a constant, in our ever-changing daily expedition. Or so we thought. Near Homosassa Springs, we stumbled into a motel that doubled as a Christian bookshop.

Just like being forced through the duty free selection of alcohol and perfumes at the airport to lure your interest before you can get to the lounge, here you had to navigate the tightly packed and meandering bookshop before you could check in for the motel at the cash desk. And it wasn't just books - I had never seen so many images and effigies of Jesus and Mary, and in so many forms - wood, porcelain and, wait, was that a woolly Jesus? The manager was a skinny, pale man in his 30s. Black greasy combed-back hair, it's darkness accentuating the pockmarked whiteness of his face, and a beige polyester shirt that stuck in sweat patches to his rake-like chest. His wife stood beside him almost motionless with a mute, vacant look in her eyes. She must've still been in her teens and wore a virginal white cotton gown. The man noticed my confused look when a third woman - someone who looked like the picture dictionary definition of 'prostitute' - sauntered past them in hot pants and into their bedroom.

"I let her sleep in our room 'cos I know what it feels like to be homeless and kicked off *the program*."

I tried not to let my face reveal the layers of intrigue he had exposed.

Thankfully, he continued, "Of course, my experience of, ahem, drugs was all before I found... *The Lord*." He said this as he slid a magazine to us on the desk, with a headline that read 'Your path to heaven.' Killer picked it up and started flicking through.

His wife now nodded. She wanted to join the conversation and didn't care how.

"I like English films," she said.

They then took turns to talk at us in a way that suggested they were playing a comedy quiz show where you had to try and say something totally disconnected to your teammate or you lose a point - him telling me how the Lord saved him from destitution and her uttering whatever European flavoured thought found its way to her mouth.

"I'm afraid we ran out of tea," she concluded.

Killer couldn't handle this any longer. "I think I've read this one," he said, pushing the magazine back across the counter, "Can we take the keys now?"

We were at Homosassa Springs for a different type of creature though, the marvellous manatee. We had planned to see them at the famed King's Spring, but had overshot it on the wrong road the day before. As our only navigational aid was the entire Florida road system compressed onto one sheet of A3, it was no surprise that we did get lost a few times in those final weeks. But as Brian wisely counselled us, "Maybe *you* are not lost, maybe *the places* you seek are the ones that are in the wrong place." We had been advised that King's Spring was one of the most magical places in the whole of Florida. It must have been incredible because our substitute stop at Homosassa Springs was breathtaking.

The water was cool and clear, showing off the thick grasses that swayed in the soft current. The clearing was wide, fringed with tall moss-laden trees. We had hoped to be able to swim with the manatees there but a sign ruled it out. "No swimming here - head north to King's". Ho hum. But just watching the creatures was something magical. At one end of the park, there was a submerged viewing area with a large glass wall where you could watch the manatees, lured in for us tourists by some food handouts from the rangers.

They looked like sleek, finned cows but glided through the water like otters. Their faces were crumpled up like pugs but their bodies were as much as four metres long. They were colossal and yet you got the sense they could not hurt a spider. They held their leafy food between their prehensile front flippers as they swam and nestled into each other like loving friends. They were intelligent, beautiful and perfectly evolved for this habitat, and yet they were highly endangered.

Many of the manatees had long deep grooves along their backs, the signs of boat propellers that had cut them from above. This (which accounts for a quarter of all manatee deaths), added to extensive habitat degradation or removal for condos, and other new century problems, meant manatees were on the critical list; more candidates for extinction. In this way, the fated manatee is following the same course that many other megafauna species have since man arrived in North America. Even here at Homosassa, in the 'wild', they survive because they are protected, cared for, monitored.

"At what point," I asked Killer, "do we humans say, 'OK, we nearly killed them all now, so we'd better stop that and start protecting the few that are left as it wouldn't be right to kill *all* of them'?"

"I think we tend to say that just before we then kill *all* of them."

Looking at nature is one of the most arresting experiences of being human - you explode both with the miracle of what is there now and the tragedy of what will no longer be. I realised that I was looking more intensely at the manatee - the way it moved, ate, and played - because of its tragic population. Why wait to respect nature until it is exclusive? I vowed to go and spend some time staring at cows in fields as soon as I could.

Of all the nature at the park though, the Americans remained amongst the most fascinating.

"Look honey - they're feeding the manatees romaine lettuce. See, that's romaine. Not just any old lettuce, honey. Romaaaaaaaaine."

What is romaine lettuce? Is it like kale? Many of the Americans at the springs were retirees. They were dressed in the state uniform and talking at the prescribed extreme volume. I managed to keep several of them at bay - and secure a front row view of the manatees - given my intense gas. The devilish aromas had only intensified with the reintroduction of choodle and it hung around me, creating a pleasantly private exclusion zone. But one old man had obviously lost his sense of smell, as he sided up to me, curious.

"Have you seen the deer?" he shouted at me, searchingly.

"I've only just got here," I replied shortly, hoping that would end the matter.

"But have you *seen* the deer?"

"No. I *just* got here."

"I haven't seen any deer at all."

"OK."

Were there even any deer here ever? Weren't we all here for the manatees? I turned and left. The man then approached someone who appeared to be more on his wavelength.

"No. I've not seen any deer either. Isn't that odd! But did you see they feed the manatees romaine lettuce?"

We spent the next two nights camping in the woods, the first a little beyond Homosassa, the second by the town of Providence. Florida may have been the Sunshine state but it was also the most humid. Forget the unpleasantness of the delta, Floridian woodland humidity is hell. Choodle was cooked in the tent to avoid the biblical plague of mosquitoes, whilst being totally naked to avoid the plague of heat. Even a quick unzipping to pass the hot sauce was an open door to extreme insect activity. So, at Providence, we even attempted to play Shithead without seeing each other, just whispering out cards and imagining who was winning. I lay back and celebrated my victory by repeatedly squirting water onto my face.

When the weather broke in the morning it was a blessed release but as the storm grew closer it took on the volume of the Book of Revelation. The storm moved directly overhead, the flashes and colossal bangs occurring at precisely the same time. It was like being a lost moth in a firework display, and with every explosion a little cry of 'shit' was let out by Killer or myself.

"What's that saying about being under a tree in a lightning storm, Bone? It's the best place to hide right?"

I took the opportunity of being a prisoner in my own tent to revisit the inventory of the load I had catalogued at San Diego. Whilst I was now powering along, the Muirwood had taken over the role of letting out small, complaining groans. I noted I was carrying no fewer than five books. Five books!! On a transcontinental ride where we had once burned beloved belongings to ensure every ounce performed an essential service, I was carrying five books. I was obviously doped by a swelling confidence that I could complete the challenge whilst doubling as a mobile library. And that was only part of my hoarding.

The list I had noted before we left the west coast now also included:

- newspapers (plural)
- the travel towel (whilst also still carrying the regular towel)
- many many muesli bars (for constant snackage)
- road maps
- CDs (gifts from Wendy. I didn't even have a CD player with me)
- a small portable radio (a belated Christmas present to myself from N'awlins that I never actually used)
- more postcards
- more gas canisters
- more spare inner tubes
- a knee brace
- cap gun + ammunition
- my old diaries
- a salt shaker
- three different types of hot sauce

As the sound of the storm moved away, we packed up. The delay meant we were not on the road until after 11am, so we continued our fast pace. As the route snaked a little inland to bypass the big coastal towns, we were left with the shitty satellites and suburbs that stretched between Tampa and Orlando. They were the old prefabricated or identikit dense sprawl that was an ongoing point of contention for me with suburban America. The traffic was heavy and fast paced. In turn, this urged us to cycle faster ourselves, to try and get through to the other side safely as quickly as possible.

At one gas station stop, Rehab's doppleganger (causing us to add 'Rehab' to the Limepedia system) walked past us and shouted, "Welcome to Dade City - the fucking dead zone." But he could have been talking about any number of these towns. Lakeland was worse - we / it got lost there as its knot of identical blandness was not sufficiently captured on our map and we were forced to tack several miles East to rejoin Route 98. The connecting road was narrow, shoulderless and swollen with traffic. Twice, I was edged off onto the verge by an eager truck, resulting in excessive sweating and colourful shouting. At times, you'd see glass, rocks, potholes or sunken drains approaching but would have nowhere to go to avoid them - hold your line, brace and ride them out or face the possibility of being run over if you swerved. At one point I rode over a long nail attached to a metal base. I slowed to assess the inevitable tyre exhalation but bizarrely the nail was wedged so tight into the rubber that no air came out and I cycled on, deciding not to stop to change it until the evening. Old Silver City Mike would not have been happy with me but the result was a pleasing percussive 'clip' sound on the tarmac, and I sang along to its metronomic rhythm, slightly rearranging some Willie Nelson.

> *On the road again*
> *Goin' places that I've never been*
> *Seein' things that I hope to NEVER see again*

Often, a pleasing name was the only saving grace for these towns. Florida wasn't quite Texas when it came to its collection of places named by drunks throwing darts at a dictionary but it held its ground - Treasure Island, Hill n' Dale, Town 'n Country, Yellow Jacket, Spuds, Mango. Yep, these towns can all be found in Florida, where you'll also discover Six Mile Bend, a town that must suffer a huge inferiority complex given its proximity to its slightly boastful neighbour, Twenty Mile Bend.

And on one occasion, a bizarre marketing promotion for a convenience store was enough to give the town character, albeit a highly freaky one. On the side of a huge lorry, there was a photo of a young girl's face, looking happy and a little coy - I guess it was supposed to suggest innocence but it came across as creepy child sexualisation. Beside her, the message read in massive script-like font: *'Please shop at Cash's. I'm 14 years old and daddy really needs the business!'* We cycled quite fast out of that town.

Finding free camps in the woods between these towns was also a battle in itself. As we moved south through the state, the opportunity to move unnoticed into wild places was increasingly limited. We tried again for a third night but at one opportune opening, we found hundreds of migrant labourers sitting beside the road, after a long day attending to the citrus crops, waiting for their ride back to the shared worker camps. At another, we found a chain gang, weeding and tidying the roadside as if they had been expecting us the next day instead and were preparing the way. I thought chain gangs were something that only resided in history books and Laurel and Hardy movies but here was the line of hard cases in orange jumpsuits toiling by the side of the road as the guard walked between them. They all turned as we cycled past and we gave them a merry wave and rang our bells, although for some reason they didn't seem to appreciate this.

"Send them to Alcatraz," said Killer to the guard. They liked that even less.

We pressed on into the night. There followed another ten miles along a road worse than at Lakeland, although now with the added fun of being in the dark. Our puny bike lights proved as effective as matches at lighting our way - and lighting up our presence - and we were again edged into the verge. It was ghastly. I wrote in my diary, 'The horror, the horror.'

Perhaps it was stress or the sun - or more likely one too many gas station coffees - but having started the day in a storm with simply a vocal expression of 'shit' the day ended with a physical one. I lost my last pair of cycling shorts, as well as my outer, grey, zip-legged shorts, to a violent pantual eruption moments after we pulled into the campsite at Wauchula. I was forced to ride the rest of the trip in my yellow swimming shorts and yellow Tour de France jersey, both with dark patches of dirt and road wear. I looked like a skinny, overripe banana. The horror, the horror.

Having only used the camp toilet facilities - albeit quite extensively - and only having stayed for a few short hours of darkness, we decided to do a runner the next day and set off at first light. We did feel bad about not paying but we also had little money

354

left and Miami in our sights, and we didn't care for the idea of effectively spending $20 on toilet roll. A few miles into the day and a sheriff's car slowed as it passed us and we feared we had been rumbled. *"I've been hunting you sons of bitches since Pelican Point. Now, which one of you is Sterneyperkel?"* But they moved on.

I was enjoying the opportunity and ability to push harder. The roads were still shoulderless and stressful but it felt right that the challenge should build as we neared the end, and I layered onto the forced demands of the road a self-imposed challenge of a high pace. The speed was incredible. I wanted to feel my legs burn, to wheeze breathlessly, I wanted to exhaust myself and collapse onto the beach at Miami. My body felt it could do anything and my mind was starting to feel the same. The faster we went, the faster I felt we could go. The next day we cycled 70 miles and I felt I could easily have done another 30.

"Where is Bone getting this magical power from?" asked Killer.

"The Limey Project is now powering The Limey Project," I concluded mystically.

Perhaps the effort was helping to chase the thoughts from my head. Passing Punta Gorda - after a two mile bridge over the Peace River - a girl in a cafe laughed at the way I said 'tomato' and I started to think about home. This will be over soon. This amazing challenge; four months, the lows, the incredible highs. What have I learned? How do I use this? What's next in life? Every day's diary entry notes my busy mind. *Enough*, I said. I'll deal with this when I get to Miami.

We sped through built-up streets, lined with miles of roadworks, dodging trucks and traffic cones, but somehow with no stress. The city of Naples - like its namesake, the armpit of Italy - teemed with traffic. The huge three-lane highway we had to travel down was flanked on each side by car lots, motels, advertising billboards, and fast food chains selling themselves as 'family restaurants'. But places like this were now familiar enough that they could be dealt with swiftly - they were like the end of level baddies in a video game you've played a hundred times; you know how to beat them to get to the next stage. It's a formality, especially when the weather was this glorious - blue skies, warm. We'd survive this, then turn left to take the scenic Route 41 that cut across the Everglades like a victory procession into Miami.

The gas station continued to be our greatest friend and the Floridians we met there were warm and welcoming, demonstrating the still-confusing but now-pleasing American ability to chat away openly and loudly to strangers. They were also generous - people pressed dollars into our hands at every stop and we ended the day $90 up in donations. Dr John Naples even gave us both cold bottles of Gatorade, handing them to us as if he was our trainer in a boxing ring between rounds.

"You'll need this to get through this city," he said with a slap on the shoulder.

We were familiar with the restorative and energising effects of this unnaturally flavoured and radioactively coloured beverage (maybe it contains manganese?) but these bottles were slightly different, having a small grip pattern shaped into the plastic. It was a simple change to the shape of the mould but the Americans couldn't resist turning this minute - totally functionless - design adaptation into a massive marketing story. A label explained it all:

WHY THIS UNIQUE GRIP?
The innovative bottle
design maximizes
function and flow for
enhanced rehydration.

Another local - leaning out of a camper van - warned us the road ahead still had a few surprises in store for us. He looked and sounded like Otto from *The Simpsons*; a gravelly voice with a super chilled attitude.

"Wooah, dude. You heading to Miami on the 41? Well if the 'gators don't get ya then the bugs will. Woahhh. If you are still travelling at like 5 o' clock, pull over dudes 'cos the bugs man - woahhhh - the bugs."

He then mimed an action that looked like having your face melted away, before breaking into a smile and making the bull sign with his fingers.

"Anyway, take it easy dudes."

Naples was typical of Florida in that the people we encountered across the state were at the extremes - mad ravers who had never left their neighbourhood, calm creative dreamers, younger people who wanted to change it all, older conservatives who wanted to change nothing, rich white people in golf carts, poor black people on park benches. In many ways, they reflected the divided character of the whole country. But more than that - they were also ultimately responsible for the precise nature of the country we had discovered over the past four months. It was in Florida that the Presidential race between Bush and Gore was decided in 2000. With the rest of the Electoral College votes in and tied, it came down to who would win here. There are 21 million people in Florida. In the end, Bush won by 327 votes. With more than 9,000 ballots not eligible for computer counting, Gore sought a manual recount but was denied. So despite Gore having half a million more popular votes across the country, Bush became the 43rd President. Surely such an injustice would never be repeated for the Democrats, we all thought.

Our last week of cycling started on the Monday with Martin Luther King Jr Day, a national day to celebrate racial equality across the nation. The very next day it was Bush's State of the Union address, in which he mentioned nothing of civil rights, but instead spoke of America as if already a land of equals, and that every one of its people were united in a common, higher purpose. Did they all know this? We watched snippets play out on TV in a campsite bar the next night at Everglades City.

America, this evening, is a nation called to great responsibilities. And we are rising to meet them… hundreds of thousands of American service men and women are deployed across the world in the War on Terror. By bringing hope to the oppressed and delivering justice to the violent, they are making America more secure… Our greatest responsibility is the active defense of the American people… After the chaos and carnage of September the 11th, it is not enough to serve our enemies with legal papers. The terrorists and their supporters declared war on the United States. And war is what they got… Had we failed to act, the dictator's weapons of mass destruction programs would continue to this day… We have no desire to dominate, no ambitions of empire. Our aim is a democratic peace, a peace founded upon the dignity and rights of every man and woman…The cause we serve is right, because it is the cause of all mankind... The momentum of freedom in our world is unmistakable. And it is not carried forward by our power alone. We can trust in that greater power who guides the unfolding of the years. And in all that is to come, we can know that His purposes are just and true. May God continue to bless America.

The barman turned off the TV and turned on the stereo. The sounds of Van Morrison played out as wondrous pelicans lazed in the lagoon outside.

"Funny that Bush should mention those weapons in his holy war speech," said Killer. "I mean, Saddam can't make any more now, sure, but I don't think they found any old ones yet either, did they?"

"True, but maybe we can be of some assistance there."

Killer and I played Patriot Points one final time. After I traded in my expert knowledge on everything from the Alamo to Armadillos for five virtual Patriot missiles, I fired them into every corner of the campsite, convinced I would locate Saddam's WMDs under my can of Tecate. Perhaps unsurprisingly, though, the weapons were nowhere to be found.

We had made it through the towns and cities, had turned to head east and had found the state's incredible wild nature as we raced the long, straight line to Miami. One of the most interesting Americans we met on this final push was Floyd Walker Jr. We had nearly arrived at the destination for the next day, a park we had been told about by Dr John Naples - the Collier Seminole State Park - when we saw a roadside bar and decided to toast our progress. The bar was in a woodland clearing and Floyd was alone in propping it up. He welcomed us in and before we had sat down he ordered us two cold beers. He was quiet and mild mannered, but talked with the eagerness of someone who had been waiting for some time for companionship and conversation. He moved easily from American politics - "Relax, we're not all Bush-worshipping weirdos" - to theories of Atlantis.

Floyd was a builder and handyman but longed to be a writer. As we left, he pressed a large folded piece of paper into my hands - on it was printed a poem he had written about the Everglades. His family's land here had been compulsorily purchased from his grandparents in the 50s and given over to industry. The pristine land was destroyed and chemicals now ran off into watercourses once enjoyed by panthers and manatees. It was a disaster story he was still trying to understand and an ongoing environmental issue he wanted to draw attention to. The poem was called *Last of the Free*. It wasn't Shakespeare - or even Stonegarth - but the writing was honest, and moving. As we neared Miami, I liked the way it concluded:

> *Careful what you wish for*
> *But don't shy from your dreams*
> *Never trade life's juices*
> *For life's boundaries*

We had stopped at the State Park so we could take a canoe out in the morning and explore 7,000 acres of swamps and flooded forests. We paddled slowly for two hours, the only humans out there on the still, black water. The canoe glided silently through a maze of mangroves. We saw countless birds - herons, egrets, vultures, ibis, storks, and hawks. This was a place of life's juices.

We pushed on, along the 41. At times it cut through vast open grasslands, sometimes alongside canals and through woods. On the banks of every water course we spotted alligators. Their black bodies motionless, soaking up the still dazzling winter sun. In the bushes and trees, sat scores of birds which rose up like a wind when we approached and passed. We stopped at the Big Bend Boardwalk, where - as you might expect - a boardwalk led you on a big, bendy path into the swampy woods. This was not just a wildlife sanctuary but also - it seemed - a wildlife nursery. Juvenile alligators lazed on logs and, at the top of a tall tree, a bald eagle attended to its chicks.

"Remarkable," I kept repeating to Killer, having not anticipated such bounties could exist on the doorstep of Florida's other attractions. "Why would anyone go to Disneyland when you can get the biggest smile of your life a few miles south in the Everglades?"

"Well, the animals do at least talk to you at Disneyland," Killer suggested.

"Where have you been for the past four and a half thousand miles? They talk on The Limey Project."

Killer let oh a small "huh" of realisation. "So they do."

As we walked along the big bend, we were stopped a few times by people who had seen the writing on our panniers. By now we had learned we needed to leave extra time at each break for extended Q&A sessions on the trip. But we were happy to do this - there was something easy and excited in the questioning in Florida that we hadn't experienced since the west coast; maybe there was a more open friendliness here or perhaps it was simply that a massively long trip is infinitely more interesting to others when you are either embarking or preparing to conclude it. Either way, they wanted to know eeeeeeverything and, invariably, the most ambitious in their probing were the retired, pastel-pantalooned people. Their interest charged us, although I did think to myself, 'If this is a wildlife reserve, why is everyone talking so freakishly loudly?'

"LOOK DONALD - I CAN SEE ONE THERE. THERE. NO THERE…. NO. NO THERE. ohjesusdonald. THEEEEEERE. Oh, it's gone."

Perhaps the creatures of the Everglades were used to the noise though. We were constantly passing adverts for airboat tours. These vehicles resemble a sort of wide surfboard with a jumbo jet engine mounted on the rear. They blast at high speed and even higher decibellage through the watery lands like a mobile wildlife torture device.

Thankfully, these were banned in some areas, including at our target for the next day, another nature area, called Shark Valley; a curious name for a place that was not only flat but also devoid of selachimorpha[11]. It was 40 miles there and we raced it, with just one 15 minute break half way. On the penultimate day, I wanted to push my legs to their max. Somehow, they have survived this far, so surely they were capable of more. As I saw Killer slip away in my rearview mirror I wondered unreasonably why he hadn't had the same thought.

We made it for the lunchtime two-hour Shark Valley tram tour. In an extension of the site's frivolous naming policy, the 'tram' was an open sided bus that us and about 30 other tourists climbed onto. It looped for 15 miles, the guide pausing and pointing, explaining and elaborating. I had already fallen deeply in love with the beauty of the Everglades, but here - surrounded by it on all sides - it was mesmerizing. From a viewing tower halfway along the tour, we looked out and all we saw was water, grass, birds and alligators.

The Everglades is 60 miles wide and 100 miles long. Given the scale, many people think of it as just a large stretch of flooded grasslands, but it is actually one massive, shallow river, moving at a quarter of a mile per hour. It's an incredibly delicate ecosystem and

---

[11] Do I really have to explain? Come on.

the only one of its kind in the world, but the effects of Florida's booming population are pushing it to crisis point, and what you see today is just a small taster of what it once was. It must have been amazing here in Floyd's grandparents' day, with an Audubundance of birds; everything living in balance. We have to protect these places while we still can.

Whenever the bus paused, we would walk around, passing right by the incredible alligators. They mostly lay still but when I got within arm's length of a giant 15 footer, it opened its mouth and hissed at me, as if to suggest it would easily take said arm if I got any closer. I jumped back and nearly lost another pair of shorts.

"Careful Bone - that is a *genuine* alligator, not some friend of Larry's."

I had assumed all alligators were friends of Larry, or at least of Brian. Either way, in the gift shop I found a small, rubber, replica Larry with legs that could bend around to grasp things. I placed him up on my handlebars so he could have a view of the road ahead and engage in conversation with hostile creatures if needed. He spoke to me again in his reassuringly curious accent. I knew he wasn't the *real* Larry, of course. This was a mere vessel. I'm not stupid.

We estimated that free camping in the Everglades was an adventure sport best not attempted so close to victory but the temptation offered by a quiet spot a few miles west of Shark Valley was too much. As we waited for it to get dark enough for us to set up the tents in secret, a cop car pulled up. He knew our game.

"Best not do that boys. The 'gators are hungry tonight. There's a genuine campsite five miles down that side road."

I contemplated telling him that it was all OK given our small green companion but decided to heed his advice. It was by now pitch black and our torches could hardly penetrate it. We cycled fast. We discovered that Otto was right about the bugs. They hit us squarely in the face - huge clouds of them. We spat them from our mouths as we peddled on, bouncing out of potholes, past hidden hisses. It was a very long, sweaty five miles.

The last camp, the last choodle, the last late night conversations with Brian. The last unzip of the tent to smell the morning air. The last breakfast coffee made with water boiled on a gas stove and then poured into a clanging metal camping mug. The last shaking out the shoes to check snakes and spiders hadn't taken up residence overnight. I'll miss this. I'll miss these sounds, these simple actions, this simple, peaceful existence, I thought. Soon, we'd be back in the world that we saw on the news, a less pleasant place indeed.

Lured on by the checkered flag, we raced the final 60 miles. Through gradually densing urban landscapes, we rode fast, stopping just once for coffee and snacks. We threaded our way through the streets of Miami, dodging cars that came from all angles. We kept heading east, pushing our way ahead. Over the Venetian Causeway, we crossed the long lagoon that separates the city from Miami Beach, then down Lincoln Road, across Collins Avenue, down a narrow path, and then there it was, the Atlantic Ocean opened up in front of us.

The tyres hit the sand.

17. Welcome to Miami

Someday soon this will all be someone else's dream.
Take That

In that moment, months of anticipation, planning, work, joy, gas, ass chafing, darkness, light, and millions of pedal rotations came to an end. And yet, it felt strangely normal, like another stop. There was the feeling, of course, of 'Yes, we did it, we bloody did it' and we grabbed fists of sand and threw them into the air, but there was no exodus of tears or final illumination. Not immediately. Instead, the initial normalness of being in Miami provided a kind of profound realisation in itself. Before we left Seattle, the idea of this trip was unfathomable, overwhelming in fact, but arriving in Miami felt so natural. We had cycled for 4,500 miles, pushed on through the pain, and over the last three and a half weeks we had averaged over 60 miles a day and paused for only one day off the bikes. The me that left Seattle would have found the achievement extraordinary, the me that arrived in Miami found it perfectly in line with the new expectations I had of myself.

The feeling of finality, that we had actually completed the challenge and could start to make sense of it, came in stages, in the various events that unfolded over the next few days, and through the conversations we had as we waited for our flight home. The first came as we cycled to find the nearest bar, and we passed in front of the Miami Convention Centre. Inside, the entire Limenagerie were having a convention to network and discuss their involvement in The Limey Project and to celebrate our arrival. Larry the Lizard, Bernard the Bull, Mr Camp Coyote, Mr Randy Rattlesnake, Arnie, Gordon, Walter, Dr John, Rehab… they were all there.

"Oh, *you're* Larry," cooed Bernard over the choodle canapes, "I've heard *so* much about you. So good to finally put a face to the name."

And Brian was providing a very beautiful keynote speech. He told our friends that our trip had shown that "we are all more than a result of the past, we are the guardians of our own future." It was oddly beautiful and I was about to thank him when he also described us as 'a poor man's Lewis and Clark'. Ah well, I'll take that, I thought. I wouldn't miss Brian because he was coming home with us but I would miss the rest of the troupe, and I would miss *the Americans*. From James and Sharon to Bill and Patsy, from homeless Dedric to millionaire Ernest, every one of them had welcomed us warmly, and their diversity - like that of the incredible landscapes they occupy - is what makes America. And somehow The Limey Project had connected all these unlikely ingredients.

Cycling gave us access to an America few people get to see, at an extraordinary period in its history. And it gave us access to ourselves; freeing up parts within us that had also been yet undiscovered. Indeed, the simple bicycle is a powerful tool for transformation: turning towns into communities, turning individuals into happier and healthier humans. Life still scared me, but I could now see that's precisely the beauty of it. I was looking forward to getting home, to that beautiful Sherborne, and taking life on. I later wrote a letter to Slavomir to thank him for the way he had inspired us. I never heard back from him and a month later I read that he died. Perhaps my letter was one of the last things he saw. In his long obituary it mentioned that some people still questioned whether his journey by foot all really took place.

"Does it matter?" Brian immediately asked. "If it is real to you then it is real enough." My imaginary friend had me there.

At Lincoln Road, we found our watering hole. We enjoyed a special Limey toast, and pressed our pinky fingers together. The other bar patrons asked us about the trip etched on the bikes.

"Have you seriously *just* done that?' they asked, pointing at the words 'Seattle to Miami'. They cheered 'Way to go guys'. And as we moved on to find the hostel the whole bar stood and started applauding.

"Aren't they wonderful, these Americans," I said to Killer.

There were two more at our hostel, two retired fishermen from Cape Cod called Mack and Jack who bought us a beer as soon as we arrived. These two splendid old buggers had worked in a job known for its brutal intensity and their stories backed it up, and yet they slapped *us* on the back with their big, grizzly man hands.

"I am utterly impressed with you guys. Many would have failed or given up and headed home," said Mack.

But would they? I always knew failure was a possibility, but I had never considered giving up as being an option. Perhaps I had seen *The Goonies* too many times, perhaps being curious about that secret place that resides in all of us - the one that holds our truth - helped lure me on through the toughest of times.

And we had completed it together. Even when the cycling was challenging, even when frozen, exhausted and in pain, or when drowning in thoughts, bottom vapours and rain storms, we had been a team. We had never argued, instead we had found joy everyday, laughing at things only appreciated by good friends. I still didn't *know* Killer in many ways (he was just starting to open himself up), but I understood him, and that's the rock on which great friendships are built. And after four months on the road, we had also become attuned to each other. We looked the same, we could complete each other's thoughts, and our bodies even craved the same food at the same time.

That last connection was confirmed the day after we arrived in Miami. We had become separated in our celebrations - partying 'in the city where the heat is on', as Will Smith puts it - and had woken up in different parts of Miami. I found myself a little lost and more than a little hungover. In my confused wanderings I bought a bright red 'Miami Beach Lifeguard' T-shirt (in case I was required to help with some rescuing) and a crisp white Panama hat. I then ducked into Subway for a foot-long meatball sandwich to soak up any lingering alcohol. As I was about to take the first bite, I saw Killer walk past the window and then stop abruptly. Something had caught his olfactory attention. He took a visible sniff of the air as if he recognised something. He turned to the shop sign to confirm his suspicions of its emanance and then checked his watch to see if it was an acceptable hour for sandwiching. He looked again at the sign and back at his watch and then nodded to himself decisively before opening the door and walking in.

"Oh, hi Killer", I said, as if I was expecting him, which of course I was.

"Oh, hi Bone," he replied, unflustered.

Miami was a gem, or at least it was where we were on South Beach, or SoBe as the locals and marketeers have it. The sea was azure, the beach wide and white. The large pastel-painted beachfront hotels held strong art deco lines. There was an eclectic mix of cultures and looks and, as a whole, the people of SoBe were all beautiful. It was like Melrose-on-sea. They jogged, rode fat-wheeled cruiser bikes along the sand or congregated in coffee shops.

It was no surprise, therefore, that Jessica was in Miami in abundant multiplicity. Just as we were recovering from the unique spectacle of a sextuple Jessica situation inside Starbucks, we were immediately confronted by a supplementary double Jessica sighting outside, and they appeared to be walking straight towards us. They were in loose, flowing dresses. They looked athletic and had dazzling white smiles. It seemed impossible that they wanted to talk to *us*. Then we noticed that one was holding a microphone, and there was a cameraman and director in tow. In a final twist of Limey fate, they announced themselves as cheerleaders for the Miami Marlins baseball team - we would have seen these very two women dancing on the pitch when, in a bar in San Francisco three months before, we watched their team unbelievably win the World Series. But on this day they were guest hosting a special programme for 'Fashion

Avenue', a lifestyle channel buried deep in the cable network (that I am surprised we never found while desperately hunting out motel TV trash). They wanted to know if they could interview us. But of course...

"So, we've found these two guys down here at South Beach, Miami. Two guys from England, right?"

"That's right, Cynthia," I said confidently, flashing an Austin Powers-esque grin and dialing up my British accent and eccentricities.

"So guys, we have to know... what were you *thinking* when you got dressed today?"

Ah ha. We hadn't so much been stopped for a casual chat but, rather, so they could expose us as curiosities. We were like Jessica Simpson, we had become the Wild Boyz of Miami, we had climbed through the screen and our world was now inside the TV world we had been poking fun at. We had finally arrived *inside* America and - as the phrase from the infomercials almost goes - 'side effects might include irony'. Someone, somewhere was watching this in a motel room and then repeating my odd, English words for comic effect.

The reason for her question was clear, though - we were wearing our brownishy-black jeans with flip flops. Killer was wearing a dusky green T-shirt he'd bought at the Shark Valley gift shop and had his 'New Mexico is HOT' cap on. I was wearing my new T-shirt and hat purchases. Our clothes hung around our skinny frames like we were toddlers playing in our parents' wardrobe. The colours clashed, the sizes were all wrong.

"These are all the clean clothes I have left," said Killer, wondering what was so interesting about it.

The girls' attention turned to me, apparently the only person in Miami wearing a Panama hat. Ernest's style leadership in LA had not reached the east coast yet, it seemed.

"What's with the hat? We are *loving* the hat!"

"Oh this, yes it's a new addition to my ensemble - it seems to crown my attire well. I just bought it." I was keen to give them a little context. "You see, we have just cycled for…"

But they wanted to press on.

"OK, next question - boxers or briefs?"

Well, they did ask. As all my pants were dirty, I really was wearing all I could. I undid my belt and dropped my trousers to reveal I was in fact wearing thermal long johns that extended all the way down to my ankles. It was 28 degrees out. This was madness. The girls, naturally, gasped.

"I'm afraid this is all I have left. You see, we have just arrived here having cycled 4,500 miles from Seattle, Washington." I said this line slowly, straight into the camera.

The girls reacted with the audible enthusiasm I had hoped for. They lost their initial tack entirely and just wanted to know more about the trip - and we were very pleased to furnish them with the facts.

"No, we never really felt in danger - we had an imaginary band of animals and Americans with us that reflected the characteristics that already existed, unknown, within us," I said.

Even lines like that didn't put them off. The director started signalling for them to close the interview but the girls kept asking questions and we recalled the details of the journey for them fondly. Once we had finally covered everything from the discovery of choodle to the joys of free camping, the interview was concluded and, with it, the journey itself felt complete.

Talking about the trip - and immortalising it on TV, albeit without the full cast of *The Limey Project: the TV show* - made us nostalgic for what we had only just finished. As much as getting to Miami was the goal, the journey was always the real prize. Killer and I sat on the beach, allowing the rays to colour in some of the Limey tan lines. We would occasionally offer a reflection on the adventure, in a strangely acceptable sincerity. We sat there until the sun went down.

"What if this is the greatest thing we ever do?" asked Killer, offering the last thought for the day. "What if this was it, and now it's finished? What do we look forward to now?"

I thought about that.

"What if this is just the start, though," I replied, "the thing that makes all the rest possible?"

- UT UT -

375

Thanks

After trying to write this book for many years, I had almost given up thinking I would ever finish it. So my first thanks is to my wife Sylvia for giving me the encouragement, love and time needed to write this. And while we are on the subject of family, thank you to my son Noah for being my greatest inspiration to complete this book and my all round proudest achievement. This adventure led to you. Thanks also to my parents who didn't flinch when I said I was quitting my promising job to cycle across a continent with no idea of where I would actually be going. You have always been there to support me.

Thank you to Killer for making the adventure what it was, for the years of music and laughter, and for your help with this book. I unashamedly 'borrowed' some of your best lines from your diaries and this book is all the better for it. Anyone in need of a seriously talented voice actor, check out nickcracknell.com.

Thank you to everyone who read drafts of this book, spotted typos, encouraged its progress or generally advised on how to get it out into the world. This includes Rebecca Evans, Susan Elderkin, Felix Lowe, Anna Luten, Rory MacLean, Daniel Mead, Nick Parker, James Spackman, Roos Stallinga and Romily Withington.

Thanks to Tom Kirkendall and Vicky Spring, not only for your inspiration on the journey itself but also for reading this and for giving your blessing to the embarrassingly imbalanced references. Vicky does the majority of the writing for their books, I now know, but our boyish hero worship of Tom meant he got most of the mentions in our diaries, and therefore in this book also. Check out kirkendall-spring.com.

The last thanks is to you, dear reader. Thank you for getting your hands on this book. If you have enjoyed it, please pass it on to someone else. The world needs more people on bicycles right now.

ABS

About the author

Adam Stones is an award-winning writer and communications consultant. His work focuses on supporting organisations addressing social and environmental issues, and on building the skills of changemakers. He grew up in Sherborne, Dorset and read Classics at Birmingham University. He is also the author of 'And other stories', a collection of flash fiction. After nearly a decade in London, in 2016 he moved to Amsterdam - the city of bikes - where he lives with his wife, son and an invisible bear called Brian. He continues to ride his bike every day. Even when it rains.

More of Adam's writing and photos of TLP at adamstones.co

Lightning Source UK Ltd.
Milton Keynes UK
UKHW011315260820
368860UK00001B/66